Starting a Business For Dummies®

KU-692-638

Making great business plans

Follow these tips to make your business plan stand out from the crowd:

- Hit them with the facts
- Make your projections believable
- Say how big the market is
- Introduce yourself and your team
- Include non-executive directors
- Provide financial forecasts
- Demonstrate the product or service
- Spell out the benefits to your potential investor

Will you make money?

Will your business idea leave you rolling in used tenners? To find out, you need to establish:

- Day-to-day operating costs
- How long it will take to reach break-even
- How much start-up capital is needed
- The likely sales volume
- The profit level required for the business not just to survive, but also to thrive
- The retail price of your product or service

Researching the market

To understand business areas that are new to you, factors to research include:

- Your customers
- Your competitors
- Your product or service
- The price
- The advertising and promotional material
- Channels of distribution
- Your location

Selecting a distribution channel

If your customers don't come to you, then you have the following options in getting your product or service to them:

- Retail stores
- Wholesalers
- Cash & carry
- Internet and mail order
- Door-to-door selling
- Party plan selling
- Telephone selling

Consider these factors when choosing channels of distribution for your particular business:

- Does it meet your customers' needs?
- Will the product itself survive?
- Can you sell enough this way?
- Is it compatible with your image?
- How do your competitors distribute?
- Is the channel cost-effective?
- Is the mark-up enough?

For Dummies: Bestselling Book Series for Beginners

Starting a Business For Dummies®

Cheat Sheet

Reasons to outsource

- Meeting unexpected deadlines
- Access to expertise
- Greater scalability
- More predictable costs
- Free up your time
- Economies of scale

Calculating VAT

Calculating the VAT element of any transaction can be a confusing sum. Following these simple steps can help you get it right:

1. Take the gross amount of any sum (items you sell or buy), that is the total including any VAT and divide it by 117.5 – if the VAT rate is 17.5 per cent. (If the rate is different, add 100 to the VAT percentage rate and divide by that number.)

2. Multiply the result from Step 1 by 100 to get the pre-VAT total.

3. Multiply the result from Step 1 by 17.5 to arrive at the VAT element of the bill.

Ten ways to minimise tax

- Make sure to include all allowable business expenses. When you have recently set up in business, you may not be fully aware of all the expenses that can be claimed.

- If you have made losses in any tax period, these may under certain circumstances be carried forward to offset future taxable profits or backwards against past profits.

- You can defer paying capital gains tax if you plan to buy another asset with the proceeds. This is known as 'rollover relief' and it can be used normally up to three years after the taxable event.

- Pension contributions reduce your taxable profits. You may even be able to set up a pension scheme that allows you some say over how those funds are used.

- If you do intend to buy capital assets for your business, bring forward your spending plans so as to maximise the use of the *writing down allowance*, which is the portion of the cost of the asset you can set against tax in any year.

- Identify non-cash benefits that you and others working for you could take instead of taxable salary.

- Examine the pros and cons of taking your money out of a limited company by way of dividends or salary. These routes are taxed differently and may provide scope for tax reduction.

- If your spouse has no other income from employment, they could earn a sum equivalent to their annual tax-free allowance (currently about £4,000) by working for your business.

- If you incurred any pre-trading expenses at any stage over the seven years before you started up in business, you can probably treat them as if you incurred them after trading started.

- You may be able to treat the full purchase price of business assets you bought through hire purchase in your capital allowances calculation.

For Dummies: Bestselling Book Series for Beginners

Starting a
Business
FOR
DUMMIES®

Starting a Business

FOR DUMMIES®

by Colin Barrow

JOHN WILEY & SONS, LTD

Starting a Business For Dummies®

Published by
John Wiley & Sons, Ltd
The Atrium
Southern Gate
Chichester
West Sussex
PO19 8SQ
England

E-mail (for orders and customer service enquires): cs-books@wiley.co.uk

Visit our Home Page on www.wileyeurope.com

Wiley also publishes its books in a variety of electronic formats. Some content that appears in print may not be available in electronic books.

British Library Cataloguing in Publication Data

A catalogue record for this book is available from the British Library

ISBN: 0-7645-7018-8

Printed and bound in Great Britain by Biddles Ltd, King's Lynn.

10 9 8 7 6 5 4 3

WILEY

About the Author

Colin Barrow is Head of the Enterprise Group at Cranfield School of Management, where he teaches entrepreneurship on the MBA and other programmes. He is also a visiting professor at business schools in the US, Asia, France, and Austria. His books on entrepreneurship and small business have been translated into fifteen languages including Russian and Chinese. He worked with Microsoft to incorporate the business planning model used in his teaching programmes into the software program, Microsoft Business Planner. He is a regular contributor to newspapers, periodicals and academic journals such as the *Financial Times*, *The Guardian*, *Management Today*, and the *International Small Business Journal*.

Thousands of students have passed through Colin's start-up and business growth programmes, going on to run successful and thriving enterprises, and raising millions in new capital. He is a non-executive director of two venture capital funds, on the board of several small businesses, and serves on a number of Government Task Forces.

Author's Acknowledgements

I would like to thank everyone at Wiley Publishing, especially Jason Dunne, Daniel Mersey and Samantha Clapp, for the opportunity to write this book – as well as their help, encouragement, feedback, and tireless work to make this all happen.

Publisher's Acknowledgements

We're proud of this book; please send us your comments through our Dummies online registration form located at www.dummies.com/register/.

Some of the people who helped bring this book to market include the following:

Acquisitions, Editorial, and Media Development

Executive Editor: Jason Dunne

Executive Project Editor: Caroline Walmsley

Project Editors: Daniel Mersey, Amie Tibble

Editorial Assistant: Samantha Clapp

Technical Reviewer: Paul Barrow

Cover Photos: © Steve Niedorf Photography/Getty

Cartoons: Ed McLachlan

Production

Project Coordinator: Erin Smith

Layout and Graphics: Amanda Carter, Andrea Dahl, Denny Hager, Michael Kruzil, Heather Ryan, Jacque Schneider, Rashell Smith

Proofreaders: Carl Pierce, Brian Walls

Indexer: TECHBOOKS Production Services

Publishing and Editorial for Consumer Dummies

  Diane Graves Steele, Vice President and Publisher, Consumer Dummies

  Joyce Pepple, Acquisitions Director, Consumer Dummies

  Kristin A Cocks, Product Development Director, Consumer Dummies

  Michael Spring, Vice President and Publisher, Travel

  Brice Gosnell, Associate Publisher, Travel

  Kelly Regan, Editorial Director, Travel

Publishing for Technology Dummies

  Andy Cummings, Vice President and Publisher, Dummies Technology/General User

Composition Services

  Gerry Fahey, Vice President of Production Services

  Debbie Stailey, Director of Composition Services

Contents at a Glance

How to Use This Book

Starting a Business For Dummies can help you succeed no matter what kind of business expertise you're looking for. If you have a great and proven business idea, you may want to plug straight into finding out how to raise finance. If you need more than just yourself to get your great business idea off the ground, then you may want to find out how to find great employees or perhaps a business partner to take some of the financial and emotional strain. This book is set up so that you can dip in and out of it in a number of ways depending on your situation.

- ✔ If you haven't started a business before, or been profit accountable for part of an enterprise, then you may want to start at the beginning and work your way through.

- ✔ If you are more experienced then you may start by selecting the areas you are less knowledgeable about to fill in the gaps and work outwards from there.

- ✔ If you are quite confident in the business world you could use the book as a guide and mentor to review a particular topic.

- ✔ If you learn by example, you may want to flip through the book, using the True Story icon as your guide. The text next to this icon highlights 'straight from the horse's mouth' examples of how successful entrepreneurs have tackled specific situations, be it finding a partner or getting a free grant from the government.

The next section tells you what's covered in the various parts of the book so that you can turn to a certain part for a specific need.

How This Book Is Organised

Starting a Business For Dummies is divided into five main parts based on the major elements involved in planning, launching and running a business. You don't have to read all the parts, however, and you certainly don't have to read them in order. Each chapter is devoted to a particular business start-up topic and you may need some chapters more than others. Feel free to jump from section to section and chapter to chapter; pick and choose what really matters to you and your business proposition.

Part I: Getting Started

Before you get a business off the ground you have to do all the preliminary legwork and make sure you have a viable business on your hands before you commit too much time and money. This part gets you on track right away by helping you put together your business plan, including establishing a mission for your business along with goals and objectives, and a longer-term vision of where you would ideally like to be a few years from now.

Part II: Managing the Business

To ensure that your business prospers you have to know something about the market you're going after and decide what strategy to adopt with regard to price, promotion, place, and product to beat your competitors. You also need to review the financing options to make sure you get both the right amount and type of finance for your business needs. You don't have to do all this on your own as the key organisations that offer advice and help to business starters are listed and described in the chapters in this part.

Part III: Staying in Business

A business needs controlling in much the same way as a car or plane. You need to understand what the key control documents are, and what they tell you about how your business is performing. You also need to have a sound appreciation of your income and valued-added tax liabilities and how to min-imise those liabilities legitimately.

Part IV: Making the Business Grow

Once you have your business up and running you want to see how fast you can make it go without blowing a gasket or running off the road. Part of this process is a bit like fine-tuning a car engine. But part involves substantially changing everything, including the people who work in the business, the products and services, the markets served and perhaps even the very nature of your business operations. This part covers the ins and outs of expanding your business safely and smartly.

Part V: The Part of Tens

The Part of Tens presents three chapters. One is a collection of warnings about the problems that most new business are likely to encounter and how to counteract them. Another contains details of the people you absolutely have to talk to before, during and after you have started up. The third chapter gives vital details on using e-training and development to further improve your business skills and those of people working with you.

Icons Used in This Book

To help you pinpoint vital information, I've placed these icons throughout the text to steer you to nuggets of knowledge.

This icon calls your attention to particularly important points and offers useful advice on practical topics.

This icon serves as a friendly reminder that the topic at hand is important enough for you to make a note of.

Business, like any specialist subject, is awash with specialised terms and expressions, some of which may not be familiar to you. This icon draws your attention to these.

This icon alerts you that I'm using a practical example showing how another business starter has tackled a particular topic. Often you can apply the example to your own business.

This icon alerts you to a potential danger. Proceed with caution; look left and right before crossing. In fact, think carefully about crossing at all when you see this icon.

This icon refers to specialised business facts and data, which is interesting as background data, but not essential for you to know. You can skip paragraphs marked by this icon without missing the point – but reading them might help you build credibility with outside investors and partners.

Where to Go From Here

Take a minute to thumb through the table of contents and get comfortable with the topics covered. Pick a chapter that strikes a particular chord with the aspect of starting a business that is uppermost in your mind. Read that and see where it leads you.

You could also use Chapter 6, 'Preparing the Business Plan', as a framework for gathering knowledge and diving back into the other chapters as you go.

If all else fails, start at the beginning. It's a technique with a pretty good track record.

Part I
Getting Started

"You may have spotted a gap in
the market, but ..."

In this part . . .

*B*efore you can think seriously about starting your
own business you need to make sure you are ready
for the big step. This part will let you check out your skills
and aptitude and see how they compare to the business
idea you have in mind. You can then see if your idea looks
like it will make the kind of money you're expecting. You
can then see if you should start up on your own or perhaps find others to help you.

Once the groundwork is done you can start turning your
ideas into a more concrete business plan. With the plan
done you are ready to take your business forward!

Chapter 1

Preparing for Business

*W*ould you go into the jungle without carrying out some pretty rigorous preparation? You'd need to know something about the terrain and how to navigate it, as well as the temperature, rainfall, and food supply. You would also be keen to know what predators you might meet on the way and how to defend yourself against them.

When you're starting a business, particularly your first business, you need to carry out the same level of preparation as you would for crossing the Gobi desert or exploring the jungles of South America. You are entering hostile territory.

Your business idea may be good, it may even be great, but such ideas are two a penny. The patent office is stuffed full of great inventions that have never returned tuppence to the inventors who spent much time and money filing them. It's how you plan, how you prepare and how you implement your plan that makes the difference between success and failure. And failure is pretty much a norm for business start-ups. Tens of thousands of small firms fail, some disastrously, each and every year.

In this chapter the scene is set to make sure you are well prepared for the journey ahead.

Getting in Shape to Start Up

You need to be in great shape to start a business. You don't have to diet or exercise, at least not in the conventional sense of those words, but you do have to be sure you have the skills and knowledge you need for the business you have in mind, or know how to tap into sources of such expertise.

The following sections will help you through a pre-opening check-up so you can be absolutely certain that your abilities and interests are closely aligned to those needed by the business you have in mind. It will also help you to check that a profitable market exists for your products or services. You can use this section as a vehicle for sifting through your business ideas to see if they are worth devoting the time and energy that is needed to start up a business.

You may well not have all the expertise you need to do everything yourself. In Chapter 7 you will be introduced to the zillions of agencies and advisers who can fill in the gaps in your expertise.

Assessing your abilities

Business lore claims that for every ten people who want to start their own business only one finally does so. It follows that there are an awful lot of dreamers out there who, whilst liking the idea of starting their own business, never get around to taking action. Chapter 3 looks in detail at how you can assess whether you are a dreamer or a doer when it comes to entrepreneurship. For now, see whether you fit into one of the following entrepreneurial categories.

- ✔ **Nature.** If one of your parents or siblings runs their own business, successfully or otherwise, you are highly likely to start up your own business. No big surprise here as the rules and experiences of business are being discussed every day and some of it is bound to rub off. It also helps if you are a risk-taker who is comfortable with uncertainty.

- ✔ **Nurture.** For very entrepreneur whose parents or siblings have a business there are two who don't. If you can find a business idea that excites you, has the prospect of providing personal satisfaction and wealth, then you can assemble all the skills and resources needed to succeed in your own business. You need to acquire good planning and organisational skills (Chapter 6 covers all aspects of writing a business plan) and either develop a well-rounded knowledge of basic finance, people management, operational systems, business law, marketing and selling, or get help and advice from people who have that knowledge.

- ✔ **Risk-taker.** If you crave certainty in everything you do, then running your own business may be something of a culture shock. By the time the demand for a product or service is an absolutely sure-fired thing, there may already be too many others in the market to leave much room for you. Don't confuse risk taking with a pure gamble. You need to be able to weigh things up and take a calculated risk.

- ✔ **Jack-of-all-trades.** You need to be prepared to do any business task at anytime. The buck definitely stops with you when you run your own business. You can't tell a customer their delivery will be late, just because a driver fails to show up. You will just have to put in a few more hours and do the job yourself.

Discovering a real need

You might be a great potential entrepreneur but you still need to spell out exactly what it is you plan to do, who needs it, and how it will make money. A good starting point is to look around and see if anyone is dissatisfied with their present suppliers. Unhappy customers are fertile ground for new businesses to work in.

One dissatisfied customer is not enough to start a business for. Check out and make sure that unhappiness is reasonably widespread, as that will give you a feel for how many customers might be prepared to defect. Once you have an idea of the size of the potential market you can quickly see if your business idea is a money making proposition.

The easiest way to fill an endurable need is to tap into one or more of these triggers:

- **Cost reduction and economy.** Anything that saves customers money is always an attractive proposition. Lastminute.com's appeal is that it acts as a 'warehouse' for unsold hotel rooms and airline tickets that you can have at a heavy discount.

- **Fear and security.** Products that protect customers from any danger, however obscure, are enduringly appealing. In 1998, two months after Long-Term Capital Management (LTCM), one of America's largest hedge funds, was rescued by the Federal Reserve at a cost of $2 billion, Ian and Susan Jenkins launched the first issue of their magazine, *EuroHedge*. In the aftermath of the collapse of LTCM, which nearly brought down the US financial system single-handedly, there were 35 hedge funds in Europe, about which little was known, and investors were rightly fearful for their investments. *EuroHedge* provided information and protection to a nervous market and five years after it was launched the Jenkins's sold the magazine for £16.5 million.

- **Greed.** Anything that offers the prospect of making exceptional returns is always a winner. *Competitors' Companion*, a magazine aimed at helping anyone become a regular competition winner, was an immediate success. The proposition was simple. Subscribe and you get your money back if you don't win a competition prize worth at least your subscription. The magazine provided details of every competition being run that week, details of how to enter, the factual answers to all the questions and pointers on how to answer any tiebreakers. They also provided the inspiration to ensure success with this sentence: You have to enter competitions in order to have a chance of winning them.

- **Niche markets.** Big markets are usually the habitat of big business – encroach on their territory at your peril. New businesses thrive in markets that are too small to even be an appetite wetter to established firms. These market niches are often easy prey to new entrants as they have usually been neglected, ignored or ill-served in the past.

> ✔ **Differentiation.** Consumers can be a pretty fickle bunch. Just dangle something, faster, brighter or just plain newer and you can usually grab their attention. Your difference doesn't have to be profound or even high-tech to capture a slice of the market. Book buyers rushed in droves to Waterstones' for no more profound a reason than that their doors remained open in the evenings and on Sundays, when most other established bookshops were firmly closed.

Checking the fit of the business

Having a great business idea and having the attributes and skills needed to successfully start your own business are two of the three legs needed to make your business stool balance. Without the third leg, though, your stool isn't stable at all. You need to be sure that the business you plan to start is right for you.

Before you go too far, make an inventory of the key things that you are looking for in a business. These may include working hours that suit your lifestyle; the opportunity to meet new people; minimal paperwork; a chance to travel. Then match those up with the proposition you are considering. (Chapter 3 talks more about finding a good business fit.)

Checking Viability

An idea, however exciting, unique, revolutionary, and necessary is not a business. It's a great starting point, and an essential one, but there is a good deal more work to be done before you can sidle up to your boss and tell him or her exactly what you think of them.

The following sections explore the steps you need to take so that you won't have to go back to your boss in six months and plead for your old job back (and possibly eat a large piece of humble pie at the same time).

Researching the market

However passionate you are about your business idea, it is unlikely that you already have the answers to all the important questions concerning your market place. Before you can develop a successful business strategy, you have to understand as much as possible about your market and the competitors you are likely to face.

Inflated numbers on the Internet

If you plan to advertise on an Internet site it makes sense to check out the sites you're considering. Be aware that some sites publish a fair amount of gobbledygook about the high number of 'hits' (often millions) the site scores. Millions of hits doesn't mean the site has millions of visitors. Some Internet sites increase their hit rate by the simple expedient of adding the number of pages each viewer must download to view the page.

Another mildly meaningless measure of the advertising value of a site is the notion of a 'subscriber'. In Internet parlance anyone visiting a Web site and passing over their e-mail address becomes part of that company's share price! It is rather like suggesting that anyone passing a shop and glancing in the window will turn into hard cash tomorrow.

Any real analysis of Web site use starts with 'page impression', which is a measure of how many times an individual page has been viewed. The Audit Bureau of Circulations, which started its life measuring newspaper response, has now turned its attention to auditing Web sites (www.abc.org.uk).

The main way to get to understand new business areas, or areas that are new to you at any rate, is to conduct market research. The purpose of that research is to ensure that you have sufficient information on customers, competitors, and markets so that your market entry strategy or expansion strategy is at least on the target, if not on the bull's-eye itself. In other words, you need to explore whether enough people are attracted to buy what you want to sell at a price that will give you a viable business. If you miss the target altogether, which you could well do without research, you may not have the necessary resources for a second shot.

The areas to research include:

- **Your customers:** Who will buy more of your existing goods and services and who will buy your new goods and services? How many such customers are there? What particular customer needs will you meet?

- **Your competitors:** Who will you be competing with in your product/ market areas? What are those firms' strengths and weaknesses?

- **Your product or service:** How should you tailor your product or service to meet customer needs and to give you an edge in the market?

- **The price:** What would be seen as giving value for money and so encourages both customer loyalty and referral?

- **The advertising and promotional material:** What newspapers, journals, and so forth do your potential customers read and what Web sites do they visit? Unglamorous as it is, analysing data on what messages actually influence people to buy, rather than just to click, holds the key to identifying where and how to promote your products and service.

> ✔ **Channels of distribution:** How will you get to your customers and who do you need to distribute your products or services? You may need to use retailers, wholesalers, mail order, or the Internet. They all have different costs and if you use one or more they all want a slice of the margin.
>
> ✔ **Your location:** Where do you need to be to reach your customers most easily at minimum cost? Sometimes you don't actually need to be anywhere near your market, particularly if you anticipate most of your sales will come from the Internet. If this is the case you need to have strategy to make sure potential customers can find your Web site.

Try to spend your advertising money wisely. Nationwide advertisements or blanketing the market with free disks may create huge short-term growth, but there is little evidence that the clients won by indiscriminate blunderbuss advertising works well. Certainly few people using such techniques made any money.

Doing the numbers

Your big idea looks as though it has a market. You have evaluated your skills and inclinations and you believe that you can run this business. The next crucial question is – will it make you money?

It's vital that you establish the financial viability of your idea before you invest money in it or approach outsiders for backing. You need to carry out a thorough appraisal of the business's financial requirements. If the numbers come out as unworkable you can then rethink your business proposition without having lost anything. If the figures look good, then you can go ahead and prepare cash flow projections, a profit and loss account and a balance sheet, and put together the all-important business plan. (These procedures are covered in Chapters 6 and 13.)

You need to establish for your business:

> ✔ Day to day operating costs
>
> ✔ How long it will take to reach break-even
>
> ✔ How much start-up capital is needed
>
> ✔ The likely sales volume
>
> ✔ The profit level required for the business not just to survive, but also to thrive
>
> ✔ The retail price of your product or service

Many businesses have difficulty raising start-up capital. To compound this, one of the main reasons small businesses fail in the early stages is that too much start-up capital is used to buy fixed assets. While some equipment is clearly essential at the start, other purchases could be postponed. You may be better off borrowing or hiring 'desirable' and labour-saving devices for a specific period. This is obviously not as nice as having them all to hand all the time but remember that you have to maintain every photocopier, electronic typewriter, word processor, micro-computer, and delivery van you buy and they become part of your fixed costs. The higher your fixed costs, the longer it usually takes to reach break-even point and profitability. And time is not usually on the side of the small, new business: it has to become profitable relatively quickly or it will simply run out of money and die.

Raising the money

Two fundamentally different types of money that a business can tap into are debt and equity.

- ✔ *Debt* is money borrowed, usually from a bank, and which you have to repay. While you are making use of borrowed money you also have to pay interest on the loan.

- ✔ *Equity* is the money put in by shareholders, including the proprietor, and money left in the business by way of retained profit. You do not have to give the shareholders their money back, but they do expect the directors to increase the value of their shares, and if you go public they will probably expect a stream of dividends too.

  If you do not meet the shareholders' expectations, they will not be there when you need more money – or, if they are powerful enough, they will take steps to change the board.

Alternative financing methods include raising money from family and friends, applying for grants and awards, and entering business competitions.

Check out Chapter 8 for a review of all these sources of financing.

Writing up the business plan

A *business plan* is a selling document that conveys the excitement and promise of your business to potential backers and stakeholders. These potential backers could include bankers, venture capital firms, family, friends, and others who could help you get your business launched if they only knew what you want to do. (See Chapter 8 for how to find and approach sources of finance.)

Location, location, location

Many traditional businesses entering the e-economy have kept the 'mortar' as well as acquiring 'clicks'. When international retail chain Tesco announced a separate e-commerce business, one great strength claimed for the new business was that 'Customers know and trust us and that gives us a real competitive edge.'

That trust stemmed from customers being able to physically see what the company stands for.

Using software produced by the leading UK Internet software company, Tesco plans to offer an intelligent Internet tool that reacts to customers' shopping habits and suggests different sites with related subjects or products the customer may be interested in. In that way Tesco hopes to build a similar level of trust, but over the Internet.

Getting money is expensive, time-consuming, and hard work. Having said that, it is possible to get a quick decision. One recent start-up succeeded in raising £3 million in eight days, the founder having turned down an earlier offer of £1 million made just 40 minutes after his business plan was presented. Your business plan should cover what you expect to achieve over the next three years. (See Chapter 6 for full details on how to write a winning business plan.)

Most business plans are dull, badly written, and frequently read only by the most junior of people in the financing organisations they're presented to. One venture capital firm in the US went on record to say that in one year they received 25,000 business plans asking for finance and invested in only 40. Follow these tips to make your business plan stand out from the crowd:

- ✔ **Hit them with the benefits:** You need to spell out exactly what it is you do, for whom, and why that matters. One such statement that has the ring of practical authority about it is: 'Our Web site makes ordering gardening products simple. It saves the average customer two hours a week browsing catalogues and £250 a year through discounts, not otherwise available from garden centres. We have surveyed 200 home gardeners, who rate efficient purchasing as a key priority.'

- ✔ **Make your projections believable:** Sales projections always look like a hockey stick: a straight line curving rapidly upwards towards the end. You have to explain exactly what drives growth, how you capture sales, and what the link between activity and results is. The profit margins will be key numbers in your projections, alongside sales forecasts. These will be probed hard, so show the build-up in detail.

- ✔ **Say how big the market is:** Financiers feel safer backing people in big markets. Capturing a fraction of a percentage of a massive market may be hard to achieve – but if you get it at least it's worth it. Going for 10 per cent of a market measured in millions rather than billions may come to the same number, but it won't be as interesting.

- **Introduce yourself and your team:** You need to sound like winners with a track record of great accomplishments.

- **Include non-executive directors:** Sometimes a heavyweight outsider can lend extra credibility to a business proposition. If you know or have access to someone with a successful track record in your area of business who has time on their hands, you could invite them to help. If you plan to trade as a limited company (see Chapter 4 for details on legal structures) you could ask them to be a director, without specific executive responsibilities beyond being on hand to offer their advice. But they need to have relevant experience or be able to open doors and do deals.

- **Provide financial forecasts:** You need projected cash flows, profit and loss accounts, and balance sheets for at least three years out. No one believes them after Year One, but the thinking behind them is what's important.

- **Demonstrate the product or service:** Financiers need to see what the customer is going to get. A mock-up will do or, failing that, a picture or diagram. For a service, show how customers will gain from using it. That can help with improved production scheduling and so reduce stock holding.

- **Spell out the benefits to your potential investor:** Tell them that their money will be paid back within 'x' years, even on your most cautious projections. Or if you are speaking with an equity investor, tell them what return they will get on their investment when you sell the business on in three or five years time.

Proving that small firms matter

One unusual thing to strike anyone thinking seriously about starting up their first business is just how many organisations there are around that have timely and valuable advice to offer and that appear willing and able to offer a helping hand. Enterprise Agencies, Business Link, The Small Business Service, which I tell you more about in Chapter 7, just seem to be busting a gut to help you get rich.

Whilst it would be good to believe that making sure that your venture succeeds is their only goal, it ain't necessarily so. Many of those organisations are either directly or indirectly linked to some government initiative. Apart from the obvious desire by the government types running those organisations to be seen in a favourable light by voters – and there are over 40 million owner managers with votes in the US and Europe alone – there are practical reasons to give small businesses a helping hand.

The most compelling reason why small firms matter so much was first brought to light by an

(continued)

American academic, David Birch, in the 1980s. Whilst conducting research at MIT (the Massachusetts Institute of Technology) Birch demonstrated that it was enterprises employing fewer than 20 workers that were responsible for over two-thirds of the increase in employment in the United States. This revealing statistic, which was shown to be valid for much of the developed world, was seized upon as the signal for governments and others to step up their efforts to stimulate and encourage enterprise.

Small firms had been neglected for most of the post-Second World War years. In the United Kingdom various studies, including the influential Bolton Committee Report commissioned in 1971 by the government to investigate the state of the small business sector, identified this sector as starved of equity capital and experienced management. But until Birch's paper no-one accepted quite how important new and small firms were to a country's economic well-being.

Alongside this recognition of the significance of small businesses, Birch's research also revealed their fragility. He estimated that roughly 8 million enterprises operating in America closed every year which means that 'every five to six years, we have to replace half of the entire US economy'. These findings on small firm failure rates have been repeated in study after study, throughout the world. Ultimately, only about half of all small firms survive more than five years.

In the years since Birch's research was first published, there has been a dramatic increase in new business creation. In the UK alone the small business population has more than doubled from 1.9 million in 1980 to nearly 4 million in 2000. However, the failure rates, though getting better, remain worryingly high. There is a general agreement that the two main reasons for small business failure are lack of management expertise and under-capitalisation, aside that is from the effects of macro-economic mismanagement.

Arising from these twin findings that new firms are both vital and fragile have come a plethora of government initiatives to both foster and protect small firms during their formative years. I talk more about where to go for help and advice in Chapter 7.

Going for Growth

Growth is as natural a feature of business life as it is of biological life. People, animals, and plants all grow to a set size range and then stop. A few very small and very large specimens come to fruition, but the vast majority fit within a fairly narrow size band.

Businesses follow a similar formula: most successful new businesses, those that survive that is, reach a plateau within five to seven years. At that stage the business employs five to 20 people and has annual sales of between £250,000 and £1 million. Of the 3.7 million private businesses operating in the UK, fewer than 120,000 have a turnover in excess of £1 million a year. That doesn't represent a bad result. Viewed from the position of a one-man band start-up, having a couple of hundred thousand of pounds in sales each year is admirable (and unusual) success.

The following sections demonstrate the great benefits of growth (see Chapters 15, 16, and 17 for more advice on how to make your business grow).

Gaining economies of scale

Once a business starts to grow, the overhead costs are spread over a wider base. You can buy materials and services in larger quantities, which usually means better terms and lower costs. The combination of these factors generally leads to a higher profit margin, which in turn provides funds to improve the business, which, in turn can lead to even lower costs. This *virtuous circle,* as it is known, can make a growing firm more cost competitive than one that is cautiously marking time.

Securing a competitive advantage

A new business can steal a march on its competitors by doing something vital that established businesses cannot easily imitate. For example a new hairdressing shop can locate where customers are, whilst an existing shop has to content itself with its current location, at least until its lease expires.

A growing firm can gain advantages over its slower competitors. For example, launching new products or services gives a firm more goods to sell to its existing customer base. This puts smaller competitors at a disadvantage because they are perceived as having less to offer than the existing supplier. This type of growth strategy can, if coupled with high quality standards, lead to improved customer retention and this too can lead to higher profits – a further push on the momentum of the virtuous circle.

Retaining key staff

The surest way to ensure a business fails is to have a constant churn of employees coming and going. Valuable time and money has to be invested in every new employee before they become productive, so the more staff you lose the more growth you sacrifice.

Most employers believe that their staff work for money and their key staff work for more money. The facts don't really support this hypothesis. All the evidence is that employees want to have an interesting job and be recognised and praised for their achievements. In Chapter 17 you will see how to get the best out of your staff.

By growing the business you can let key managers realise their potential. In a bigger business your staff can be trained and promoted, moving up the ladder into more challenging jobs, with higher salaries earned on merit, whilst staying with you, rather than leaving for pastures new. And if employees are good at their jobs, the longer they stay with you the more valuable they become. You save time and money on the recruitment merry-go-round and you don't have to finance new managers' mistakes whilst they learn how to work in your business.

Gaining critical business mass

Bigger isn't always better, but a growing business will have a greater presence in its market, and that's rarely a bad strategy. Large businesses are also more stable, tending to survive better in turbulent times. Bigger businesses can and do sometimes go bust, but smaller 'doing nicely' small businesses are far more likely to go bump.

A small company often relies on a handful of customers and just one or two products or services for most or all of its profits. If its main product or service comes under competitive pressure, or if a principal customer goes bust, changes supplier, or simply spreads orders around more thinly, then that company is in trouble. Breaking out of the 80/20 cycle, in which 80 per cent of the business comes from just 20 per cent of customers, by expanding the number of customers is a sensible way to make your business safer and more predictable.

One-product businesses are the natural medium of the inventor, but they are extremely vulnerable to competition, changes in fashion, and technological obsolescence. Having only one product can limit the growth potential of the enterprise. A question mark must inevitably hang over such ventures until they can broaden out their product base. Adding successful new products or services helps a business to grow and become a safer and more secure venture. This process is much like buying a unit trust rather than investing in a couple of shares. The individual shares are inevitably more volatile, whilst the spread over dozens of shares smoothes the growth path, and reduces the chances of disaster significantly.

Chapter 2

Doing the Groundwork

· ·

· ·

*I*f you have worked in a big organisation, you will know that a small and medium enterprise (SME) is a very different kind of animal from a big business. SMEs are more vulnerable to the vagaries of the economy, but are vital to its vigour.

In this chapter you will find out how to come up with a great business idea and avoid the lemons, and look at the most common mistakes made by those starting up and how you can avoid them.

Understanding the Small Business Environment

During one of the all too many periods in recent history when the business climate was particularly frigid, some bright spark claimed that the only sure-fire way to get a small business safely down the slipway was to start out with a big one and shrink it down to size. There is no denying that is one way to get started, but even as a joke it completely misses the point. Small businesses have almost nothing in common with big ones. Just because someone, you perhaps, have worked in big business, however successfully, that is no guarantee of success in the small business world.

Big businesses usually have deep pockets and even if those pockets are not actually stuffed full of cash, after years of trading under their belt, they can usually extract credit from suppliers. If all else fails they can tap their shareholders or go out to the stockmarket for more boodle – options a small business owner can only dream about. The boss of a big firm has legions of staff to carry out research, or to do all those hundred and one boring but essential jobs like writing up the books.

In contrast, the small business founder has to stay up late burning the midnight oil, poring over those figures themselves. To cap it all, they may even have to get up at dawn and make special deliveries to customers in order to ensure deadlines are met. The big business boss has a chauffeur and travels business class, after all they don't own a large proportion of the shares so however frugal they are they won't be much richer. The small firm founder, in contrast, is personally poorer every time an employee makes a phone call at work, books a business trip, or takes a client out to lunch, unless that is the call, trip, or lunch that generates extra business. The question that separates owners from employees, which is after all what the boss of a big business really is, however powerful they look from below, is: If it was your money would you spend it on that call, business trip, or lunch? Seven times out of ten the answer is no way, not with my dosh.

Defining Small Business

Small business defies easy definition. Typically, people apply the term small business to one-man bands such as shops, garages, and restaurants, and we apply the term big business to such giants as IBM, General Motors, Shell, and ICI. But between these two extremes fall businesses that may be looked upon as big or small, depending on the yardstick and cut-off point used to measure size.

There is no single definition of a small firm, mainly because of the wide diversity of businesses. One bright spark claimed a business was small if it felt it was, and there is a grain of truth in that point of view.

From a practical point of view the only reason to be concerned about a business size, age or business sector is the support and constraints imposed by virtue of those factors. The government, for example, may offer grant aid, support or even constraints based on such factors. A business with a very small annual sales turnover, less than £15,000, can file a much simpler set of accounts than a larger business.

Looking at the Types of People Who Start a Business

At one level statistics on small firms are very precise. Government collects and analyses the basic data on how many businesses start (and close) in each geographic area and what type of activity those businesses undertake.

Periodic studies give further insights into how new and small firms are financed or how much of their business comes from overseas markets. Beyond that the 'facts' become a little more hazy and information comes most often from informal studies by banks, academics, and others who may have a particular axe to grind.

The first fact about the UK small business sector is how big it is. Over 2.7 million people now run their own business, up from 1.9 million three decades ago.

The desire to start a business is not evenly distributed across the population as a whole. Certain factors such as geographic area, age group, and so forth seem to influence the number of start-ups at any one time. The following sections explore some of these factors.

Making your age an asset

Research by Barclays Bank shows that people aged between 25 and 44 are more likely than other age groups to be planning to start a business. Nearly 5 per cent of those age groups are starting a business on their own or with others. Around 3 per cent of those under 24 or between 45 and 54 also have business start-up plans. Those over 55 are the least likely to want to start up, with only 1.3 per cent heading for self-employment.

But those percentages are only showing those planning a start-up. Around three times those proportions are already running small or medium sized business.

Looking at location

More than three times as many people in London start a business, as do those in the North East. At the very least you are more likely to feel lonelier as an entrepreneur in that area, or in Wales and Scotland, than you would in, say, London or the South-East.

According to the DTI (Department of Trade and Industry), the chances of your business surviving are best in Northern Ireland, where 73 per cent are still going after 3 years and worst in London were just 63 per cent are in business at that point.

Widening business to include women

Women in Europe currently own less than a third of small businesses but women start about 35 per cent of new businesses in the UK. Businesses started by women tend to be concentrated in the labour intensive retail industries, where management skills are particularly valuable.

The British Association of Women Entrepreneurs (www.bawe-uk.org) and everywoman (www.everywoman.co.uk) are useful starting points to find out more about targeted help and advice for women starting up a business.

Self-employment, a term used interchangeably with starting a business, tends to be a midlife choice for women, with the majority starting up businesses after the age of 35. Self-employed women usually have children at home (kudos to these super-mums), and many go the self-employment route *because* they have family commitments. In most cases, self-employment grants greater schedule flexibility than the rigors of a 9–5 job.

The types of businesses women run reflect the pattern of their occupations in employment. The public administration, education, and health fields account for 22 per cent of self-employed women, and distribution, hotels, and restaurants another 21 per cent.

In financing a new business, women tend to prefer using personal credit cards or re-mortgaging their home, while men prefer bank loan finance and government and local authority grants.

Being educated about needing education

A popular myth states that under-educated self-made men dominate the field of entrepreneurship. Anecdotal evidence seems to throw up enough examples of school or university drop-outs to support the theory that education is unnecessary, perhaps even a hindrance, to getting a business started. After all, if Bill Gates and Richard Branson can give higher education a miss, it can't be that vital.

However, the facts, such as they are, show a rather different picture. Research shows the more educated the population, the more likely entrepreneurship takes place. Educated individuals are more likely to identify gaps in the market or understand new technologies. So if you are in education now, stay the course. After all, a key characteristic of successful business starters is persistence and the ability to see things through to completion. See Chapter 3 for more on entrepreneurial attributes.

Coming Up with a Winning Idea

Every business starts with the germ of an idea. The idea may stem from nothing more profound than a feeling that customers are getting a raw deal from their present suppliers.

In this section you can find out about some tried and tested ways to help you come up with a great idea for a new business.

Ranking popular start-up ideas

The government's Small Business Service produces periodic statistics on the types of businesses that people start up.

In terms of the sheer number of start-up enterprises, it would appear that the UK is more a nation of estate agents than of small shopkeepers, as demonstrated in the following list that shows the types of businesses being operated in the UK in 2002.

Smaller firms (under 50 employees) by sector:

- ✔ Estate agencies and related property services 22 per cent
- ✔ Construction 18 per cent
- ✔ Wholesale and retail 14 per cent
- ✔ General social and personal services 11 per cent
- ✔ Manufacturing 9 per cent
- ✔ Transport services 6 per cent
- ✔ Health and social work 6 per cent
- ✔ Agriculture and horticulture 5 per cent
- ✔ Hotels and restaurants 4 per cent
- ✔ Education 3 per cent
- ✔ Financial services 2 per cent

You can take one of two views on entering a particularly popular business sector. Either it represents a great idea you would be mad to resist, or it's a business already awash with competition. In practice, the best view to take is that if others are starting up there is at least a market opportunity. Your task is to thoroughly research the market, using Chapter 5 as your guide.

Going with fast growth

Mintel, the market research and intelligence company, produces an annual report on lifestyle and consumer spending identifying the fastest growing business sectors.

Not surprisingly, home improvements were the biggest growth sector in recent years, followed closely by garden products and health and fitness. But history, as they say, is bunk ... or at least it can be. Fortunately Mintel's study does not merely confine itself to the past, but peers into the future as well. Table 2-1 shows their hot list of business sectors for the coming few years.

Table 2-1	Hot Businesses for the Future
Industry	*Five year percentage growth projection*
Health and fitness	59 per cent
Life assurance	50 per cent
Accident and health	47 per cent
Cinema	43 per cent
Overseas travel	41 per cent
Personal pensions	37 per cent
Private medical insurance	32 per cent
Convenience foods	32 per cent
Fast food	30 per cent
House purchase	28 per cent
Medicines	20 per cent
Domestic and garden help	16 per cent
Cleaning and laundry services	16 per cent

Source: Mintel.

You can use this information to help pick a fast growing business area to start-up in. Getting started with the current flowing strongly in the direction you want to travel makes things easier to begin with.

Mintel argues that spending patterns are changing to reflect adjustments to such factors as longer working hours and the desire to balance work and home life. With four out of every ten adults now living alone and the number of over-sixties about to overtake the number of under-fives for the first time, Mintel certainly seems to have a point!

Spotting a gap in the market

The classic way to identify a great opportunity is to see something that people would buy if only they knew about it. The demand is latent, lying beneath the surface, waiting for someone, you hopefully, to recognise that the market is crying out for something not yet being supplied.

These are some of the ways to go about identifying a market gap.

- ✔ **Timing.** Are customers happy with current opening hours? If you opened later, earlier, or longer would you tap into a new market?

- ✔ **Size.** If you made things a different size, would that appeal to a new market? Anita Roddick of The Body Shop fame found that she could only buy the beauty products she wanted in huge quantities. By breaking down the quantities and sizes of those products she unleashed a huge new demand.

- ✔ **Adapting.** Can you take an idea that is already working in another part of the country or abroad, and bring it to your own market?

- ✔ **Locating.** Do customers have to travel too far to reach their present source of supply? This is a classic route to market for shops, hairdressers and other retail based businesses.

The case example in the 'Filling Needs' sidebar nearby show how one business founder identified such a gap and successfully launched his own business.

Revamping an old idea

A good starting point is to look out for products or services that used to work really well, but have stopped selling. Ask yourself why they seem to have died out and then see if you can see if, and how, that problem could be overcome. Or you could look overseas or into other markets at products and services that have worked well for years in their home markets but have so far failed to penetrate into your area.

Sometimes with little more than a slight adjustment an old idea can be given a whole new lease of life. For example, the Monopoly game, with its emphasis on the universal appeal of London street names, has been launched in France with Parisian *rues* and in Cornwall using towns rather than streets.

Winning on the net

Harold had worked in a car salvage business for five years when he decided he would like to be his own boss. The salvage business consists largely of broken-down cars, rusty puddles of water, and lots of used notes changing hands – an unlikely e-business environment.

His employer had two sites situated strategically at motorway junctions to cover as much of the country as possible. Once recovered from an accident, the insurance company assesses the vehicle – those that are beyond repair are sold for scrap after the spare parts have been salvaged. His employer, or one of his competitors, sold the rest at auction. Historically, all vehicles were held and sold at the company's premises, which effectively acts as a car showroom. Prospective purchasers would visit, view, and buy vehicles in the traditional way, much like a second-hand car dealership. This meant that traders who were located in prime positions had access to both the best buys and the best customers. Some customers from out of the area would visit occasionally, but not often because it was too time-consuming to take a day out browsing on the off chance of finding a good deal.

But for Harold, having a prime site was too expensive a proposition. He had read about e-business and felt that it offered the possibilities of opening up the market so more buyers could be enticed into an auction. Also if the auctions could be conducted online, Harold could use a less expensive site to store the vehicles, as access was less important to buyers, who could have their purchases delivered to them.

Harold bought an off-the-shelf software package which enabled him to come up with a no mess, no fuss Web site. He had all the features of an online auction up and working within six weeks and ran a promotional campaign including advertising in local and trade publications. He e-mailed his network of business contacts to start spreading the news by word-of-mouth.

Over 100 serious buyers attend Harold's online auctions, which compares with a comparable physical auction, which would be lucky to attract fifty. Having a wider and larger audience ensures better prices, too.

Harold started small with just a dozen cars for sale, but quickly built up his stock. He was able to do this because all his vehicles were sold and paid for in a matter of days. His previous employer took up to three months to get his money back after buying in stock.

Using the Internet

Many of the first generation of Internet start-ups had nothing unique about their offer, the mere fact that the business was 'on the net' was thought to be enough. Hardly surprising that most of them went belly-up in no time at all.

All the basic rules of business apply to Internet businesses. You need a competitive edge – something better and different about your product or service that will make you stand out from the crowd.

However, you also need something about the way you use the Internet to add extra value over and above the traditional ways in which your product or service is sold. Online employment agencies, for example, will add value to their Web sites by offering clients and applicants useful information such as interview tips, prevailing wage rates and employment law updates.

But using the Internet to take an old idea and turn it into a new and more cost-efficient business can be a winner. Check out the case example in the nearby 'Winning on the net' sidebar.

Solving customer problems

Sometimes customers are just not having their needs met by existing suppliers. Big firms very often don't have the time to pay attention to all of their customers properly as it is just not economic. Recognising that there are enough people with needs and expectations that are not being met could constitute an opportunity for a new small firm to start up.

TRUE STORIES

Giving readers what they like

For Tim Waterstone the basic concept of his bookshop chain, Waterstone's, came from wandering around Manhattan bookshops on his frequent trips to the US. They were brilliant places: lively and consumer-led with huge stocks, accessible staff, and long opening hours. He felt book buyers in Britain were frustrated at not being able to browse outside normal working hours, as bookshops in Britain stuck pretty much to regular shop opening times. Also, shop assistants who knew about merchandising but little or nothing about books staffed them. This meant that unless a customer knew exactly what book they were looking for, they were unlikely to get much help to find it.

Although Waterstone felt he was on to a winning idea, at the time he did nothing about it as he had a job. But after he was made redundant, a trip to the dole office acted as a catalyst. It was the most horrific experience of his life. Not waiting for his turn, he rushed out and sat in his car. Instead of trying to get a new job, he formulated the Waterstone's concept. High street banks turned him down. He then went to a finance house and struck lucky. He pledged his house and committed £6,000 savings and £10,000 borrowed from his father-in-law, and raised the rest through the Government Small Firms Loan Guarantee Scheme (SFLG). Three months later, the first Waterstone's opened.

Based on a simple store plan an art student sketched out for £25, Waterstone filled the shop with the type of books that appeal to book lovers, not best-seller buyers. Late hours, Sunday trading (where possible) and bonus schemes for his highly literate staff led to dazzling sales. Within eight years, Waterstone's had some 40 shops employing 500 people, with a turnover of £35 million plus. He sold the business out to WH Smith for nearly £60 million and was invited to stay on and run it less than a decade after his dole queue experience.

Start by recalling the occasions when you have had reason to complain about a product or service. You can extend that by canvassing the experiences of friends, relatives, and colleagues. If you spot a recurring complaint, that could be a valuable clue about a problem just waiting to be solved.

Next you could go back over the times when firms you have tried to deal with have put restrictions or barriers in the way of your purchase. If those restrictions seem easy to overcome, and others share your experience, then you could well be on the trail of a new business idea.

Creating inventions and innovations

Inventions and innovations are all too often almost the opposite of either identifying a gap in the market or solving an unsolved problem. Inventors usually start by looking through the other end of the telescope. They find an interesting problem and solve it. There may or may not be a great need for whatever it is they invented.

The Post-it Note is a good example of inventors going out on a limb to satisfy themselves rather than to meet a particular need or even solve a burning problem. The story goes that scientists at 3M, the giant American company, came across an adhesive that failed most of their tests. It had poor adhesion qualities as it could be separated from anything it was stuck to. There was no obvious market but they persevered and pushed the product onto their marketing department, saying the new product had unique properties in that it would stick 'permanently, but temporarily'. The rest, as they say, is history.

Never go down the lonely inventor's route without getting all the help and advice you can get. See Chapter 7 for details of organisations that can smooth your path from the bench to the market. You should also make sure someone else hasn't already grabbed your innovation, and if they haven't that you can put a legal fence around it to keep rustlers out. I deal with copyrights, patents, and the like in Chapter 10.

Marketing other people's ideas

You may not have a business idea of your own, but nevertheless feel strongly that you would like to work for yourself. There is nothing unusual about this approach. Sometimes an event such as redundancy, early retirement, or a financial windfall may prompt you into searching for a business idea.

Business ideas themselves very often come from the knowledge and experience gained in previous jobs, but often take time to come into focus. Usually you need a good flow of ideas before one arrives that appeals to you and that appears viable.

You can trawl for ideas and opportunities any number of ways:

- ✔ **Read business magazines:** Periodicals such as *Business Opportunity Digest* (www.hhc.co.uk/businessopportunitiesdigest) present the bones of a number of ideas each month, as the name suggests.

- ✔ **Scan papers and periodicals:** Almost all papers and many general magazines too, have sections on opportunities and ideas for small businesses.

- ✔ **Browse Web sites:** The Internet is a great source of business ideas. Try Entreprenurs.com (www.entrepreneur.com/bizoppzone), who list hundreds of ideas for new businesses, together with information on start-up costs and suggestions for further research. They also have a series of checklists to help you evaluate a business opportunity to see if it's right for you. Home Working (www.homeworkinguk.com) lists dozens of current business ideas exclusively aimed at the UK market.

When answering advertisements for other people's business ideas, do take precautions to ensure that you are not about to become a victim of someone's fraudulent venture. The Advertising Standards Authority (ASA) warns that not all 'Get rich quick' offers are genuine. These advertisements can lure even quite sophisticated people into bogus schemes. The ASA believes that 'fooling all of the people all of the time' is entirely possible when the product or service is interesting or persuasive enough. Recent complaints include a mail shot saying: 'No more telephone bills for you – ever.' For £7.50, GP Services of Huntingdon offered to disclose details of a technique which had been 'tried, tested and proven', which required no equipment or capital and which was 'currently being used throughout the UK'. The method was just to contact British Telecom's customer services department and ask to be disconnected. Upholding complaints against the firm, the authority ruled that it 'exploited consumers' credulity'.

The ASA (www.asa.org.uk) publishes a quarterly list of complaints that they have or are investigating.

Being better or different

To have any realistic hope of success every business opportunity must pass one crucial test. The idea or the way the business is to operate must be either different from or better than any other business in the same line of work. In other words you need a USP (*Unique Selling Proposition*), or its Internet equivalent, a *Killer Application*.

The thinking behind these two propositions is that your business should have a near unbeatable competitive advantage if your product or service offers something highly desirable that others in the field cannot easily copy.

Something that only you can offer. Dyson's initial USP was the bagless cleaner, and Amazon's was 'one-click' shopping, a system for retaining customer details that made buying online a more painless experience.

The trick with USPs and Killer Applications is not just with developing the idea in the first place, but making it difficult for others to copy it. (See Chapter 9 for ways to protect your USP.)

If neither you nor the product or service you are offering stands out in some way, then why on earth would anyone want to buy from you? Now don't run off with the idea that only new inventions have any hope of success. Often just doing what you say you will do, when you say you will do it, is enough to make you stand out from the crowd.

That was all Tom Farmer did when he founded Kwik-Fit. He put his finger on the main criticisms people had of garages. The experience of getting an exhaust fitted or tyres changed was made seriously unpleasant simply because you couldn't rely on the garage's cost estimate or be sure when your car would be ready. The message always was, ring us at 4 p.m. and we'll let you know.

Farmer's big idea was simply to make promises he could keep; to meet deadlines and keep to estimated costs. And wow, that was enough to build a business that the Ford Motor Company thought was worth the billion pounds they paid for it. I point out ways to test the feasibility of your business idea in Chapter 5.

Banning Bad Reasons to Start a Business

You may have any number of good reasons to start a business, just make sure you're not starting a business for the wrong reasons – some of which I explore in the following sections.

Steering clear of bad assumptions

You need to be sure your business idea isn't a lemon. No one can be sure they have a winning idea on their hands, but you can take some steps to make sure you avoid obvious losers. Much as you want to start a business, it won't serve you if you get in over your head because you start from a bad premise, such as those in the following list:

  ✔ **The market needs educating.** A situation in which the market doesn't yet realise it can't live without your product or service. Many early Internet businesses fitted this description and look what happened to them. If you think customers have to be educated before they'll purchase your product, walk away from the idea and leave it to someone with deep pockets and a long time horizon; they'll need them.

✔ **We'll be first to market.** Gaining 'first mover advantage' is a concept used to justify a headlong rush into a new business. This principle is one of the most enduring in business theory and practice. Entrepreneurs and established giants are always in a race to be first. Research from the 1980s appeared to show that market pioneers have enduring advantages in distribution, product-line breadth, product quality and, especially, market share. Beguiling though the theory of first mover advantage is, it is probably wrong. A thorough review of the research studies that supported this theory, published in the *Sloan Management Review*, found the findings to be flawed. Amongst the many errors in the earlier research, the authors of the Sloan paper revealed that the questions used to gather much of the data were at best ambiguous, and perhaps dangerously so. In fact the only compelling evidence from all the research was that nearly half of all firms pursuing a first to market strategy were fated to fail, whilst those following fairly close behind were more likely to succeed.

✔ **If we can get just one per cent of the market we are onto a winner.** There are no markets with a vacant percentage or two just waiting to be filled. Entering almost any market involves displacing someone else, even if your product is new. Po Na Na, the chain of late night souk bars, failed despite being new and apparently without competitors. If they had captured just one per cent of the dining market instead of 100 per cent of the souk-eating student market they may have survived. But the dining market had Italian, Indian, Greek, and French competitors already in place. This, when combined with the vastly improved range of ready-to-eat meals from the supermarket means that every hundredth of a per cent of this market is fought over bitterly.

Whilst every business begins with an idea, it does not necessarily have to be your own idea. It has to be a viable idea, which means there have to be customers out in the market who want to buy from you. And there have to be enough of them to make you the kind of living you want. It may be an idea you have nursed and investigated for years, or it may be someone else's great idea that is just too big for them to exploit on their own. A franchised business is one example of a business idea that has room for more than one would-be business starter to get involved with. Franchises can be run at many levels ranging from simply taking up a local franchise, through to running a small chain of two to five such franchises covering neighbouring areas.

Avoiding obvious mistakes

Your enthusiasm for starting a business is a valuable asset as long as you don't let it blind you to some practical realities. The following list contains some reasoning to resist:

✔ **Starting in a business sector about which you have little or no previous knowledge or experience.** The grass always looks greener, making business opportunities in distant lands or in technologies with which you have only a passing acquaintance seem disproportionately attractive. Going this route leads to disaster. Success in business depends on superior market knowledge from the outset and sustaining that knowledge in the face of relentless competition.

✔ **Putting in more money than you can afford to lose, especially if you have to pay up front.** You need time to learn how business works. If you have spent all your capital and exhausted your capacity for credit on the first spin of the wheel, then you are more a gambler than an entrepreneur. The true entrepreneur takes only a calculated risk. Freddie Laker, who started the first low-cost no-frills airline, bet everything he could raise on buying more planes than he could afford. To compound the risk he bet against the exchange rate between the pound and the dollar, and lost. You would be wise to learn from Mr Laker's mistake.

✔ **Pitting yourself against established businesses before you're strong enough to resist them.** Laker also broke the third taboo. He took on the big boys on their own ground. He upset the British and American national carriers on their most lucrative routes. There was no way that big entrenched businesses with deep pockets would yield territory to newcomers without a fight to the death. That's not to say Laker's business model was wrong. After all, RyanAir and EasyJet have proved it can work. But those businesses tackled the short haul market to and from new airfields, and, in the case of EasyJet, at least started out with tens of millions of pounds of family money that came from a lifetime in the transportation business.

Recognising that the Economy Matters

The state of the economy in general has an effect both on the propensity of people to start a business and their chances of survival.

In 1989–90 and 1996–97, both periods of strong economic growth in the UK, the quarterly business start-up rate was 130,000 and 140,000 new businesses, respectively. In 1991–92 and 1999–2000, both periods now seen as recession troughs, start-ups ran at around 80,000 per quarter. The business closure rates during the economic troughs were also about 15 per cent higher, so the small business population as a whole shrank.

There are two schools of thought on whether starting a business is more difficult when the economy is contracting – corresponding to whether you subscribe to the belief that a glass is half-full or half-empty. On the one hand there are fewer competitors in the market, as many will have failed, whilst on the other hand those remaining are both seasoned warriors and more desperate to keep what small amount of business there is to themselves.

In real life most people start a business when they want to and not at a favourable stage in the economic cycle. That, however, does not mean that you can just ignore the economy. In much the same way as a prudent sailor pays attention to the state of the tide, you need to see if the general trend of the economy is working with or against you.

If you have a choice of when to start-up it's usually best to have the current working for you rather than against, so choose to open your business during an economic upswing, if possible.

Preparing to Recognise Success

To be truly successful in running your own business you have to both make money and have fun. That's your pay-off for the long hours, the pressure of meeting tough deadlines, and the constant stream of problems that accompany most start-up ventures.

One measure of success for any business is just staying in business. That's not as trite a goal as it sounds, nor is it easily achieved, as you can see by looking at the number of businesses that fail each year.

But survival is not enough. Cash flow, which I talk about in Chapter 8, is the key to survival, but becoming profitable and making a worthwhile use of the assets you employ determines whether staying in business is really worth all your hard work.

Measuring business success

No-one in their right mind sets out to run an unsuccessful business, however that's exactly what millions of business founders end up doing. Answering the following questions can act as a check on your progress to keep you on track to success.

- ✔ Are you meeting your goals and objectives? In Chapter 6, I talk about setting down business goals. Achieving those goals and objectives is both motivational and ultimately the reason you are in business.

- ✔ Are you making enough money? This sounds like a daft question, but it might well be the most important one you ask. The answer comes out of your reply to two subsidiary questions:

  - • Could you do better by investing your time and money elsewhere? If the answer to this question is yes, then it's time to go back to the drawing-board with your business idea.

- Can you make enough money to invest in growing your business? The answer to this question will only become clear when you work out your profit margins, which is covered in Chapter 13. But the evidence that many businesses do not make enough money to re-invest in themselves is pretty evident when you see scruffy run-down premises, and old worn-out equipment and the like.

✔ Can you work to your values? Anita Roddick's Body Shop has a clearly articulated set of values which she and every employee buys into. Every aspect of the business from product and market development down to the recruitment process promotes this value system – if you're not green you do not join. Ms Roddick's philosophy may be a little higher than you feel like going, but values can help guide you and your team when the going gets tough.

Exploring the myth and reality of business survival rates

There is considerable misinformation in circulation about the number of failing businesses. The most persistent and wrong statistic is that 70 per cent (some even quote 90 per cent) of all new businesses fail. The failure rate is high, but not that high, and in any case the term 'failure' itself, if the word is used to mean a business closing down, has a number of subtly different nuances.

Efficiency versus effectiveness

Effectiveness is often described as 'doing the right thing', whereas *efficiency* can be described as 'doing things right'. Doing the right thing has a great deal to do with choosing the right goals to pursue. For example, if your business's mission statement emphasises becoming customer-focused and market-driven, then to be effective you must set goals that encourage everyone who works for you to be in touch with your customers *first* and to be aware of market demands *before* they start, for example designing and creating new products.

Efficiency – doing things right – is concerned more with how well the business is applying resources in pursuit of its goals. To be efficient your employees must have objectives that ensure that the business can achieve its goals of becoming customer-focused and market-driven. Among other things, these objectives should lead to a proper allocation of the research budget among design, product development, and market testing. Resources are always scarce, and no business can afford to squander them.

Successful organisations are not just one or the other – either effective or efficient. The best businesses are both efficient and effective on a consistent basis. These businesses get that way by taking goal setting and the development of clear, measurable objectives seriously in the relentless pursuit of the business's mission.

Studying the statistics

One comprehensive study of all 814,000 firms started up in the US in a particular year followed their destinies for eight years. That research indicated that only 18 per cent were failures, in that the founders had no real say in the final event. A higher proportion (28 per cent) opted for a voluntary closure, usually when they discovered that the business they had started was losing money, or that in some other way the venture was unsatisfactory. Of the remaining 54 per cent, about half sold out or in some other way changed their ownership, perhaps moving from a partnership to trading through a limited company.

Some of these ownership changes were no doubt symptoms of success brought about by business growth, but some would indubitably have been rescue operations in which a stronger competitor saved a drowning firm. Only 28 per cent of all the start-ups in this study survived as independent entities, which after all is the primary goal of most people starting a business.

The European Observatory study carried out a few years later using a smaller sample came to a similar conclusion on survival rates. However this study added one important extra fact: the failure rate in the early years is much higher than in later years and by year five of a firm's life the failure curve is flattening off.

Whilst there are millions of small businesses starting up, many of these survive only a relatively short time. Over half of all independently-owned ventures cease trading within five years of starting up. However, if you can make it for five years, the chances of your business surviving increase dramatically from earlier years. The nearby sidebar 'Studying the statistics' relates the results of a long-term study in the US.

The office of the Official Receiver lists the following causes for business failures:

- ✓ **Insufficient turnover:** This can happen if the fixed costs of your business are too high for the level of sales turnover achieved. See Chapter 6, which shows how to calculate your break-even point and so keep sales levels sufficient to remain profitable.

- ✓ **Poor management and supervision:** You may well know how your business works, but sharing that knowledge and expertise with those who you employ is not always that easy. In Chapter 11 you will see how to manage, control and get the best employees to give of their best.

- ✓ **Lack of proper accounting:** Often business founders are too busy in the start-up phase to keep track of the figures. Invoices and bills are often piled up to await a convenient moment when they can be entered in the accounts. But without timely financial information key signals are missed or wrong decisions made. In Chapter 13 you can read how to keep on top of the numbers.

✔ **Competition:** Without a sound strategy for winning and retaining customers your business will be at the mercy of the competition. In Chapter 10 you can see how to win the battle for the customer.

✔ **Not enough capital:** You, along with most business start-ups, may hope to get going on a shoestring. But you need to be realistic about how much cash is needed to get underway and stay in business until sales volumes build up. In Chapter 8 you will see how to plan the cash flow so you can survive.

✔ **Bad debts:** Unfortunately having great products and services and customers keen to buy them is only half the problem. The other half is making sure those customers pay up on time. One or two late or non-payers can kill off a start-up venture. In Chapter 13 you will see how to make sure you get paid and are not left in the lurch.

✔ **Excessive remuneration to the owners:** Some business owners mistake the cash coming into the business for profit and take that money out as drawings. They forget that periodic bills for tax, VAT, insurance and replacement equipment have to be allowed for, before you can calculate the true profit, and hence what can be safely drawn out. In Chapter 13 you will see how to tell profit from cash and how to allow for future bills.

Chapter 3

Can You Do the Business?

In This Chapter

▶ Understanding if being your own boss is right for you

▶ Taking a skills inventory to identify any gaps

*I*t's fairly clear why governments are so keen to foster entrepreneurship. New businesses create jobs for individuals and increased prosperity for nations, which are both primary goals for any government. If those new firms don't throw people out of work when recessions start to bite, supporting them becomes doubly attractive.

But people, you included, don't start businesses or grow existing ones simply to please politicians or to give their neighbours employment. There are many reasons for considering self-employment. Most people are attracted by the idea of escaping the daily grind of working for someone else and being in charge of their own destiny. But despite the many potential benefits there are real challenges and problems, and self-employment is not a realistic career option for everyone.

The questions you need to ask yourself are: – Can I do it? Am I really the entrepreneurial type? What are my motivations and aims? How do I find the right business for me? This chapter can help you discover the answers to these questions.

Deciding What You Want From a Business

See whether you relate to any of the following most common reasons people give for starting up in business.

- ✔ Being able to make your own decisions
- ✔ Having a business to leave to your children
- ✔ Creating employment for the family
- ✔ Being able to capitalise on specialist skills

- Earning your own money when you want
- Having flexible working hours
- Wanting to take a calculated risk
- Reducing stress and worry
- Having satisfaction of creating something truly of your own
- Being your own boss
- Working without having to rely on others

The two central themes connecting all these reasons seem to revolve around gaining personal satisfaction, which can be seen as making work as much fun as any other aspect of life, and creating wealth, which is essential if an enterprise is going to last any length of time.

Even when your personality fits and your goals are realistic, you have to make sure that the business you're starting is a good fit for your abilities.

The following sections explore each of these reasons in more detail.

Gaining personal satisfaction (or, entrepreneurs just wanna have fun)

No one particularly enjoys being told what to do and where and when to do it. Working for someone else's organisation brings all those disadvantages.

The only person to blame if your job is boring, repetitive, or takes up time that should perhaps be spent with family and friends is yourself.

Another source of personal satisfaction comes from the ability to 'do things my way'. Employees are constantly puzzled and often irritated by the decisions their bosses impose on them. All too often managers in big firms say that they would never spend their own money in the manner they are encouraged or instructed to by the powers that be. Managers and subordinates alike feel constrained by company policy, which seems to set out arbitrary standards for dealing with customers and employees in the same way.

The high failure rate for new businesses would suggest that some people are seduced by the glamour of starting up on their own, when they might be more successful and more contented in some other line of endeavour.

Running your own firm allows you to do things in a way that you think the market, and your employees, believe to be right for the time. Until, of course, you become big and successful yourself!

Taxing wealth in the UK

Business starters have something else going for them today when it comes to creating wealth. Most countries have recognised the value of entrepreneurship and vie with each other to make their business climate more friendly towards small businesses, or in many cases to actually woo entrepreneurs themselves to emigrate to their more favourable regime.

In the UK, for example, the Labour government under Callaghan during the 1970s presided over a punitive income and capital gains tax system that made it all but impossible to create personal wealth. Whilst various Conservative governments whittled these taxes down, by the turn of the century entrepreneurs still faced a 40 per cent capital gains tax when they sold their business, unless they took drastic (and not necessarily reliable) measures such as selling up all their UK assets (including their home) and moving overseas.

The current climate is improving radically. From April 2002 the capital gains tax on the sale of most businesses trading as limited companies that are at least two years old is just 10 per cent. This very low level of capital gains tax is designed to encourage more people to start up businesses, to sell them once they have reached either the level of wealth that they aspire to or their level of managerial and business competence, and then to either start up again or to finance other entrepreneurial ventures.

Making money

Apart from winning the lottery, starting your own business is the only possible way to achieve full financial independence. That is not to say it is not without risks. In truth most people who work for themselves do not become mega rich. But many do and many more become far wealthier than they would probably have become working for someone else.

You can also earn money working at your own pace when you want to and even help your family to make some money too.

Running your own business means taking more risks than you do if you're working for someone else. If the business fails, you could stand to lose far more than your job. If, like most owner managers, you opt for *sole trader status*, that is someone working usually on their own without forming a limited company (find more on business categories in Chapter 4), you could end up personally liable for any business debts incurred. This could mean having to sell up your home and other assets to meet your obligations. In these circumstances, not only will all your hard work have been to no avail, you could end up worse off than when you started. Also winding up a business is far from fun or personally satisfying.

Running a business is never easy and on an hourly wage basis is often less well paid than working for someone else. So why do people set up their own business, and do your aims seem realistic in that context?

If you want to strike out on your own because you think you'll make millions, consider this: on an hourly wage basis, you'll probably make less than you do now. And, if you think, 'well, at least I'll be working for myself', consider for how long. The harsh reality is that most start-ups fail.

I don't want to discourage you, just to apply a reality check. The truth is that running your own business is hard work that often doesn't pay well at first. You have to be OK with those facts in order to have a chance of success.

Assessing Yourself

Business is not just about ideas or about market opportunities. Business is about people too, and at the outset it is mostly about you. You need to make really sure that you have the temperament to run your own business and the expertise and understanding required for the type of business you have in mind to start.

The test at the end of this section requires no revision or preparation. You will find out the truth about yourself and whether or not running a business is a great career option or a potential disaster.

Discovering your entrepreneurial attributes

The business founder is frequently seen as someone who is bursting with new ideas, highly enthusiastic, hyperactive, and insatiably curious. But the more you try to create a clear picture of the typical small business founder, the fuzzier that picture becomes. Many efforts have been made to define the characteristics of people who are best suited to becoming small business founders with limited success. In fact, the most reliable indicator that a person is likely to start a business is whether he or she has a parent or sibling who runs a business – such people are highly likely to start businesses themselves.

That being said, some fairly broad characteristics are generally accepted as being desirable, if not mandatory. Check whether you recognise yourself in the following list of entrepreneurial traits:

- **Totally committed:** You must have complete faith in your business idea. That's the only way that you can convince all the doubters that you are bound to meet on the way. But blind faith is not enough. That commitment has to be backed up with a sound business strategy.

- **Hard working:** Hard work should not be confused with long hours. There will be times when an owner-manager has to put in 18-hour days, but that should not be the norm. But even if you do work long hours and enjoy them, that's fine. Enthusiasts can be very productive. Workaholics, on the other hand, have a negative kind of black, addictive driven quality where outputs (results) become less important than inputs. This type of hard work is counterproductive. Hard work means sticking at a task however difficult until it is completed. It means hitting deadlines even when you are dead-beat. It means doing some things you don't enjoy much to work your way through to the activities that are really what you enjoy most.

✔ **Accepting of uncertainty:** An essential characteristic of someone starting a business is a willingness to make decisions and to take risks. This does not mean gambling on hunches. It means carefully calculating the odds and deciding which risks to take and when to take them.

Managers in big business tend to seek to minimise risk by delaying decisions until every possible fact is known. There is a feeling that to work without all the facts is not prudent or desirable. Entrepreneurs, on the other hand, know that by the time the fog of uncertainty has been completely lifted too many people will be able to spot the opportunity clearly. In point of fact an entrepreneur would usually only be interested in a decision that involved accepting a degree of uncertainty and would welcome, and on occasion even relish, that position.

✔ **Healthy:** Apart from being able to put in long days, the successful small business owner needs to be on-the-spot to manage the firm every day. Owners are the essential lubricant that keeps the wheels of the small business turning. They have to plug any gaps caused either by other people's sickness or because they just can't afford to employ anyone else for that particular job. They themselves cannot afford the luxury of sick leave. Even a week or so's holiday would be viewed as something of a luxury in the early years of a business life.

✔ **Self-disciplined:** The owner manager needs strong personal discipline to keep him or her and the business on the schedule the plan calls for. This is the drumbeat that sets the timing for everything in the firm. Get that wrong and wrong signals are sent to every part of the business, both inside and out.

One of the most common pitfalls for the novice business man or woman is failing to recognise the difference between cash and profit. Cash can make people feel wealthy and if it results in a relaxed attitude to corporate status symbols such as cars and luxury office fittings, then failure is just around the corner.

✔ **Innovative:** Most people recognise innovation as the most distinctive trait of business founders. They tend to tackle the unknown; they do things in new and difficult ways; they weave old ideas into new patterns. But they go beyond innovation itself and carry their concept to market rather than remain in an ivory tower.

✔ **Well-rounded:** Small business founders are rarely geniuses. There are nearly always people in their business who have more competence, in one field, than they could ever aspire to. But they have a wide range of ability and a willingness to turn their hands to anything that has to be done to make the venture succeed. They can usually make the product, market it, and count the money, but above all they have the self-confidence that lets them move comfortably through uncharted waters.

✔ **Driven to succeed:** Business founders need to be results-oriented. Successful people set themselves goals and get pleasure out of trying to achieve them as quickly as possible and then move on to the next goal. This restlessness is very characteristic.

Taking a skills and knowledge inventory

The self-evaluation questions in this section probe only those areas that you can control or affect. Do the evaluation and get one or two people who know you well to rate you too.

A high score is not a guarantee of success and a poor score does not necessarily bode failure. But the combination of answers should throw up some things to consider carefully before taking the plunge.

If the statement is rarely true, score 1; if usually true, score 2; and if nearly always true, score 3.

1. I know my personal and business objectives.
2. I get tasks accomplished quickly.
3. I can change direction quickly if market conditions alter.
4. I enjoy being responsible for getting things done.
5. I like working alone and making my own decisions.
6. Risky situations don't alarm me.
7. I can face uncertainty easily.
8. I can sell my business ideas and myself.
9. I haven't had a day off sick for years.
10. I can set my own goals and targets and then get on with achieving them.
11. My family is right behind me in this venture – and they know it will mean long hours and hard work.
12. I welcome criticism – there is always something useful to learn from others.
13. I can pick the right people to work for me.
14. I am energetic and enthusiastic.
15. I don't waste time.

A score of 30 plus is good; 20–30 is fair; below 20 is poor. A high score won't guarantee success but a low one should cause a major re-think.

Working out a business idea that's right for you

Take some time to do a simple exercise that can help you decide what type of business is a good match with your abilities. Take a sheet of paper and draw up two columns. In the left-hand column, list all your hobbies, interests, and skills. In the right-hand column, translate those interests into possible business ideas. Table 3-1 shows an example of such a list.

Table 3-1	Matching a Business Idea to Your Skills
Interest/skills	*Business ideas*
Cars	car dealer/repair garage/home tuning service
Cooking	restaurant/home catering service/bakery shop providing produce for freezer outlets
Gardening	supplier of produce to flower or vegetable shop/running a nursery/running a garden centre/landscape design
Using a computer	typing authors' manuscripts from home/typing back-up service for busy local companies/running a secretarial agency/web design/book-keeping service

Having done this exercise, balance the possibilities against the criteria important to you in starting a business.

Figuring out what you're willing to invest

I'm not just talking about money here. How much are you willing to invest of your time, your interest, and your education, as well as your (and your investors') money?

Spending time

How much time are you willing to devote to your business? That may sound a basic enough question, but different business done in different ways can have quite different time profiles. One business starter I know started a French bakery in London. He was determined to make his own croissants and did so for the first three months. But making his own bread meant starting work at 4 a.m. As he didn't close until city workers passed his door on their way home, by the time he cleaned up and took stock, he had worked a fifteen-hour day. But he still had the books to do, orders to place and plans to prepare. He eventually settled for a ten-hour day, which meant he had to buy in croissants already baked.

Furthering your education

You may have identified a market opportunity that requires skills over and above those that you currently have. There may, for example, be a gap in the market for Teaching English as a Foreign Language (TEFL), but to do so requires a month of intensive study plus a £1,000 course fee.

Doing the TEFL certificate may involve you in more skill upgrading than you want to commit to, at the outset at least. So either you need to find customers who don't require you to have that qualification, or you need to think about a less educationally challenging business.

Keeping things interesting

If you want to start a restaurant, and have never worked in one, get a job in one. That's the best way to find out if you would like a particular type of work. You may find that a restaurant looks very different from behind the chair as opposed to on it. Some businesses are inherently repetitive, with activities that follow a predictable pattern. If that suits you fine, but if not then perhaps you need to consider a business venture with a shifting range of tasks.

Weighting your preferences

After you have an idea of some of the businesses you may want to start, you can rank those businesses according to how closely they match what you want from starting a business.

Go through the standards you want your business to meet and assign a weight between 1 and 5 to each on a range from not important at all to absolutely must have. Next, list your possible business opportunities and measure them against the graded criteria.

Table 3-2 shows a sample ranking for Jane Clark, an imaginary ex-secretary with school-aged children, who needs work because her husband has been made redundant and is busy looking for another job. Jane isn't in a position to raise much capital, and she wants her hours to coincide with those of her children. She wants to run her own show and she wants to enjoy what she does. The criteria she selected were:

Table 3-2	**Weighing Up the Factors**
Criteria	*Weighting*
Minimal capital required	5
Possibility to work hours that suit lifestyle	5
No need to learn new skills	4
Minimal paperwork	3
Work satisfaction	2
Opportunity to meet interesting people	1

Since minimal capital was a very important criterion for Jane she gave it a weight of five, whereas the opportunity to meet interesting people, being far less important to her, was only weighted one.

Jane then gave each of her three business ideas a rating, in points (out of five) against these criteria. A secretarial agency needed capital to start so was given only one point. Back-up typing needed hardly any money and was allocated five points.

Her worked-out chart is shown in Table 3-3.

Table 3-3		**Scoring Alternatives**					
		Secretarial agency		*Back-up typing*		*Authors' manuscripts*	
	Weighting factor	Points	Score	Points	Score	Points	Score
Criteria							
Minimal capital	5 _	1	= 5	5	25	4	20
Flexible hours	5 _	1	= 5	3	15	5	25
No new skills	4 _	2	= 8	5	20	5	20
Work satisfaction	3 _	4	= 12	1	3	3	9
Minimal paperwork	2 _	0	= 0	4	8	5	10
Meeting people	1 _	4	= 4	3	3	4	4
Total score			34		74		88

The weighting factor and the rating point multiplied together give a score for each business idea. The highest score indicates the business that best meets Jane's criteria. In this case, typing authors' manuscripts scored over back-up typing since Jane could do it exactly when it suited her.

Chapter 4
Structuring Your Business

In This Chapter

▶ Finding the right form

▶ Exploring working on your own

▶ Going into partnership with others

▶ Starting a larger company

*W*hen you start your business you will have to make a decision more or less from the outset on the legal structure you will use to trade. Whilst that is an important decision luckily it is not an irrevocable one. You can change structures, though not without some cost and paperwork, as your business grows.

The simplest structure is to make all the business decisions yourself and take all the risk personally. You don't have to shoulder all the responsibilities when you start a business, though most people initially do so. It may be great doing everything your way, at last, after the frustrations of working for someone else. But it can be lonely, or even scary with no one to talk over the day-to-day problems and share the responsibility of decision-making with.

If your business requires substantial investment, or involves other people who will have a more or less equal hand in the venture alongside you then your decision as to the legal structure of the business is a bit more complicated. In this chapter you will see all the important factors to consider when deciding on the legal structure for your business.

Choosing the Right Structure

There are different legal frameworks for the ownership of a business and not all are equally appropriate for everyone.

Most small businesses in the UK trade as sole proprietorships, as the figures in Table 4-1 show. However, if the larger businesses are included, then you can see that limited companies and partnerships are very popular ways to structure a business.

Table 4-1	Popular Business Structures	
	All businesses	*Businesses with fewer than 50 employees*
Sole proprietorships	578,505	189,345
Partnerships	358,330	64,550
Limited companies	657,215	94,405

One of the many factors you have to consider when deciding on the legal structure of your business is the tax implications, and I talk about how to manage your tax position in Chapter 14.

But there may be even more compelling reasons than tax to choose one structure over another. Not all sources of finance are open to every type of business. When you know how much money you need either to start up or to grow a business and what that money is needed for, you're in a better position to make an informed choice as to the best way to structure your business. If you need to raise large sums of money from the outset for research and development, for example, then a limited company may be your only realistic option, with its access to risk capital. If you are nervous of embroiling your finances with other people's, a partnership isn't an attractive option.

In general, the more money required and the more risky the venture, the more likely it is that a limited company is the appropriate structure.

The good news is that you can change your legal structure at more or less any time. Even if you go the full distance and form a company and get it listed on the stock exchange you can de-list and go private. Richard Branson (Virgin) and Alan Sugar (Amstrad) have both done this. That's not to say it's easy to dissolve partnerships or shut down companies, but it can be done.

Both your accountant and lawyer can help you with choosing your legal form. The types of business structures and some of their advantages and disadvantages are shown in Table 4-2.

Table 4-2	Pros and Cons of Various Organisational Structures	
Type of entity	*Main advantages*	*Main drawbacks*
Sole proprietorship	Simple and inexpensive to create and operate.	Owner personally liable for business debts.
	Profit or loss reported on owner's personal tax return.	No access to outside capital.
		Life of business restricted to life of owner.
		Limited potential for value creation.
General partnership	Simple and inexpensive to create and operate.	Partners personally liable for business debts.
	Partners' share of profit or loss reported on personal tax returns.	The business is dissolved when a partner dies.
	Potential for some value creation.	Only partners can raise out side capital.
Limited Partnership	Non-managing partners have limited personal liability for business debts.	General partners personally liable for business debts.
	General partners can raise cash without involving outside investors in management of business.	More expensive to create than general partnership.
	Wider access to outside capital than for a sole proprietor.	Life of business restricted to life of first partner to die.
	Potential for some value creation.	
Limited company	Owners have limited personal liability for business debts.	More expensive to create and run than partnership or sole proprietorship.
	Some benefits (such as pensions) can be deducted as a business expense.	Owners must meet legal requirements for stock registration, account filing, and paperwork.

(continued)

Table 4-2 *(continued)*

Type of entity	Main advantages	Main drawbacks
	Owners can share out the profit and could end up, paying less overall.	
	Access to full range of outside capital.	
	Business can live on after founder's death.	
	Potential for value creation.	
	Separate taxable entity.	
Co-operative	Owners have limited personal liability for business debts.	More expensive to create than a sole proprietorship.
	Owners' share of corporate profit or loss reported on personal tax returns.	requirements for account filing, registration, and paperwork.
	Owners can use corporate loss to offset income from other sources.	Restricted access to outside capital.
		Limited potential for value creation.

Going into Business by Yourself

You may want to develop your own unique ideas for a product or service, and if so setting up your own business from the drawing board may be your only option. You may want to start a home-based business that you can run on your time. You may want to start a business because you want to do things the right way, after working for an employer who goes about things in the wrong way.

It is much easier to do things your own way if you're working alone, rather than, say, buying someone else's business that already has its routines and working practices established.

Advantages

Working for and by yourself has several things going for it:

- ✔ It may be possible to start the business in your spare time. This will allow you to gain more confidence in the future success of your proposed venture before either giving up your job or pumping your life savings into the venture.

- ✔ If you have limited money to invest in your new venture, you may not need to spend it all at the start of the project. This also means that if things do start to go wrong, it will be easier to restrict the losses.

- ✔ Starting a business is not just about money. Setting up and running a successful business has the potential to give you a feeling of personal achievement which may not be there to quite the same extent if you buy someone else's business, for example.

Disadvantages

Going it alone isn't all fun and games. Some of the disadvantages are:

- ✔ Your business will take time to grow. It may not be able to support your current personal financial obligations for many months or years.

- ✔ There is a lot of one-off administration involved in setting up a new business such as registering for VAT and PAYE, getting business stationery, setting up phone, fax, and Internet connections at your trading premises, and registering your business name, in addition to actually trading.

  These tasks can be very time-consuming and frustrating in the short term, and very costly in the long run if you get them wrong. Unfortunately, these tasks are often not easily delegated and can be expensive if you get other people to do them. If you buy a business or take up a franchise, these basic administrative tasks should have already been dealt with.

- ✔ There is no one to bounce ideas off, or to share responsibility with when things go wrong.

- ✔ As a result of this perceived riskiness it is generally more difficult to borrow money to fund a start-up than to borrow to invest in an established profitable business.

Settling on sole trader status

The vast majority of new businesses are essentially one-man (or woman) bands. As such they are free to choose the simplest legal structure, known by terms such as sole trader or sole proprietor. This structure has the merit of being relatively formality free and having few rules about the records you have to keep. As a sole proprietor you don't have to have your accounts audited or file financial information on your business.

As a sole trader there is no legal distinction between you and your business. Your business is one of your personal assets, just as your house or car is. It follows from this that if your business should fail your creditors have a right not only to the assets of the business, but also to your personal assets, subject only to the provisions of local bankruptcy rules (these often allow you to keep only a few absolutely basic essentials for yourself and family). It may be possible to avoid the worst of these consequences by distancing your assets (see Chapter 12 for how to deal with business failure).

The capital to start and run the business must come from you, or from loans. In return for these drawbacks you can have the pleasure of being your own boss immediately, subject only to declaring your profits on your tax return and if necessary applying for a trade license. (In practice you would be wise to take professional advice before starting up.)

Often people who start up on their own do not have enough money to buy into an existing operation, so the do-it-yourself approach is the only alternative.

Building Up to Network Marketing

Network marketing, multilevel marketing (MLM), and *referral marketing* are the names used to describe selling methods designed to replace the retail outlet as a route to market for certain products. Although referral marketing has been around since the early part of the last century, for many people it is still unfamiliar territory.

Network marketing is one way of starting a profitable, full-time business with little or no investment. It is also a method of starting a second or part-time business to run alongside your existing business or career. It is also one of the fastest growing business sectors. Industry turnover has grown from £700 million ten years ago to £1,700 million today.

In most cases network marketing involves selling a product or service produced and supplied by a parent company. You take on the responsibilities of selling the products and introducing other people to the company. You get paid commission on the products/services you sell yourself and a smaller commission on the products/services sold by the people you have introduced to the company. In addition to this, you often get a percentage commission based on the sales of the people introduced to the company by the people you introduced to the company, and on and on.

Advocates of network marketing maintain that, when given identical products, the one sold face to face (without the cost of maintaining a shop and paying employees and paying insurance) is less expensive than the same product sold in a store. Additionally, network marketing fans believe that it makes more sense to buy a product from someone you know and trust than from a shop assistant behind a retail counter. There are a wide variety of good quality network marketing companies from all over the world to choose from. They offer products and services from a wide range of industries: health, telecommunications, household products, technology, e-commerce, adult industry etc. Household names include: Amway, Avon, Betterware, Herbalife, Kleeneze, and Mary Kay Cosmetics. It would be advisable to choose a product or service that you are interested in because, when it comes to sales, nothing beats enthusiasm and confidence in the product.

Evaluating the pros and cons

Like any other type of business, network marketing has its upside and its downside. Some of the positives are:

- Little or no start-up costs: With most companies the investment in a business kit and a range of sample products rarely exceeds £100. The law governing MLM does not allow an investment of more than £200 in the first seven days.

- The potential to build a substantial business: By recruiting more and more people to join the company and by those people recruiting more people, your percentages of their sales grows and grows. And, of course, you're still selling at a high rate yourself.

- A proven business formula: Network marketing has been around since the early 1900s.

- Low risk: Unlike a brand new business idea that you may have uncovered, MLM products and services are usually tried and tested business concepts. That doesn't mean they can't fail, but if you follow the rules you are less likely to hit the buffers than you would on your own.

- A great deal of support and advice is often given: The parent company and the person who brought you into the company have a vested interest in helping you succeed because the more you sell, the more money they make.

- Flexible hours: You can sell on a full-time or part-time basis during the hours that suit you and your customers.

- Highly expandable: You don't have territory restrictions like conventional salespeople and with e-commerce capabilities, most parent companies can supply to many countries.

- Business can be run from your own home.

- Builds your confidence and increases your communication skills.

Again, as with any business, network marketing isn't all good. The following lists some of the disadvantages:

- ✔ There may be restrictions on your business practices, for example recruitment, advertising etc.

- ✔ Your business heavily relies on the success of one parent company and its ability to deliver its products/services on time.

- ✔ You may not feel comfortable selling to your friends or to strangers.

- ✔ Even the best network marketing companies may be thought of as pyramid schemes – see the next section.

One characteristic of network marketing that leads to its all-too-frequent excesses is that everyone can get in for very little money up front; thus, everyone does get in.

Distinguishing pyramids from network marketing

Pyramid selling schemes are sometimes disguised to look like network marketing schemes but commonly have the following characteristics:

- ✔ They encourage participants to make substantial investments in stocks of goods, by offering rewards to participants for getting others to do the same.

- ✔ They make little reference to direct selling, and the need to achieve consumer sales. Instead, they imply that the main source of rewards comes from getting others to make substantial initial investments.

- ✔ They do not offer contracts to participants, nor cancellation rights or the opportunity to buy back unsold goods – all of which are required under UK law.

Be sceptical of multilevel marketing systems, especially if the company promises outrageous incomes for very little work. Also, be wary if the company is a lot more interested in telling you how to sign up new recruits than how to sell its products. That's a red flag for a pyramid scheme.

Legitimate network marketing companies put as much emphasis, if not more, on the products or services they offer, and they don't claim that you'll make a killing without working hard to find new customers. Although not shy about advertising the big earnings its successful salespeople make, legitimate companies don't hype the income potential.

Quality network marketing companies make sense for people who really believe in a particular product and want to sell it but don't want to, or can't, tie up a lot of money buying a franchise or other business, or don't have a great idea of their own. Just remember to check out the network company using trade associations such as the Direct Selling Association (www.dsa.org.uk). You won't get rich in a hurry, or probably ever, but you probably won't lose your shirt either.

Working with a Limited Number of Other People

Unless you are the self-contained type, who prefers going it alone, you will have to work alongside other people to get your business going. Not just suppliers or employees and bankers and the like. Everyone in business has to do that to a greater or lesser extent.

The upside of going into business with others is that you have someone on your side to talk to when the going gets tough, and it will do from time to time. Two heads are very often better than one. Also you will have the advantage of extra physical and mental resources, when they matter most, from the very outset.

However it is not a one-sided equation, unfortunately. With other people come other points of view, other agendas and the opportunity to disagree, argue, and to misunderstand.

Taking on an existing business

If you don't have a solid business idea of your own, with a clear vision and strategy, you could consider using someone else's wholly formed business. You could think of such ventures as virtually a business-in-a-box. Just buy it, take it home, open it up, and start trading. Of course it's not always quite that easy, but in broad principle that is what network marketing, franchising, and co-operative ventures are all about.

Forming a partnership

A *partnership* is effectively a collection of sole traders or proprietors. There are very few restrictions to setting up in business with another person (or persons) in partnership, and several definite advantages.

✔ Pooling your resources means you have more capital.

✔ You bring several sets of skills to the business, hopefully, instead of just one.

✔ If one of you is ill or disabled, the business can still carry on.

Partnerships are a common structure used by people who started out on their own, but want to expand.

The legal regulations governing partnerships in essence assume that competent businesspeople should know what they are doing. The law merely provides a framework of agreement, which applies 'in the absence of agreement to the contrary'. It follows from this that many partnerships are entered into without legal formalities and sometimes without the parties themselves being aware that they have entered a partnership! Just giving the impression that you are partners may be enough to create an implied partnership under the law.

In the absence of an agreement to the contrary these rules apply to partnerships:

✔ All partners contribute capital equally.

✔ All partners share profits and losses equally.

✔ No partner shall have interest paid on his or her capital.

✔ No partner shall be paid a salary.

✔ All partners have an equal say in the management of the business.

It is unlikely that all these provisions will suit you, so you would be well advised to get a partnership agreement drawn up in writing before opening for business.

Partnerships have three serious financial drawbacks that merit particular attention:

✔ If one partner makes a business mistake, perhaps by signing a disastrous contract without your knowledge or consent, every member of the partnership must shoulder the consequences. Under these circumstances your personal assets could be taken to pay the creditors even though the mistake was no fault of your own.

✔ If a partner faces personal bankruptcy, for whatever reason, their creditors can seize their share of the partnership. As a private individual you are not liable for your partner's private debts, but having to buy them out of the partnership at short notice rather than gain unwanted replacements could put you and the business in financial jeopardy.

✔ If one partner wants to quit the partnership, that partner will want to take the value of their part of the business with them. The remaining partner(s) will, in effect, have to buy out the partner that is leaving.

The agreement you have on setting up the business should specify the procedure and how to value the leaver's share, otherwise resolving the situation will be costly. Several options for addressing this issue exist. A few are:

- The traditional route to value the leaver's share is to ask an independent accountant. This is rarely cost-effective. The valuation costs money and worst of all it is not definite and consequently there is room for argument.

- Another way is to establish a formula, say eight times the last audited pre-tax profits, for example. This approach is simple but difficult to get right. A fast-growing business is undervalued by a formula using historic data unless the multiple is high; a high multiple may overvalue 'hope' or goodwill thus unreasonably profiting the leaver.

The multiplier can be arrived at by looking up the performance of a business, similar to the one in question that is listed on a stock market. Such a business will have a _P/E ratio_ published in both its accounts and the financial sections of national newspapers. The P/E ratio is calculated by dividing the share price into the amount of profit earned for each share. For example, if a business makes £100,000 profit and has 1000 shares, the profit per share is £100. If the share price of that company is £10, then its P/E ratio is 10 (100/10). So much for the science, now for the art. As any business quoted on a stock market is big and its shares are liquid, that is easy to buy and sell, it is considered more valuable than a small private company. In any event private firms don't have a published share price. To allow for that it is usual to discount the P/E ratio by a third to compensate. So this example a private firm in the same line of work as the one listed on a stock market would be given a P/E of approximately seven ($2/3 \times 10$).

- Under a third option, the assets of the business can be valued and that could be used as a basis for dividing the spoils.

Even death may not release you from partnership obligations and in some circumstances your estate can remain liable for the partnerships' obligations. Unless you take public leave of your partnership by notifying your business contacts, and legally bringing your partnership to an end, you remain liable indefinitely.

Looking at limited partnerships

One option that can reduce the more painful consequences of entering a partnership is to have your involvement registered as a limited partnership. A limited partnership is very different from a general partnership. It is a legal animal that, in certain circumstances, combines the best attributes of a partnership and a corporation.

Going into partnership

Jane, Stephanie, and Anne, librarians all, planned to open an electronic information searching business with an emphasis on information of special interest to women. They would hold on to their daytime jobs until they could determine if their new business could support all three.

At a planning meeting to discuss buying personal computers and modems, Jane said she wanted the business to be run as professionally as possible, which to her meant promptly incorporating. The discussion about equipment was put off, and the three women tried to decide how to organise the legal structure of their business. After several frustrating hours, they agreed to continue the discussion later and to do some research about the organisational options in the meantime.

Before the next meeting, Jane conferred with a small business adviser who suggested that the women refocus their energy on the computers and modems and getting their business operating, keeping its legal structure as simple as possible. One good way to do this, she suggested, was to form a partnership, using a written partnership agreement. Each partner would contribute equally to buy equipment and share the workload fairly. Profits would be divided equally.

Later, if the business succeeded and grew, it might make sense to incorporate and consider other issues, like a health plan, pensions, and other benefits. But for now, real professionalism meant getting on with the job, not consuming time and money forming an unneeded corporate entity.

A limited partnership works like this: there must be one or more general partners with the same basic rights and responsibilities (including unlimited liability) as in any general partnership, and one or more limited partners who are usually passive investors. The big difference between a general partner and a limited partner is that the limited partner isn't personally liable for debts of the partnership. The most a limited partner can lose is the amount that he or she:

✔ Paid or agreed to pay into the partnership as a capital contribution; or

✔ Received from the partnership after it became insolvent.

To keep this limited liability, with very few exceptions a limited partner may not participate in the management of the business. A limited partner who becomes actively involved in the management of the business risks losing immunity from personal liability and having the same legal exposure as a general partner.

The advantage of a limited partnership as a business structure is that it provides a way for business owners to raise money (from the limited partners) without having to either take in new partners who will be active in the business, or having to form a limited company. Often, a general partnership that's been operating for years creates a limited partnership to finance expansion.

Checking out co-operatives

If making money is much lower on your list of priorities for starting up in business than being involved in the decisions of an ethical enterprise, then joining a co-operative or starting your own is an idea worth exploring.

A *co-operative* is an autonomous association of persons united voluntarily to meet their common economic, social, and cultural needs and aspirations through a jointly owned and democratically controlled enterprise.

You must have at least seven members at the outset, though they do not all have to be full-time workers at first.

Like a limited company, a registered co-operative has limited liability for its members and must file annual accounts.

Although the most visible co-operatives are the high street shops and supermarkets, pretty well any type of business can operate as a co-operative.

There are over 1,500 co-operatives in the UK, with over 40,000 people working in them. In the US there are 47,000 co-operatives, generating over $100 billion in sales output. There are co-ops that sell bicycles, furniture, camping equipment, appliances, carpeting, clothing, handicrafts, and books. There are co-operative wholesalers like those in the hardware, grocery, and natural foods businesses. There are co-operatives that disseminate news and co-operatives for artists. There are co-operative electric and telephone utilities. There are co-operatively managed banks, credit unions, and community development corporations. There are thousands of farm co-ops, along with co-ops that provide financing to farm co-ops. There are subscriber-owned cable TV systems and parent-run day-care centres. There are co-operatively organised employee-owned companies, co-operative purchasing groups for fast food franchises, and, of course, various kinds of co-operative housing.

There are co-ops that provide healthcare, such as health maintenance organisations and community health clinics. There are co-operative insurance companies. There are co-operative food stores, food-buying clubs, and discount warehouses. You get the idea. There are co-ops in virtually every area of business you could possibly imagine.

If you choose to form a co-operative, you can pay from £90 to register with the Chief Registrar of Friendly Societies. Not all co-operatives bother to register as it is not mandatory, but if you don't register, your co-operative is regarded in law as a partnership with unlimited liability.

Finding Your Way to Franchising

Franchising can be a good first step into self-employment for those with business experience but no actual experience of running a business – often the case with those who are looking for something to do following a corporate career.

Franchising is a marketing technique used to improve and expand the distribution of a product or service. The franchiser supplies the product or teaches the service to you, the franchisee, who in turn sells it to the public. In return for this, you pay a fee and a continuing royalty, based usually on turnover. You may also be required to buy materials or ingredients from the franchiser, which gives them an additional income stream. The advantage to you is a relatively safe and quick way of getting into business for yourself, but with the support and advice of an experienced organisation close at hand.

The franchising company can expand its distribution with minimum strain on its own capital and have the services of a highly motivated team of owner managers. Franchising is not a path to great riches, nor is it for the truly independent spirit, as policy and profits will still come from on high.

Franchising in the UK and Europe is a relatively young industry. The whole franchise concept spread only slowly in the decades after the first really major British franchise, Wimpy, got going in the mid-1950s. Since then, however, development has been very rapid; more rapid, perhaps, than most people realise. Now there are few sectors of the economy be it babysitting, fast food, or knitwear that don't have a franchise operation working in them.

According to the latest annual franchise survey produced by the National Westminster Bank and the British Franchise Association (www.british-franchise.org), in 2003 the number of franchised units rose to 35,200, representing big overall growth since the beginning of the 1990s. The turnover of the industry in 2003 – up by 20 per cent to £8.9 billion – is well over the rise in inflation over this period. The number of people employed in it, directly and indirectly, is estimated to be 316,900. London and the Southeast, the Southwest, Northwest, West and East Midlands are the main regions for franchising activity. London and the Southeast alone account for 29 per cent of all franchise units. Table 4-3 shows the sectors that are most popular for franchising, with the number of franchise chains operating in each sector.

Table 4-3	Popular Franchise Areas
Sector	*Number of franchises*
Business and communication services	148
Hotel and catering	100
Personal services	111
Property services	114
Store retailing	94
Transport and vehicle services	68

Although franchising eliminates some of the more costly and at times disastrous bumps in the learning curve of working for yourself, it is not an easy way to riches. Whilst 90 per cent of franchisees report they are trading profitably, the number of those claiming high levels of profitability remains low at under 10 per cent.

Wild claims are made about how much safer a franchise is when compared to a conventional start-up. Whilst it is true that the long-established big franchise chains are relatively safe, though a few big names have got into trouble, the smaller and newer ones are as vulnerable as any other venture in their early formative years.

Looking at franchise types

Franchises can be clustered under these three main headings:

- **Job franchises:** This is where you are buying the rights to operate what is essentially a one-person business, such as plumbing, building services or a recruitment business. These require a financial investment in the £7,000–£20,000 range and could be described as 'buying a job'. However, with back-up in the way of training, customer leads, advertising etc. from the franchiser these are suitable for someone with little capital but having a specific area of expertise or willing to be trained in it such as cleaning or vehicle repair and maintenance services.

- **Business franchises:** These businesses typically have premises and employees. These require a higher level of investment, typically in the range of £20,000–£120,000 in stock, equipment, and premises. There are large numbers of business franchises available in such areas as retailing, food services, and business services such as high street printing shops.

✔ **Investment franchises:** Here, you are talking about initial investments of over £120,000. Hotels and some of the larger and more established fast food outlets come into the top range of this category at around £750,000.The essence of this type of franchise is that the franchisee is unlikely to work in the business day to day. People operating investment franchises typically operate several similar franchises in nearby areas.

Defining a franchise

A franchise agreement is just like any business contract in that it sets out what each party is expected to do and what could happen if they don't.

The main ingredients of the franchise agreement are:

✔ Permission to use a business name and so be associated with that bigger enterprise

✔ The right for the franchiser to set and enforce business and product standards, such as the use of ingredients, cooking processes, opening times, staff uniforms and so forth

✔ An obligation for the franchiser to provide help, training and guidance in all aspects of operating the business

✔ A definition of the way in which the rights to operate the franchise are to be paid for, for example, royalties on sales, initial purchase fee, marketing levy, mark-up on goods and services provided and so forth.

The British Franchise Association (BFA) agreement, though helpful, does not cover everything you need to know to make a sound decision. For example though running a pilot scheme is a condition of membership of the BFA, that in itself is no guarantee that the business model is fully tried and tested. Neither does the BFA standard contract mention that the business, once set up, is the property of the franchisee, nor does it warn him or her of the degree of control that they might be subjected to from the franchisor. Further, it gives no indication of the extent of the back-up services that the franchisee might reasonably expect to get for his money. In other words, the BFA definition is not a sufficient standard against which to check the franchise contract.

The British Franchise Association expects its members to follow its code of practice, and you can find out more on their website: www.british-franchise.org.

Whilst membership of the BFA and adhering to a code of practice is helpful it is not a guarantee of success for your franchise. You should be looking for a shortlist of as many as six opportunities, acquiring as much advice as you can get from franchisers, from franchisees, from your bank, and from other professional advisers.

Before deciding on a particular franchise it is essential that you consult your legal and financial advisers, as well as ask the franchiser some very searching questions:

- ✔ Has the franchiser operated at least one unit for a year or so as a pilot unit in the UK? This is an essential first step before selling franchises to third parties. Otherwise, how can they really know all the problems, and so put you on the right track?

- ✔ What training and support is included in the *franchise package,* the name given to the start-up kit provided by the franchiser? This package should extend to support staff over the launch period and give you access to back-up advice.

- ✔ How substantial is the franchise company? Ask to see the balance sheet (take it to your accountant if you cannot understand it). Ask for the track record of the directors (including their other directorships).

Sometimes a major clearing bank offers financial support to buy a particular franchise, which is an encouraging sign that the company is in good financial health. At least you know the concept is tried and tested and to some extent the business is reputable. However, as with everything to do with starting up a business, the buck stops with you.

Founding a Larger Company

If your business looks like it will need a substantial amount of money from the outset and will be taking on the risk of customers owing money, as with any manufacturing venture, then the legal structures looked at so far may not be right for you.

In this section you can find out about the advantages and disadvantages of going for a limited company, or buying out a company already in business.

Opting for a limited company

As the name suggests, in this form of business your liability is limited to the amount you contribute by way of share capital.

Limiting liability through the ages

The concept of limited liability, where the shareholders are not liable in the last resort for the debts of their business, can be traced back to the Romans. However it was rarely used, only being granted as a special favour to friends by those in power.

Some two thousand years later the idea was revived when in 1811 New York State brought in a general limited liability law for manufacturing companies. Most American states followed suit and eventually Britain caught up in 1854. Most countries have a legal structure incorporating the concept of limited liability.

Two shareholders, one of whom must be a director, can form a limited company. A company secretary must also be appointed, who can be a shareholder, director, or an outside person such as an accountant or lawyer.

The company can be bought 'off the shelf' from a registration agent, then adapted to suit your own purposes. This will involve changing the name, shareholders, and articles of association and take a couple of weeks to arrange. Alternatively, you can form your own company.

A limited company has a legal identity of its own, separate from the people who own or run it. This means that, in the event of failure, creditors' claims are restricted to the assets of the company. The shareholders of the business are not liable as individuals for the business debts beyond the paid-up value of their shares. This applies even if the shareholders are working directors, unless of course the company has been trading fraudulently. In practice, the ability to limit liability is restricted these days as most lenders, including the banks, often insist on personal guarantees from the directors. Other advantages include the freedom to raise capital by selling shares.

Disadvantages include the legal requirement for the company's accounts to be audited and filed for public inspection.

A *Ltd company* can be started with, say, an authorised share capital of £1,000. This is then divided into 1,000 £1 shares. You can then issue as few or as many of the shares as you want. As long as the shares you have issued are paid for in full, if the company liquidates, the shareholders have no further liabilities. If the shares have not been paid for, the shareholders are liable for the value; for example, if they have 100 £1 shares they only are liable for £100.

A *PLC* (Public Limited Company) is a public company and may be listed on the Stock Exchange. Before a PLC can start to trade it must have at least £50,000 of shares issued and at least 25 per cent of the value must have been paid for. A PLC company has a better status due to its larger capital.

A company must have on its notepaper the company's full name, the address of its registered office, the fact that it's registered in England or Scotland etc., and the company number. However, the names of the directors need not be stated but, if any are (other than as signatory), all must be stated.

When a company is first registered it must send to Companies House, (www.companies-house.org.uk), the place where all business details and accounts are kept, a copy of its memorandum and articles of association and form 10, which contains the address of the company's registered office and details of its directors and company secretary. The directors' details are: current names, any former names, date of birth, usual residential address (currently under review), occupation, nationality, and other directorships. For the secretary only the names and address are required.

Buying out a business

Buying out an existing business is particularly well suited to people who have extensive experience of general business management but lack detailed technical or product knowledge.

When you buy an established business, you not only pay for the basic assets of the business, but also the accumulated time and effort that the previous owner spent growing the business to its present state. This extra asset can be thought of as *goodwill*. The better the business, the more the 'goodwill' will cost you.

Advantages of buying a business include:

- You acquire some of the experience and expertise you do not have. It is much easier, and almost invariably less costly, to learn from the mistakes that other people have made in the past, rather than making all these mistakes yourself.

- You gain both access to your potential customers and the credibility of a trading history from the outset, which can save months if not years of hard work in building relationships.

- If the business you buy is already profitable, you could pay yourself a living wage from the outset.

- Bank financing may be easier to acquire for an established business than for a riskier start-up business.

Disadvantages of buying a business include:

- ✔ You run the risk of acquiring the existing unsolved problems and mistakes of the person who is selling it.

- ✔ Identifying the right potential acquisition and negotiating purchase can take a very long time, and there is no guarantee that you will succeed at your first attempt.

- ✔ The professional fees associated with buying a business can be a significant, though necessary, cost. If you buy a very small business, the total professional fees associated with the transaction will be a major percentage of the total cost of your investment, perhaps as much as 15 or 20 per cent. Experienced solicitors and accountants are vital to this process. They are your safeguards to ensure that you know exactly what you are buying.

Chapter 5

Testing Feasibility

. . . .

. . . .

*Y*ou need to decide whether or not starting up your own business is for you. Maybe you have reached some tentative decision on whether to go it alone or to join forces with others with valuable resources or ideas to add to your own and now have the bones of an idea of what type of business you will start, buy into, franchise or in some other way get into.

So all you have to do now is wait for the customers to turn up and the cash to roll in. Right? Wrong, regrettably. Although you are beyond square one, there are still a good few miles to cover before you can be confident your big business idea will actually work and make money. This chapter gives you the right questions to ask to make you as sure as you can be that you have the best shot at success.

Finding Enough Product or People

The first test of feasibility is whether you can get enough goods to sell or enough people to provide the service you're offering. You need to be sure that you can get your product manufactured at the rate and quantity to meet your needs. Likewise, if you're starting a service business, you need to be sure that you can hire the people with the skills you need, whether you need housecleaners or Web page designers.

Of course, if you're buying into a franchise or joining an existing business or co-operative, these issues are already addressed for the most part. Still, it never hurts to do your own assessment of the supply chain if only to familiarise yourself with the process.

How much is enough?

The amount of goods or services you need depends in part on the scale of your ambitions and also on what you believe the market will bear. If the restaurant you plan to open has a total population of 100 people within a fifty mile radius, that fact alone will limit the scale of your venture.

It makes sense to work backwards to answer this question. For example if you want to make at least as much money from your business as you have in wages in your job, then that figure can be used to work out the initial scale of your level of output. As a rough rule of thumb if you want to make £10,000 profit before tax, a business involved in manufacturing or processing materials will need to generate between £80,000 and £100,000 worth of orders. Taking away your anticipated profit from the sales target leaves you with the value of the goods and services you need to buy in.

Buying in equipment and supplies

In this area there are four main areas to check out:

- **Premises:** Finding the right premises can be the limiting factor for some businesses. If, for example you need to be in a particular type of area, as with restaurants, coffee shops, and night clubs, it could take months for the right place to come on the market and even longer to get planning or change of use consent if those are required. Once you have a clear idea of the type of premises you want, check out all the commercial estate agents in the area. It will make sense to have a few alternative locations in your plans too.

- **Equipment:** If you are going to make any or all of your products yourself then you need to check out suppliers, delivery times, payment terms and so forth for the equipment needed for the production processes. You will first need to check out the output levels and quality standards of any equipment you want, to make sure it will meet your needs. You can find equipment suppliers in either *Kelly's Directories* (www.kellys.co.uk) or *Kompass* (www.kompass.com). Between these two directories there is information on hundreds of thousands of branded products and services from suppliers in over 70 countries. These directories are available both in your local business library or, to a limited extent, online.

- **Finished goods:** It is usually a better use of scarce cash for a new business to buy in product in as close to finished state as possible, leaving you to complete only the high value-added tasks to complete. Few niche mail-order catalogue businesses make any of their own product; their key skills lie in merchandise selection, advertising copy, web design or buying in the right mailing lists. Kelly's and Kompass directories list almost every finished good supplier.

✔ **Consumable materials:** If you are making things yourself then you will need to check out suppliers of raw materials. Even if, like mail-order firms, you are buying in finished product you will need to check that out too. You can search in Google, Ask Jeeves or any of the major search engines for almost any product or service. However unless the quantities are large and significantly better terms can be had elsewhere it is better to stick to local suppliers for consumables. This is an inexpensive way to build up goodwill in the local community and may even create business for you. See *Kelly's* and *Kompass* directories for details of suppliers of consumables.

Hiring in help

Unless you plan to do everything yourself on day one, you will need to check out that people with the skills you need are available at wage rates you can afford in your area. Start by looking in the situations vacant section of your local newspaper under the appropriate headings. If you need kitchen staff for your new restaurant and the paper has 20 pages of advertisers desperately looking for staff, then you could well have a problem on your hands. In Chapter 10 we look at finding employees for your business.

Sizing Up the Market

You need to ensure that there are enough customers out there, with sufficient money to spend, to create a viable marketplace for your products or services. You must also see who will be competing against you for their business. In other words, you need to research your market.

Market research is something that potential financial backers – be they banks or other institutions – will insist on. And in this they are doing you a favour. Many businesses started with private money fail because the founders don't thoroughly research the market at the outset.

Whatever your business idea, you must undertake some well thought out market research before you invest any money or approach anyone else to invest in your venture.

You don't have to pay professional companies to do your research, although sometimes it may make good sense to do so. You can often gather information effectively (and cheaply) yourself.

Market research has three main purposes:

✔ **To build credibility for your business idea:** You must prove, first to your own satisfaction and later to outside financiers, that you thoroughly understand the marketplace for your product or service. This proof is vital to attracting resources to build the new venture.

✔ **To develop a realistic market entry strategy:** A successful marketing strategy is based on a clear understanding of genuine customer needs and on the assurance that product quality, price, promotional and distribution methods are mutually supportive and clearly focused on target customers.

✔ **To gain understanding of the total market, both customers and competition:** You need sufficient information on your potential customers, competitors, and market to ensure that your market strategy is at least on the target, if not on the bull's-eye itself. If you miss the target altogether, which you could well do without research, you may not have the necessary cash resources for a second shot.

The military motto 'Time spent in reconnaissance is rarely time wasted' holds true for business as well.

Researching the market need not be a complex process, nor need it be very expensive. The amount of effort and expenditure needs to be related in some way to the costs and risks associated with the business. If all that is involved with your business is simply getting a handful of customers for products and services that cost little to put together, then you may spend less effort on market research than you would for, say, launching a completely new product or service into an unproven market that requires a large sum of money to be spent up front. However much or little market research you plan to carry out the process needs to be conducted systematically.

Before you start your research:

✔ **Define your objectives:** Figure out what you vitally need to know. For example, how often do people buy and how much?

✔ **Identify the customers to sample for this information:** Decide who you want to sample and how you can best reach them. For example, for DIY products, an Ideal Home Exhibition crowd might be best.

✔ **Decide how best to undertake the research:** Choose the research method best suited to getting the results you need. For example, face-to-face interviews in the street may allow you direct access to potential customers.

✔ **Think about how you will analyse the data:** If your research involves complex multi-choice questions, or a large sample size, you may need to plan in advance to use a computer and the appropriate software to help you process the data, which in turn means coding the questions. An even better idea is to keep it so simple you don't need a computer!

The raw market research data can be analysed and turned into information to guide your decisions on price, promotion, location, and the shape, design, and scope of the product or service itself.

The following sections cover the areas you need to consider to make sure you have properly sized up your business sector.

Figuring out what you need to know

Before embarking on your market research, set clear and precise objectives. You don't want just to find out interesting information about the market in general, and you don't want to spend the time and money to explore the whole market when your target is just a segment of that market. (I talk about segmenting the market in the 'Finding your segment of the market' section coming up in a bit.)

You have to figure out who your target customer is and what you need to know about him or her. For example, if you are planning to open a shop selling to young fashion-conscious women, your research objective could be to find out how many women between the ages of 18 and 28, who make at least £25,000 p.a., live or work within two miles of your chosen shop position. That would give you some idea if the market could support a venture such as this.

You also want to know what the existing market is for your product and how much money your potential customers spend on similar products. You can get a measure of such spending from Mintel reports (www.mintel.com). Mintel publishes over 400 reports every year examining nearly every consumer market from baby foods to youth holidays.

Figuring out the size of the market may require several different pieces of information. You may want to know the resident population of a given area, which may be fairly easy to find out, and also something about the type of people who come into your area for work, for leisure, on holiday, or for any other purpose. A nearby hospital, library, railway station, or school, for example, may pull potential customers into your particular area.

You also want to know as much as you can about your competitors – their share of the market, their marketing strategy, their customer profile, product pricing schemes, and so on.

You need to research in particular:

✔ **Your customers:** Who will buy your goods and services? What particular customer needs will your business meet? How many of them are there, are their numbers growing or contracting, how much do they spend and how often do they buy?

✔ **Your competitors:** Which established businesses are already meeting the needs of your potential customers? What are their strengths and weaknesses? Are they currently failing their customers in some way that you can improve on?

✔ **Your product or service:** Could, or should, it be tailored to meet the needs of particular groups of customers? For example if you are starting up a delivery business, professional clients may require a 'same day service', whilst members of the public at large would be happy to get goods in a day or two, provided it was less costly.

✔ **The price you should charge:** All too often small firms confine their research on pricing to seeing what the competition charges and either matching it or beating it. That may be a way to get business, but it is not the best route to profitable business. You need to know what price would be perceived as being too cheap, what would represent good 'value for money' and what would be seen as a rip off, so you can pitch in at the right price for your offering.

✔ **Which promotional material will reach your customers:** What newspapers and journals do they read and which of these is most likely to influence their buying decision?

✔ **Your location:** From where could you reach your customers most easily and at minimum cost?

✔ **Most effective sales method:** Can you use telesales, the Internet, or a catalogue, or will customers only buy face to face either from a salesperson or from a retail outlet?

Research is not just essential in starting a business but should become an integral part in the on-going life of the business. Customers and competitors change; products and services don't last forever. Once started, however, on-going market research becomes easier, as you will have existing customers (and staff) to question. It is important that you regularly monitor their views on your business (as the sign in the barber shop stated: 'We need your head to run our business') and develop simple techniques for this purpose (for example, questionnaires for customers beside the till, suggestion boxes with rewards for employees).

Finding your segment of the market

Market segmentation is the process whereby customers and potential customers are organised into clusters of similar types, such as age, sex, education level or location.

The starting point for your business may be to sell clothes, but every person who buys clothes is too large and diverse a market to get a handle on. So you divide that market into different segments – clothes for men, women, and children, for example – and then further divide those segments into clothes for work, leisure, sports, and social occasions. You just segmented your market.

Most businesses end up selling to several different market segments, but when it comes to detailed market research you need to examine each of your main segments separately.

Above all it is customers who increasingly want products and services tailored to their needs and will pay for the privilege.

Grouping market segments

Some of the tried-and-tested ways by which markets can be segmented follow:

- **Demographic segmentation** groups customers together by such variables as age, sex, interest, education, and income. Some companies have made their whole proposition age focused. Live4now.com was only interested in those aged between 18 and 35, for example.

- **Psychographic segmentation** divides individual consumers into social groups such as Yuppie (young, upwardly mobile, professional), Bumps (borrowed-to-the-hilt upwardly mobile professional show off) and Jollies (jet-setting oldies with lots of loot). These categories try to explain how social behaviour influences buyer behaviour.

- **Benefit segmentation** recognises that different people get different benefits from the same product or service. The Lastminute.com bargain travel site claims two quite distinctive benefits for its users. Initially it aims to offer people bargains, which appeals because of price and value. But lately the company has been laying more emphasis on the benefit of immediacy. The theory is rather akin to the impulse buy products placed at checkout tills that you never thought of buying until you bumped into them on your way out. Whether ten days on a beach in Goa, or a trip to Istanbul, is the type of thing people pop in their baskets before turning off their computer screens, time will tell.

- **Geographic segmentation** recognises that people in different locations have different needs. For example, an inner city store might sell potatoes in 1kg bags, recognising its customers are likely to be on foot. An out of town shopping centre sells the same product in 20kg sacks, knowing their customers have cars.

- **Industrial segmentation** groups together commercial customers according to a combination of their geographic location, principal business activity, relative size, frequency of product use, urgency of need, loyalty, order size and buying policies. Using this approach a courier service would price its overnight delivery service higher than its 48 hour service.

> ✔ **Multivariant segmentation** uses a combination of segments to get a more precise picture of a market than using just one factor.

Use the following guidelines to help determine whether a market segment is worth trying to sell into:

> ✔ **Measurability:** Can you estimate how many customers are in the segment? Are there enough to make it worth offering something different for?
>
> ✔ **Accessibility:** Can you communicate with these customers, preferably in a way that reaches them alone? For example you could reach the over 50s through advertising in a specialist magazine, with reasonable confidence that young people will not read it. So if you are trying to promote a large-print edition of a game, you might prefer young people did not hear about it, so that they don't think of the game as strictly for old folks.
>
> ✔ **Open to profitable development:** The customers must have money to spend on the benefits you propose offering. Once upon a time oldies were poor, so that market wasn't a good target for upscale, expensive products. Then they became rich and everyone had products aimed at older markets.

Seeing natural market subsegments

Even after you determine your target market segments, your growth may not come through as fast as you were hoping. You have to realise that every market segment is itself made up of sub-segments. Everett M Rogers, in his book *Diffusion of Innovations* (New York Free Press, 1962) broke markets into the following sub-segments:

> ✔ Innovators, the adventurous types who try out new things early on represent 2.5 per cent of the average market.
>
> ✔ The Early Adopters make up 13.5 per cent of the average market. This type of customer only starts buying when the service has the seal of approval from the Innovators.
>
> ✔ Early Majority and Late Majority buyers, each 34 per cent of the market, follow on, after the Early Adopters have shown the way.
>
> ✔ Laggards, 16 per cent of the average market, follow well behind, perhaps taking years and some significant price drops before they can be tempted to put down their cash.

One further issue that has a profound effect on marketing strategy is that Innovators, Early Adopters, and all the other sub-segments don't necessarily read the same magazines or respond to the same images and messages. So they need to be marketed to in very different ways. This makes the blitz approach to market penetration taken by some new ventures look a bit suspect. Blitz marketing with a single message may work in stimulating a mature market, but how much use is it in a market that is still looking for the signal of approval from further up the chain?

You need to identify the innovators who will buy from you first. Whilst your product or service may not be earth shatteringly new, you and your business may well present a mature market with established competitors with a situation that looks much similar to a new innovation.

Budgeting for your research

Market research isn't free even if you do it yourself. At the very least, you have to consider your time. You may also spend money on journals, phone calls, letters, and field visits. And, if you employ a professional market research firm, your budgeting needs shoot to the top of the scale.

For example, a survey of 200 executives responsible for office equipment purchasing decisions cost one company £12,000. In-depth interviews with 20 banking consumers cost £8,000.

Doing the research in-house may save costs but limit the objectivity of the research. If time is your most valuable commodity, it may make sense to get an outside agency to do the work. Another argument for getting professional research is that it may carry more clout with investors.

Whatever the cost of research, you need to assess its value to you when you are setting your budget. So if getting it wrong will cost £100,000, then £5,000 spent on market research may be a good investment.

Doing the preliminary research

Research methods range from doing it all from your desk to getting out in the field yourself and asking questions – or hiring someone to do it for you. The following sections explore the various methods you can use to find out what you need to know.

If you are a member of a chamber of commerce, a trade association, small business association, or are or have taken a small business course, the chances are you can access some market data for free.

Even if it does cost something in time and money, getting the data you need helps you make better decisions. If you think knowledge is expensive, you should try ignorance!

Doing research behind your desk

Once you know the questions you want answers to, the next step is finding out if someone else has the answers already. Much of the information you need may well be published, so you can do at least some of your market research in a comfortable chair either in your home or in a good library.

Even if you use other research methods, it is well worth doing a little desk research first.

Gathering information at the library

There are thousands of libraries in the UK and tens of thousands elsewhere in the world that between them contains more desk research data than any entrepreneur could ever require. Libraries offer any number of excellent information sources. You can either take yourself to your local library or bring the library's information to you via the Internet if you're dealing with one of the reference libraries in a larger city or town.

As well as the fairly conventional business books, libraries contain many hundreds of reference and research data bases. For example, the official Census of Population supplies demographic data on size, age, and sex of the local populace. You can also find a wealth of governmental and other statistics that enable you to work out the size and shape of the market nationwide and how much each person spends.

Details of every journal, paper, and magazines readership are to be found in *BRAD* (British Rate and Data) and every company has to file details of its profits, assets, liabilities, and directors at Companies House, the place where all business details and accounts are kept (www.companies-house.org.uk).

Sources of Unofficial UK Statistics published by Gower (www.gowerpub.com) gives details of almost 900 publications (including electronic publications) and services produced by trade associations, professional bodies, banks, consultants, employers' federations, forecasting organisations and others, together with statistics appearing in trade journals and periodicals. Titles and services are listed alphabetically by publisher and each entry contains information, where available, on subject, content, and source of statistics, together with frequency, availability and cost, and address, telephone, and fax details for further information.

Some market information data costs hundreds of pounds and some is available only to subscribers who pay thousands of pounds to have it on tap. Fortunately for you, your library (or an Internet link to a library) may have the relevant directory, publication, or research study on its shelves.

Librarians are trained, amongst other things, to archive and retrieve information and data from their own libraries and increasingly from Internet data sources as well. Thus, they represent an invaluable resource that you should tap into early in the research process. You can benefit many times from their knowledge at no cost, or you may want to make use of the research service some libraries offer to business users at fairly modest rates.

Apart from public libraries, there are hundreds of university libraries, specialist science and technology libraries, and government collections of data that can be accessed with little difficulty.

Connecting to the world's libraries

The 123 World.com Web site (www.123world.com/libraries) claims to be the ultimate source of authentic and reliable information about the library resources of the world on the net. Their list of libraries includes public and state libraries, national archives, research, university, and other educational libraries, agricultural, science, and technical libraries, business libraries, and many other specialist libraries. The links in this directory guide you to the official sites of the libraries you choose. Using 123 World.com you can find out about all the libraries in your vicinity and anywhere else in the world.

Using the Internet

The Internet can be a powerful research tool. However, it has some particular strengths and weaknesses that you need to keep in mind when using it.

Strengths of the Internet include:

- ✔ Access is cheap and information is often free
- ✔ Provides good background information
- ✔ Information is produced quickly
- ✔ Covers a wide geographic scope

Weaknesses of the Internet include:

- ✔ The bias is strongly toward the US
- ✔ Coverage of any given subject may be patchy
- ✔ Authority and credentials are often lacking

It would be a brave or foolhardy entrepreneur who started up in business or set out to launch new products or services without at least spending a day or two surfing the Internet. At the very least this will let you know if anyone else has taken your business idea to market. At best it might save you lots of legwork around libraries, if the information you want is available online.

You can gather market research information on the Internet two main ways:

- ✔ Use directories, search engines, or telephone directories to research your market or product.
- ✔ Use bulletin or message boards, newsgroups, and chat rooms to elicit the data you require.

These three useful search engines can help get you started:

- ✔ **Business.com** (`www.business.com`)**:** Contains some 400,000 listings in 25,000 industry, product, and service sub-categories. Useful for general industry background or details about a particular product line.

- ✔ **Easy Searcher 2** (`www.easysearcher.com`) is a collection of 400 search engines, both general and specialist, available on drop down menus, listed by category.

- ✔ **The Small Business Research portal** (`www.smallbusinessportal. co.uk/index.php`) links Internet sites of interest to small business researchers, policy-makers, and support agencies. The site is a valuable portal for small business research.

Getting to the grass roots

If the market information you need is not already available, and the chances are that it won't be, then you need to find the answers yourself.

Going out into the marketplace to do market research is known as *field research*, or sometimes *primary research*, by marketing professionals.

Field research allows you to gather information directly related to your venture and to fine-tune results you get from other sources. For example, entrepreneurs interested in opening a classical music shop in Exeter aimed at young people were encouraged when desk research showed that of a total population of 250,000, 25 per cent were under 30. However, it did not tell them what percentage of this 25 per cent was interested in classical music nor how much money each potential customer might spend. Field research showed that 1 per cent was interested in classical music and would spend £2 a week, suggesting a potential market of only £65,000 a year (250,000 × 25% × 1% × £2 × 52)! The entrepreneurs sensibly decided to investigate Birmingham and London instead. But at least the cost had been only two damp afternoons spent in Exeter, rather than the horror of having to dispose of a lease of an unsuccessful shop.

Most field research consists of an interviewer putting questions to a respondent. No doubt you've become accustomed to being interviewed while travelling or resisting the attempts of an enthusiastic salesperson on your doorstep posing as a market researcher ('slugging' as this is known has been illegal since 1986).

The more popular forms of interviews are:

- ✔ Personal (face-to-face) interview (especially for consumer markets)

- ✔ Telephone (especially for surveying businesses)

- ✔ Postal survey (especially for industrial markets)

    ✔ Test and discussion groups

    ✔ Internet surveys

Personal interviews and postal surveys are clearly less expensive than getting together panels of interested parties or using expensive telephone time. Telephone interviewing requires a very positive attitude, courtesy, an ability not to talk too quickly and listening while sticking to a rigid questionnaire. Low response rates on postal surveys (normally less than 10 per cent) can be improved by including a letter explaining the purpose of the survey and why respondents should reply; by offering rewards for completed questionnaires (small gift); by associating the survey with a charity donation based on the number of respondents; by sending reminder letters and, of course, by providing pre-paid reply envelopes.

Internet surveys using questionnaires similar to those conducted by post or on the telephone are growing in popularity. On the plus side, while the other survey methods involve having the data entered or transcribed at your expense, with an Internet survey, the respondent enters the data. Internet survey software also comes with the means to readily analyse the data turning it into useful tables and charts. Such software may also have a statistical package to check out the validity of the data itself and so give you some idea how much reliance to place on it.

Whilst buying the software to carry out Internet surveys may be expensive, you can rent it and pay per respondent for each survey you do.

Another negative aspect of using the Internet is that, at present at any rate, the sample of users is heavily biased. Students, big companies, and university academics would be well represented in any sample you chose, but other sectors, for example the over 70s (up to a fifth of the population), may not.

Conducting the research

Field research means that you have to do the work yourself. Decide the questions, select the right people to ask those questions and then interpret the data once you have it. This is completely different from desk research where all that work has been done for you. But field research can be worth every ounce of sweat that goes into it. You get information that no one else is likely to have at their finger tips, and knowledge in the business start-up arena is definitely power. When you come to writing up your business plan (see Chapter 6) you will have the evidence to support your belief in your business.

Setting up a sample

It is rarely possible or even desirable to include every potential customer or competitor in your research. Imagine trying to talk to all pet owners before launching petfeed.com! Instead you select a sample group to represent the whole population.

Sampling saves time and money and can be more accurate than surveying an entire population. Talking to every pet owner may take months. By the time you complete your survey, the first people questioned may have changed their opinions, or the whole environment may have changed in some way.

You need to take care and ensure you have included all the important customer segments that you have targeted as potential users or buyers of your products or services in your research sample.

The main sampling issue is how big a sample you need to give you a reliable indication as to how the whole population will behave. The accuracy of your survey increases with the sample size, as Table 5-1 shows. You need to ensure that each of your main customer segments, for example, the over 50s, people earning between £20,000 and £30,000 a year or those without university degrees, if those are groups of people whose views are important to your strategy, are included in sample in numbers sufficient to make your sample reasonably reliable.

Table 5-1	Sample Size and Accuracy
Number in sample	*Percentage accuracy of 95% of surveys*
250	6.2
500	4.4
750	3.6
1000	3.1
2000	2.2
6000	1.2

For most basic research a small business will find the lower sample sizes accurate enough given the uncertainty surrounding the whole area of entering new markets and launching new products.

Asking the right questions

To make your field research pay off you have to ask the questions whose responses tell you what you need to know. Writing those questions is both an art and a science – both aspects of which you can master by using the following tips:

✔ Keep the number of questions to a minimum. A dozen or so should be enough – 25 is getting ridiculous.

✔ Keep the questions simple. Answers should be either Yes/No/Don't Know or somewhere on a scale such as Never/Once a Month/Three or Four Times a Month/Always.

✔ Avoid ambiguity. Make sure the respondent really understands the question by avoiding vague words such as 'generally', 'usually', 'regularly'. Seek factual answers; avoid opinions.

✔ Make sure you have a cut-out question at the beginning to eliminate unsuitable respondents. You don't want to waste time questioning people who would never use your product or service.

✔ Put an identifying question at the end so that you can make sure you get a suitable cross-section of respondents. For example, you may want to identify men from women, people living alone from those with children, or certain age groups.

The introduction to a face-to-face interview is important; make sure you are prepared, either carrying an identifying card (maybe a student card or watchdog card) or with rehearsed introduction (such as 'Good morning, I'm from Cranfield University [show card] and we are conducting a survey and would be grateful for your help'). You may also need visuals of the product you are investigating (samples, photographs), to ensure the respondent understands. Make sure these are neat and accessible.

Try out the questionnaire and your technique on your friends prior to using them in the street. You may be surprised to find that questions that seem simple to you are incomprehensible at first to respondents!

Remember, above all, however, that questioning is by no means the only or most important form of fieldwork. Another form of fieldwork market research you should undertake is to get out and look at your competitors' premises, get their catalogues and price lists, go to exhibitions and trade fairs relevant to your chosen business sector, and get information on competitors' accounts and financial data. One would-be business starter found out from the company's accounts, obtained from Companies House (www.companies-house.org.uk) that the 'small' competitor near to where he planned to locate was in fact owned by a giant public company that was testing out the market prior to a major launch themselves.

All methods can be equally valid depending only on the type of market data you need to gather. The results of each piece of market research should be carefully recorded for subsequent use in presentations and business plans.

Once the primary market research (desk and field research) and market testing (stalls and exhibitions) are complete, if you are investing a substantial amount of money up front in your venture, then pilot testing of the business should take place in one location or customer segment before launching fully into business. Only then can you make a reasonably accurate prediction of sales and the cash flow implications for your business.

Finding test subjects

Now you need someone to ask your questions to. If you're doing a street survey then you will have to make do with whoever comes along. Otherwise to carry out a survey, your best bet is to buy or rent a mailing list. Typically, you'll pay a fee to the list owner, such as a magazine with its list of subscribers. You'll negotiate a fee for how many times you are allowed to use the list. Note that you are not the owner of the list.

There are several individual freelancers who specialise in brokering lists and building lists You may want to consider hiring an individual for a consultation or to manage the entire process. Marketing professionals claim there's a science to buying lists, but it's quite possible to master this science on your own, especially if you are trying to reach a local or regional market. Think of publications, organisations, and businesses whose lists would most likely contain people who could buy your product or service. Don't overlook trade magazines, regional magazines, or non-competing businesses with a similar customer base. You can then select and narrow your lists by looking at nearly any demographic variable to arrive at as close to your description of your target market as possible. Listbroker.com (www.listbroker.com) and List-Link International Limited (www.list-link.com) between them can provide lists of all types.

Determining whether you have enough information

Use Table 5-2 to check out whether you know enough about your market yet. Complete the questionnaire by entering the score in the box that most closely describes your knowledge. For example in the first question below if you don't know the likely age, sex or income group of your prospective or actual customers, put a zero in the left-hand column. Try to be honest and perhaps get someone else who knows your business area well to answer the questions also.

Table 5-2	Evaluating Your Results		
	No (0)	*Have some idea (1)*	*Yes, have detailed information (2)*
Do you know the likely age, sex, or income group of your prospective (or actual) customers?			
Do you know your customers' buying habits and preferences?			
Do know what other related products and services your customers buy?			
Do you know which of your competitors they also use?			
Do you know how much of your competitors' business you want or have?			
Do you know who else operates in this marketplace?			
Do you know how successful they are in terms of sales and profits?			
Do you know how they promote their goods and services?			
Do you know how satisfied their customers are with their service?			
Do you know how much your competitors charge?			
Do you know the overall size of your market?			
Do you know if your market is growing or contracting, and by how much?			
Do you know what papers, journals, and magazines your customers read?			
Do you know which other Web sites your customers are most likely to visit?			
Do you know how your competitors recruit their best staff?			

Add up all your scores and rate whether or not you know enough about your market yet.

- ✔ Less than 10: It seems unlikely that you know enough to start up yet.

- ✔ 10–15: You still have a lot more to find out, but at least you have made a start.

- ✔ 15–25: You have got a handle on the basic information, but there are still a few more important bits of data to research.

- ✔ Over 25: A high score is no guarantee of success, but you seem to have the right level of sector knowledge to start a business. Superior information can in itself be a source of competitive advantage, so keep up the good work.

Working Out Whether You Can Make Money

There isn't much point in trying to get a new business off the ground if it is going to take more money than you can raise or take longer to reach break-even and turn in a profit than you can possibly survive unaided. I look in more detail at financial matters such as profits and margins in Chapter 13, but you can't start looking at the figures soon enough. Doing some rough figures at the outset can save you a lot of time pursuing unrealistic or unprofitable business opportunities.

Estimating start-up costs

Setting up a business requires money – there is no getting away from that. You have rent to pay, materials and equipment to purchase, and all before any income is received. Starting a business on the road to success involves ensuring that you have sufficient money to survive until the point where income continually exceeds expenditure.

Raising this initial money and the subsequent financial management of the business is therefore vital, and great care should be taken over it. Unfortunately, more businesses fail due to lack of sufficient day-to-day cash and financial management than for any other reason.

The first big question is to establish how much money you need. Look at every possible cost and divide them into one-off, fixed, or variable categories.

The *fixed costs* are those that you have to pay even if you make no sales (rent, rates, possibly some staff costs, repayments on any loans, and so on) as well as some *one-off costs,* or one-time purchases such as buying a vehicle or computer, which will not be repeated once the business is up and running. *Variable costs* are those that vary dependent on the level of your sales (raw materials, production and distribution costs, and so on).

Your finance requirements will be shown very clearly on your cash flow forecast, which is a table showing, usually on a monthly basis, the amount of money actually received into the business, and the amount of money paid out.

According to the Bank of England's report on small business finance published in March 2002, the average start-up cost for a new business in the UK is just over £18,000. However that average conceals some wide variations. Some start-ups, particularly those in technology or manufacturing, may require hundreds, thousands, or even millions of pounds, whilst others, such as those run from home may cost very little or nothing.

Six out of every ten people starting up a businesses use personal funds as their initial source of finance. Naturally, using your own money, your savings, your un-mortgaged property, your life insurance, and your other assets, is a logical starting point. You may not feel you can put all of your worth behind a business because of the risks involved, but whichever route you go down you will normally be expected to invest some of your own assets. Banks seek personal guarantees; venture capitalists like to see owners taking risks with their own money – why should they risk their clients' money if you will not risk yours?

If you can fund the project from your own resources there are attractions to doing so. Only in this way do all of the rewards of success flow to you. As soon as you bring in other sources of finance they slice off some of the reward, be it interest, share of the value on the sale of the business, or dividends. They may also constrain the business through the use of covenants, borrowing limits, and the placement of financial obligations on the business – potentially not only carving off part of your rewards but also capping them by restricting your operation. But if not at the outset, at some stage in their growth, most firms require outside finance to realise their full potential.

Forecasting sales

While all forecasts may turn out to be wrong, it is important to demonstrate in your strategy that you have thought through the factors that will impact on performance. You should also show how you could deliver satisfactory results even when many of these factors work against you. Backers and employees alike will be measuring the downside risk, to evaluate the worst scenario and its likely effects, as well as looking towards an ultimate exit route.

Here are some guidelines to help you make an initial sales forecast:

- **Credible projections:** Your overall projections have to be believable. Most lenders and investors have an extensive experience of similar business proposals. Unlike you they have the benefit of hindsight, being able to look back several years at other ventures they have backed, and see how they fared in practice as compared with their initial forecasts.

  You could gather some useful knowledge on similar businesses yourself by researching company records (at Companies House, where the accounts of most UK companies are kept), or by talking with the founders of similar ventures, who will not be your direct competitors.

- **Market share:** How big is the market for your product or service? Is it growing or contracting and at what rate, percentage per annum? What is the economic and competitive position? These are all factors that can provide a market share basis for your forecasts. An entry market share of more than a few percent would be most unusual. But beware of turning this argument on its head. Unsubstantiated statements such as 'In a market of £1 billion per annum we can easily capture 1 per cent, which is £1 million a year', will impress no investor.

- **Customers:** How many customers and potential customers do you know who are likely to buy from you, and how much might they buy? Here you can use many types of data on which to base reasonable sales projections. You can interview a sample of prospective customers, issue a press release or advertisement to gauge response, and exhibit at trade shows to obtain customer reactions. If your product or service needs to be on an approved list before it can be bought, then your business plan should confirm that you have that approval, or less desirably, show how you will get it.

  You should also look at seasonal factors that might cause sales to be high or low at certain periods in the year. This will be particularly significant for cash flow projections. You should then relate your seasonal, customer-based, forecast to your capacity to make or sell at this rate. Sometimes your inability to recruit or increase capacity may limit your sales forecasts.

- **Market guidelines:** Some businesses have accepted formulas you can use to estimate sales. This is particularly true in retailing where location studies, traffic counts, and population density are known factors.

- **Desired income:** This approach to estimating sales embraces the concept that forecasts may also accommodate the realistic aims of the proprietor. Indeed, you could go further and state that the whole purpose of strategy is to ensure that certain forecasts are achieved. In a mature company with proven products and markets, this is more likely to be the case than with a start-up.

Nevertheless, an element of 'How much do we need to earn?' must play a part in forecasting, if only to signal when a business idea is not worth pursuing.

One extreme of the 'desired income' approach to forecasting comes from those entrepreneurs who think that the forecasts are the business plan. Such people cover the business plan with a mass of largely unconnected numbers. With reams of computer printout covering every variation possible in business, complete with sensitivity analysis, these people are invariably a big turn-off with financiers.

Calculating break-even

So far I've taken certain decisions for granted and ignored how to cost the product or service you're marketing, and indeed, how to set the selling price. These decisions are clearly very important if you want to be sure of making a profit.

At first glance the problem is simple. You just add up all the costs and charge a bit more. The more you charge above your costs, provided the customers will keep on buying, the more profit you make. Unfortunately as soon as you start to do the sums the problem gets a little more complex. For a start, not all costs have the same characteristics. Some costs, for example, do not change however much you sell. If you are running a shop, the rent and rates are relatively constant figures, completely independent of the volume of your sales. On the other hand, the cost of the products sold from the shop is completely dependent on volume. The more you sell, the more it costs you to buy in stock. You can't really add up those two types of costs until you have made an assumption about how much you plan to sell. You can find out more detail about this subject in Chapter 10.

Becoming lean and mean

Paradoxically, one of the main reasons small businesses fail in the early stages is that too much start-up capital is raised and used to buy fixed assets. While clearly some equipment is essential at the start, other purchases can be postponed until later in the day. This may mean that you rent or borrow desirable and labour-saving devices for a while. This is not quite as convenient but may mean the difference between surviving in business and going bust.

Suppose you are producing widgets and decide to rent bigger premises from the outset, with room to store your widgets, rather than keeping them in your spare garage space. The rent and business rates on these larger premises are set at £3,500, which becomes your new fixed cost. Your break-even sales figure now becomes 1,000 (£3,500 fixed cost divided by £3.50 contribution per widget sold). In other words, you have to sell an extra 285 widgets, or 60 per cent more, just to cover the cost of having the extra storage space, which you had for free in your garage. Only you will know if the benefit of having the extra space is worth the cost.

One other very good reason for keeping fixed costs as low as possible is that you may not know what you really need until you actually start trading. You may find that your suppliers are so reliable that you need only carry a couple of days' stock in hand rather than the month you anticipated that called for the extra space. In which case you will have spent the extra money for no gain whatsoever.

In any event, you need to keep your fixed costs low enough to break-even within six to nine months of starting up.

Chapter 6

Preparing the Business Plan

. . . .

In This Chapter

▶ Turning your ideas into plans

▶ Satisfying financiers' concerns

▶ Making your plan stand out

▶ Using software

▶ Preparing for an elevator pitch

. . . .

*P*erhaps the most important step in launching any new venture or expand-ing an existing one is the construction of a *business plan*. Such a plan must include your goals for the enterprise, both short and long term; a description of the products or services you offer and the market opportunities you antici-pate; finally, an explanation of the resources and means you need to achieve your goals in the face of likely competition.

Preparing a comprehensive business plan along these lines takes time and effort – The Cranfield School of Management estimates anywhere between 200 and 400 hours, depending on the nature of your business and how much data you have already gathered. Nevertheless, such an effort is essential if you are both to crystallise and focus your ideas, and test your resolve about starting or expanding your business.

The core thinking behind business plans and their eventual implementation is strategic analysis. The strategic analysis refines or confirms your view of what is really unique about your proposition. Or to put it another way, 'Why on earth would anyone want to pay enough for this to make me rich?'

Once completed, your business plan will serve as a blueprint to follow which, like any map, improves the user's chances of reaching their destination.

Finding a Reason to Write a Business Plan

There are a number of other important benefits you can anticipate arising from preparing a business plan. All these benefits add up to one compelling reason. Businesses that plan make more money than those that don't and they survive longer too.

The research on planning generally shows a positive relationship between planning and business performance. Businesses that follow a well thought out plan generally out perform businesses with no plans or informal plans in every relevant category. Businesses that continue to update their plans throughout the life of the business enjoy significantly more success than businesses that don't.

Key reasons for writing up your business plan are covered in the following sections.

Building confidence

Completing a business plan makes you feel confident in your ability to set up and operate the venture because you put together a plan to make it happen. It may even compensate for lack of capital and experience, provided of course you have other factors in your favour, such as a sound idea and a size-able market opportunity for your product or service.

Testing your ideas

A systematic approach to planning enables you to make your mistakes on paper, rather than in the marketplace. One potential entrepreneur made the discovery while gathering data for his business plan that the local competitor he thought was a one-man band was in fact the pilot operation for a proposed national chain of franchised outlets. This had a profound effect on his market entry strategy!

Another entrepreneur found out that, at the price he proposed charging, he would never recover his overheads or break even. Indeed 'overheads' and 'break even' were themselves alien terms before he embarked on preparing a business plan. This naive perspective on costs is by no means unusual.

Showing how much money you need

Your business plan details how much money you need, what you need it for, and when and for how long you need it.

As under-capitalisation and early cash flow problems are two important reasons why new business activities fail, it follows that if you have a soundly prepared business plan, you can reduce these risks of failure. You can also experiment with a range of alternative viable strategies and so concentrate on options that make the most economic use of scarce financial resources.

It would be an exaggeration to say that your business plan is the passport to sources of finance. It will, however, help you to display your entrepreneurial flair and managerial talent to the full and to communicate your ideas to others in a way that will be easier for them to understand and to appreciate the reasoning behind your ideas. These outside parties could be bankers, potential investors, partners, or advisory agencies. Once they know what you are trying to do they will be better able to help you.

Providing planning experience

Preparing a business plan gives you an insight into the planning process. It is this process itself that is important to the long-term health of a business, and not simply the plan that comes out of it. Businesses are dynamic, as are the commercial and competitive environments in which they operate. No-one expects every event as recorded on a business plan to occur as predicted, but the understanding and knowledge created by the process of business planning helps prepare the business for any changes that it may face, and so enables it to adjust quickly.

Satisfying financiers' concerns

If you need finance, it is important to examine what financiers expect from you if you are to succeed in raising those funds.

It is often said that there is no shortage of money for new and growing businesses, the only scarce commodities are good ideas and people with the ability to exploit them. From the potential entrepreneur's position this is often hard to believe. One major venture capital firm alone receives several thousand business plans a year. Only 500 or so are examined in any detail, less than 25 are pursued to the negotiating stage, and only six of those are invested in.

To a great extent the decision whether to proceed beyond an initial reading of the plan depends on the quality of the business plan used in supporting the investment proposal. The business plan is your ticket of admission, giving you your first and often only chance to impress prospective sources of finance with the quality of your proposal.

It follows from this that to have any chance at all of getting financial support, your business plan must be the best that can be written and it must be professionally packaged. The plans that succeed meet all of the following requirements.

Presenting evidence of market orientation and focus

You need to demonstrate that you recognise the needs of potential customers, rather than simply being infatuated with an innovative idea. Business plans that occupy more space with product descriptions and technical explanations than with explaining how products will be sold and to whom usually get cold-shouldered by financiers. They rightly suspect that these companies are more of an ego trip than an enterprise.

But market orientation is not in itself enough. Financiers want to sense that the entrepreneur knows the one or two things their business can do best and that they are prepared to concentrate on exploiting these opportunities.

Demonstrating customer acceptance

Financiers like to know that your new product or service will sell and is being used, even if only on a trial or demonstration basis.

The founder of Solicitec, a company selling software to solicitors to enable them to process relatively standard documents such as wills, had little trouble getting support for his house conveyancing package once his product had been tried and approved by a leading building society for their panel of solicitors.

If you are only at the prototype stage, financiers have no immediate indication that, once made, your product will appeal to the market. They have to assess your chances of succeeding without any concrete evidence that you will. Under these circumstances you have to show that the problem your innovation seeks to solve is a substantial one that a large number of people will pay for.

One inventor from the Royal College of Art came up with a revolutionary toilet system design that used 30 per cent less water per flush and had half the number of moving parts of a conventional product, all for no increase in price. Although he had only drawings to show, it was clear that with domestic metered water for all households a distinct possibility and a United Kingdom market for 500,000 new units per annum, a sizeable acceptance was reasonably certain.

As well as evidence of customer acceptance, you need to demonstrate that you know how and to whom your new product or service must be sold, and that you have a financially viable means of doing so.

Owning proprietary position

Exclusive rights to a product through patents, copyright, trade mark protection, or a licence helps to reduce the apparent riskiness of a venture in the financiers' eyes, as these can limit competition, for a while at least.

One participant on a Cranfield enterprise programme held patents on a revolutionary folding bicycle he designed at college. While no financial institution was prepared to back him in manufacturing the bicycle, funds were readily available to enable him to make production prototypes and then license the design to established bicycle makers throughout the world.

However well-protected legally a product is, marketability and marketing know-how generally outweigh 'patentability' in the success equation. A salutary observation made by an American Professor of Entrepreneurship revealed that less than 0.5 per cent of the best ideas contained in the *US Patent Gazette* in the last five years have returned a dime to the inventors.

Making believable forecasts

Entrepreneurs are naturally ebullient when explaining the future prospects for their businesses. They frequently believe that the sky's the limit when it comes to growth, and money (or rather the lack of it) is the only thing that stands between them and their success.

It is true that if you are looking for venture capital, then the providers are also looking for rapid growth. However, it is as well to remember that financiers are dealing with thousands of investment proposals each year, and already have money tied up in hundreds of business sectors. It follows, therefore, that they already have a perception of what the accepted financial results and marketing approaches currently are for any sector. Any new company's business plan showing projections that are outside the ranges perceived as acceptable within an industry will raise questions in the investor's mind.

Make your growth forecasts believable; support them with hard facts where possible. If they are on the low side, then approach the more cautious lending banker, rather than venture capitalists. The former often see a modest forecast as a virtue, lending credibility to the business proposal as a whole.

Benefiting your business

Despite many valuable benefits, thousands of would-be entrepreneurs still attempt to start without a business plan. The most common among these are entrepreneurs who think that they need little or no capital at the outset, or those who have funds of their own. Both types of entrepreneurs may believe that they don't need a business plan because they don't need to expose their project to harsh financial appraisal.

The former type may believe the easily exploded myth that customers will all pay cash on the nail and suppliers will wait for months to be paid. In the meantime, the proprietor has the use of these funds to finance the business. Such model customers and suppliers are thinner on the ground than optimistic entrepreneurs think. In any event, two important market rules still apply: Either the product or service on offer fails to sell like hot cakes and mountains of unpaid stocks build up, or the product or service does sell like hot cakes and more financially robust entrepreneurs are attracted into the market. Without the staying power that adequate financing provides these new competitors will rapidly kill the business off.

Those would-be entrepreneurs with funds of their own, or worse still borrowed from friends and relatives, tend to think that the time spent in preparing a business plan could be more usefully (and enjoyably) spent looking for premises, buying a new car, or installing a computer. In short, anything that inhibits them from immediate action is viewed as time wasting.

As most people's initial perception of their business venture is flawed in some important respect, it follows that jumping in at the deep end is risky, and unnecessarily so. Flaws can often be discovered cheaply and in advance as, when preparing a business plan, they are almost always discovered.

Writing Up Your Business Plan

In these sections, I give you some guidelines to make sure your plan attracts attention and succeeds in the face of some fierce competition. More than a thousand businesses start up in the UK each day, and many of those are looking for money or other resources that they are hoping their business plan will secure for them. Making your business plan the best it can be gives it a chance to stand out.

Defining your readership

Clearly a business plan will be more effective if it is written with the reader in mind. This will involve some research into the particular interests, foibles, and idiosyncrasies of those readers. Bankers are more interested in hearing about certainties and steady growth, whilst *venture capitalists*, who put up risk capital on behalf of institutions such as pension funds, are also interested in dreams of great things to come. *Business angels*, who put their own money at risk, like to know how their particular skills and talents can be deployed in the business.

It is a good idea to carry out your reader research before the final editing of your business plan, as you should incorporate something of this knowledge into the way it is presented. You may find that slightly different versions of the business plan have to be made for different audiences. This makes the reader feel the proposal has been addressed to them rather than just being the recipient of a 'Dear Sir or Madam' type of missive. However, the fundamentals of the plan remain constant.

Choosing the right packaging

Appropriate packaging enhances every product and a business plan is no exception. Most experts prefer a simple spiral binding with a clear plastic cover front and back. This makes it easy for the reader to move from section to section, and it ensures the document will survive the frequent handling that every successful business plan is likely to get.

A letter quality printer, using size 12 typeface, double-spacing and wide margins, will result in a pleasing and easy to read plan.

Deciding on layout and content

There is no such thing as a universal business plan format. That being said, experience has taught us that certain styles have been more successful than others. Following these guidelines will result in an effective business plan, which covers most requirements. Not every sub-heading will be relevant, but the general format is robust.

The following list contains the elements of an effective business plan, one that covers most requirements. You may not need all of these sections, and you may need others to cover special requirements.

- ✔ The **cover** should show the name of your business, its address, phone and fax numbers, e-mail address, Web site, contact name, and the date on which this version of the plan was prepared. It should confirm that this is the current view on the business's position and financing needs.

- ✔ The **title page,** immediately behind the front cover, should repeat the above information and also give the founder's name, address, and phone number. A home phone number can be helpful, particularly for investors, who often work irregular hours too.

- ✔ The **executive summary** is ideally one page, but certainly no longer than two, and contains the highlights of your plan.

Writing this summary is a difficult task but it is the single most important part of your business plan. Done well it can favourably dispose the reader from the outset. Done badly, or not at all, then the plan may not get beyond the mail-room. This one page (or two pages) must explain:

- The current position of the company, including a summary of past trading results.

- A description of the products or services, together with details on any rights or patents and details on competitive advantage.

- The reasons why customers need this product or service, together with some indication of market size and growth.

- A summary of forecasts of sales and profits, together with short- and long-term aims and the strategies to be employed.

- How much money is needed to fund the growth and how and when the provider will benefit.

Write the executive summary only after you complete the business plan itself. Read the real-life example executive summary to get a feel for how this vital task can be successfully carried out.

✔ The **table of contents,** with page numbers, is the map that guides readers through the business plan. If that map is obscure, muddled, or even missing, then you are likely to end up with lost or irritated readers who are in no mind to back your proposal. Each main section should be listed, numbered, and given a page identity. Elements within each section should also be numbered: 1, 1.1, 1.2, and so on.

✔ Details of the **business and its management** should include a brief history of the business and its performance to date and details on key staff, current mission, legal entity, capital structure, and professional advisers.

✔ A description of **products and services,** their applications, competitive advantage, and proprietary position. Include details on state of readiness of new products and services and development cost estimates.

✔ The **marketing** section should provide a brief overview of the market by major segment showing size and growth. Explain the current and proposed marketing strategy for each major segment, covering price, promotion, distribution channels, selling methods, location requirements, and the need for acquisitions, mergers, or joint ventures, if any.

✔ Information on **management and staffing** should give details on current key staff and on any recruitment needs. Include information on staff retention strategies, reward systems, and training plans.

✔ The **operations** section describes how your products and services are made, how quality standards are assured, and how output can be met.

✔ A summary of the key **financial data,** including ratios together with a description of the key controls used to monitor and review performance.

✔ **Financing requirements** needed to achieve the planned goals, together with how long you will need the money for. You should also demonstrate how the business would proceed using only internal funding. The difference between these two positions is what the extra money will help to deliver.

✔ **E-commerce** isn't just about selling goods and services online, though that is important. It covers a range of activities that can be carried out online to make your business more efficient. These solutions extend across the supply chain from ordering your raw materials right through to after-sales service. It can incorporate market intelligence gathering, customer relationship management, and a whole range of back office procedures. Your business plan should show how you plan to tackle this area.

✔ Include **major milestones** with dates. For example: get prototype for testing by 20 December, file patents by 10 January, or locate suitable premises by such and such a date.

✔ **Risk assessment** features high on your reader's list of concerns, so it's best to anticipate as many as you can, together with your solution. For example: Our strategy is highly dependent on finding a warehouse with a cold store for stock. But if we can't find one by start date we will use space in the public cold store 10 miles away. Not as convenient but it will do.

✔ Detail an **exit route** for venture capitalists and business angels. Typically, they are looking to liquidate their investments within three to seven years, so your business plan should show them how much money they can make and how quickly.

If you think you need long-term investment (see Chapter 8 for more about equity financing) then you need to say something about who might buy the business and when you might be able to launch it on a stock market.

✔ **Appendixes** include CVs of the key team members, technical data, patents, copyrights and designs, details on professional advisers, audited accounts, consultants' reports, abstracts of market surveys, details of orders on hand, and so on.

Writing and editing

The first draft of the business plan may have several authors and it can be written ignoring the niceties of grammar and style. The first draft is a good one to talk over the proposal with your legal adviser to keep you on the straight and narrow, and with a friendly banker or venture capitalist. This can give you an insider's view as to the strengths and weaknesses of your proposal.

When the first draft has been revised, then comes the task of editing. Here grammar, spelling, and a consistent style do matter. The end result must be a crisp, correct, clear, complete plan no more than 20 pages long. If you are not an expert writer you may need help with editing. Your local librarian or college may be able to help here.

Maintaining confidentiality

Finding an investor or a bank to lend to your business may take weeks or months. During that time, potential investors diligently gather information about the business so that they won't have surprises later about income, expenses, or undisclosed liabilities. The business plan is only the starting point for their investigations.

If you and the prospective financiers are strangers to one another, you may be reluctant to turn over sensitive business information until you are confident that they are serious. (This is not so sensitive an issue with banks as it is with business angels and venture capital providers.) To allay these fears, consider asking for a confidentiality letter, or agreement.

A confidentiality letter will suffice in most circumstances. But if substantial amounts of intellectual property are involved you may prefer a longer, more formal confidentiality agreement drafted by a lawyer. That's okay, but you (and perhaps your lawyer as well) should make sure that the proposed document contains no binding commitment on you. The confidentiality letter should be limited to their agreement to treat the information as strictly confidential and to use the information only to investigate lending or investing in the business, and to the other terms set out in the letter. Figure 6-1 shows a sample confidentiality agreement.

Doing due diligence

Don't be surprised if the investor wants to learn about your personal financial status, job, or business history. They are interested in your financial stability, your reputation for integrity, and your general business savvy because they will, in effect, extend credit to you until you deliver them the interest or return they are expecting on their money. That is what the *due diligence* process is all about.

Usually the due diligence process, which involves a thorough examination of both the business and its owners, takes several weeks, if not longer. But that depends on how much money your plan calls for and from whom you are trying to raise it. (I cover raising finance in Chapter 8.)

WHEREAS

1. The purpose of communication between the Parties to this Agreement is for the investor/lender to evaluate the suitability as an investment or lending proposition, the business proposition as set out in the business plan

2. The information to be communicated in strict confidence between the Parties to this Agreement includes the business plan, demonstrations, commercial and technical information, all forms of intellectual property and includes material for which patent or similar registration may have been filed.

THEREFORE THE PARTIES HEREBY UNDERTAKE AS FOLLOWS:

FIRST: Each Party hereto agrees to maintain as confidential and not to use any of the information directly or indirectly disclosed by the other Party until or unless such information becomes public knowledge through no fault of the recipient Party, or unless the Parties to the Agreement complete a further Agreement making provision for utilisation of information disclosed. Each Party undertakes to prevent the information disclosed from passing to other than those representatives who must be involved for the purpose of this Agreement.

SECOND: In the event that no further Agreement on utilisation or publication of information is concluded each Party hereto undertakes to return to the other all confidential items submitted and to furnish certification that no copies or other records of those items have been retained.

THIRD: In the event that either Party requires the assistance of a further party in pursuing the purposes of the Agreement the approval of the other Party to this Agreement shall be secured.

FOURTH: Any information which either Party can prove was in his possession prior to disclosure hereunder and was not acquired from the other Party or his representatives is excepted from this Agreement.

FIFTH: The construction, validity and performance of this Agreement shall be governed in all respects by Law and the Parties hereto submit to the jurisdiction of the Courts.

SIGNED for
First Party..

Position:..

For and on behalf of:

....

In the presence of:

....

SIGNED for
Second Party..

Position:..

For and on behalf of:

....

In the presence of:

....

Figure 6-1:
A confidentiality agreement.

Accountants and lawyers will usually subject your track record and the business plan to detailed scrutiny. You will then be required to warrant that you have provided *all* relevant information, under pain of financial penalties. The cost of this due diligence process, rarely less than a big five-figure sum and often running into six, will have to be borne by the firm raising the money, but will be paid out of the money raised, if that is any consolation.

Using Business Planning Software

You may consider taking some of the sweat out of writing your business plan by using one of the myriad of software programmes on the market. You need to take some care in using such systems as the end result can be a bland plan that pleases no one and achieves nothing worthwhile.

Don't buy a package with several hundred business plans covering every type of business imaginable. The chances are that the person who wrote the plans knows far less than you do about your business sector and will add little or no value to your proposition. Worse still there is at least an even chance that the reader of your plan will have seen the fruits of these packaged plans before and may be less than enthusiastic to see yet another one.

You may well find it useful to use the test shown in Figure 6-2 as an uncomplicated form of self-assessment, before becoming bogged down in number-crunching software.

Recognising the limits of software

Good business planning software provides a useful structure to drop your plan in to and may provide a few helpful spreadsheets and templates for financial projections and market analysis. It also provides a valuable repository for your work-in-progress as you assemble the evidence to convince yourself and others that your business will succeed.

What software does not do is write a convincing business proposition by itself. The maxim, 'garbage in garbage out' applies to business planning software just as it does to everything to do with computers.

The other danger is that you end up with spreadsheet solutions – numbers just pumped into the financials – without any evidence of the underlying logic to support them.

Use business planning software as an aid and not a crutch. Go beyond that and you may end up worse than if you had started with a blank sheet of paper.

By answering the questions below you will get some idea of how well your business plan is progressing. Score 1, 2, or 3 following the key below for each of the questions. Mark the options closest to your instincts, and be honest. Then add up your scores and refer to the results at the end of the questionnaire to see how you scored and to check the potential of your plan.

Whatever your score, remember that this type of self-assessment test is broad brush. It is designed only to give an indication of whether you have the basic attitude, instincts, and capabilities to make a success of launching a home-based business.

If your score is low, the chances are that you do not. If it is high, the opposite is true.

1 = Made a start   2 = Some data only   3 = Comprehensive

Title page   ☐1 ☐2 ☐3

   Name of business contact details, date of business plan, contents

Executive summary   ☐1 ☐2 ☐3

   Your details; summary of key strategies; why you are better or different; summary of profit projections; summary of financial needs

The business and its management   ☐1 ☐2 ☐3

   You and your team's relevant experience; business goals and objectives; legal structure of the business

The marketing strategy   ☐1 ☐2 ☐3

   Market segment analysis; pricing strategy; promotion plans; product mix and range; e-commerce strategy; location; selling strategy

Management and staffing   ☐1 ☐2 ☐3

   Staff numbers; roles and responsibilities; recruitment needs

Operations   ☐1 ☐2 ☐3

   What facilities and equipment are needed; what services will be brought in?

Legal issues   ☐1 ☐2 ☐3

   What intellectual protection do you have as a barrier to entry; what other legal issues affect your business?

Financial forecasts   ☐1 ☐2 ☐3

   Summary of financial projections; monthly cash flows; profit and loss accounts; balance sheets; break-even analysis

Financing requirements   ☐1 ☐2 ☐3

   How much money do you need; what is it needed for; how much money can you provide; how much do you need to raise from outside; what security is available?

Figure 6-2:
Assessing
the content
of Your
business
plan.

Results:

9 points or less
You still have a lot more information to gather or decisions to make. No serious plan can be drawn up at this stage.
Between 10 and 20 points:
You have made progress, but still have a few gaps to fill. Concentrate your efforts on completing your plan.
More than 20 points:
Your plan is now complete and ready for final editing.

Reviewing systems

This section provides reviews of some business planning software packages that have been used to good effect.

- ✔ American Express (home3.americanexpress.com/smallbusiness/tool/biz_plan/index.asp): American Express run something they call the Small Business Exchange Business Plan Workshop. This workshop will help you write a business plan using their 'Toolboxes' of samples, worksheets, and glossaries. You can experiment on someone else's business in the 'Try It Yourself' section by testing your skills on a fictional business plan and be rated on how prepared you are to create your own.

- ✔ BizPlanIt.Com (Web site: www.bizplanit.com; e-mail: biz@bizplanit.com): BizPlanIt.Com's Web site has free resources offering information, advice, articled links to other useful sites and a free monthly newsletter, the *Virtual Business Plan* to pinpoint information. They also have an email service, providing answers to business plan questions within 24 hours.

- ✔ Royal Bank of Canada (www.royalbank.com): This site has a wide range of useful help for entrepreneurs. At www.royalbank.com/sme/index.html you can have access to their business plan writer package and three sample business plans.

- ✔ National Federation of Enterprise Agencies (NFEA) (www.smallbusinessadvice.org.uk): The Web site of NFEA has a step-by-step business planning guide with free downloads to help with the financial calculations.

Presenting Your Plan

Anyone backing a business does so primarily because they believe in the management. They know from experience that things rarely go according to plan so they must be confident that the team involved can respond effectively to changing conditions. You can be sure that any financier you are presenting to will have read dozens of similar plans, and will be well rehearsed. They may even have taken the trouble to find out something of your business and financial history.

Starring in show time

When you present your business plan to financial backers, your goal is to create empathy between yourself and your listeners. Whilst you may not be able to change your personality you could take a few tips on presentation skills. Eye contact, tone of speech, enthusiasm, and body language all have a part to play in making a presentation go well.

Wearing a suit is never likely to upset anyone. Shorts and sandals could just set the wrong tone! Serious money calls for serious people and even the Internet world is growing up.

Rehearse your presentation beforehand, having found out how much time you have. Explain your strategy in a business-like manner, demonstrating your grasp of the competitive market forces at work. Listen to comments and criticisms carefully, avoiding a defensive attitude when you respond.

Use visual aids and if possible bring and demonstrate your product or service. A video or computer-generated model is better than nothing.

Allow at least as much time for questions as you take in your talk. Make your replies to questions brief and to the point. If they want more information, they can ask. This approach allows time for the many different questions that must be asked either now or later, before an investment can proceed.

Making an 'elevator pitch'

You never know when the chance to present your business plan may occur – maybe even in a lift between floors (hence the term *elevator pitch*). You need to have every aspect of your business plan in your head and know your way around the plan backwards, forwards, and sideways. It's as well to have a five-, ten- and 20-minute presentation ready to run at a moment's notice.

One entrepreneur was given a chance to make a presentation of her business plan to the most powerful and influential person in her industry. This person could make or break new businesses and frequently did. The opportunity was a ten-minute ride in a chauffeur-driven car between the Dorchester hotel and Harrods. She had no room to demonstrate the product, set up flip charts or PowerPoint presentations or to involve the team. That was just enough space and time for a handful of powerful facts to be conveyed with passion, conviction, and authority. Fortunately the entrepreneur concerned had rehearsed her impromptu presentation and was completely prepared to seize the opportunity presented. She now has a £10 million business, eight years after taking that fateful car ride.

Stuff for Other Places?

Two friends, who eventually made it to an enterprise programme, and to founding a successful company, had great difficulty in getting backing at first. They were exceptionally talented designers and makers of clothes. They started out making ball-gowns, wedding dresses, and children's clothes –

anything the market wanted. Only when they focused on designing and marketing clothes for the mother-to-be that allowed them still to feel fashionably dressed, was it obvious that they had a winning concept. That strategy built on their strength as designers and their experiences as former mothers-to-be, and exploited a clear market opportunity neglected at that time by the main player in the marketplace.

From that point their company made a quantum leap forward from turning over a couple of hundred thousand pounds a year into the several million pound league within a few years.

Chapter 7

Getting Help

· ·

In This Chapter

▶ Locating help and advisory agencies

▶ Looking at Business Link

▶ Checking out Local Enterprise Agencies

▶ Exploring incubators

▶ Getting help for younger entrepreneurs

· ·

*J*ust because you have decided to start up your own business doesn't mean you have to do everything yourself. Even if you have rejected the idea of taking on a partner or going into a franchise chain, you can still get expert help and advice with nearly every aspect of your business, before you start up, whilst you start up, and even long after you have established your enterprise.

In taking outside help and advice you will be in good company. Each working day over 7,000 people use the services of a small business advisory organisation. Most are simple telephone enquiries but others involve face-to-face counselling sessions. There are now several hundred organisations specifically concerned with providing help, advice, and resources (including finance) for small businesses and those starting them. For the most part, these services are provided free or at a very low cost, at least at the outset.

Many of these organisations have been set up, or at least been encouraged to set up, by both national and local government who have come to realise how valuable small businesses are to communities and economies. (Chapter 2 addresses these issues in more depth.)

Although there are lots of people and organisations out there that can help you get started in business, in the end the decisions have to be made by you. That is not to knock the great advice and wisdom that many in help agencies such as Business Link or Enterprise Agencies and the like have to offer. However no one can step into your shoes and see the world through your eyes. But by the same token the final responsibility for choice of action rests with you. Listen to advice and take your own decisions.

In this chapter, I introduce some of the organisations you would be mad not to talk to if you want to get an expert outsider's view on the problems you are tussling with to get off to the best possible start.

Connecting with Business Link

The contact point for the small business support services throughout the UK, which for the most part is government-sponsored, is through a Business Link, or its equivalent outside of England. These are supported by the government through its Small Business Service. The eventual aim is for the Business Link network to be self-financing, but as business founders are mostly looking for money rather than someone to spend it on, this is more of an aspiration than a fact.

Business Link can best be seen as a gateway to a wide range of support services, some off which it delivers and some which is delivered by others. But the intention is that Business Link should be a one-stop shop for business owners and would be business owners, looking for help, advice and support on any aspect of starting and running a business.

Business Link aims to improve an entrepreneur's chances of success by encouraging them to do research and planning and to ask for help when it's needed.

The Link can provide a Personal Business Adviser (PBA), usually an experienced business person and often professionally qualified – or even a former business owner themselves – to help with business improvement and innovation, as well as with a range of other business issues.

In particular they provide pre-start-up help and advice to enable you to:

- ✔ Assess yourself against the attributes and skills needed to launch and run a business
- ✔ Decide what type of business is most appropriate
- ✔ Discover the range of issues that you need to consider in developing your business proposition
- ✔ Decide on the right sort of finance to start and grow your business
- ✔ Become aware of the regulations that apply when starting a business
- ✔ Understand the steps required for informing public authorities that they are launching your business

For in-depth advice related to your personal circumstances, your local Business Link operation offers a comprehensive business start-up service. Experienced advisers will work with you to develop your plans and help you access the full range of business support service providers who can assist you.

In England, advice on general business matters can be obtained from one of 40 or so Business Links that cover the country. These can be contacted on the Web site: www.businesslink.org.

The services on offer from Business Link England is available elsewhere in the UK through the following organisations:

- ✔ For most of Scotland, small business services are provided by the network of Scottish Business Shops. Web site: www.sbgateway.com; Tel: 0845 609 6611.

- ✔ The Highlands are covered by Highlands and Islands Enterprise-Scotland. Web site: www.hie.co.uk; Tel: 01463 715400.

- ✔ In Northern Ireland the Local Enterprise Development Unit (LEDU), whose small business portal is at www.ednet-ni.com, provides small business services.

  Alternatively, they can be contacted on 02890 491031. The Industrial Development Board (IDB) offers services in Northern Ireland. Web site: www.idbni.co.uk; Tel: 01232 233233.

- ✔ In Wales, Business Connect offers small business services. Web site: www.businessconnect.org.uk; Tel: 0845 796798.

All these sites provide links to your nearest small firms advisory service.

The Business Link Signpost at www.businesslink.org will direct you to a Business Link or you can telephone 0345 567765. Alternatively, contact the most convenient Business Link yourself, via *Yellow Pages*.

If you can't find answers to your questions on the Business Link Web site, you can email your question and expect a prompt response either via e-mail or by telephone.

Making use of Business Link financial services

Business Link can also offer advice and help on the basics of all sorts of financial needs, including accounting, bookkeeping, and managing your working capital effectively.

To be successful, a business needs a constant flow of new customers and the means to ensure they become loyal and profitable in the longer term. This means understanding customers – knowing what they want, need, and will pay for.

The experts at Business Link know that entrepreneurs need to keep abreast of changes in the market and understand how these will affect their customers. They also need to be aware of what competitors are doing and find unique ways to sell their own products and services. To help meet those needs, Business Link can provide practical help with ideas on:

✔ Finding, winning, and keeping profitable customers

✔ Developing your business by launching new products, entering new markets and starting to export

✔ Planning and using a wide variety of marketing communications, advertising, public relations (PR), direct mail, and the Internet

✔ Making use of information about competitors

✔ Exploring new markets

Depending on your circumstances and geographic area, there may be special initiatives or grants that are available and suitable for your business needs. Business Link can advise on such grants as well as helping prepare your case for bank or equity finance.

Exploring the variety of other Business Link services

Business Link offers help with nearly every aspect of running a business – I'm not sure they can advise you on a good coffee service, but I may be wrong. The following sections fill you in on programmes to help you deal with personnel, technology, taxes, and general management issues.

Making the most of your people

For most small businesses, workers are one of the most important resources. The lack of suitably skilled staff is seen as a major obstacle to small business expansion.

Business Link can help you put plans in place to develop your staff, enhance their skills, and improve their effectiveness to your business. Their *Investors In People* programme helps both the business founder and employees to perform better by ensuring adequate training. They also help you make sure that you have all the appropriate personnel requirements such as job descriptions, contracts of employment, and personal development plans in place.

Entering e-commerce and IT

If you tell people you started a business, one of the first questions you get asked is 'What's your Web site address?' Everyone, including you, doesn't even pause to ask whether you have e-mail – they assume that much automatically.

Technology can be a little intimidating, especially if you just know that you don't know enough about an aspect of running a business that is fast becoming an automatic aspect. Not to worry, Business Link can help you enter the age of *e-commerce*.

E-commerce is a term used to describe any business activity on the Internet. It is about selling things you make or have as well as being a way to speed up transactions, innovate new products and services and create more value for your business and for your customers. E-commerce covers everything along the whole value chain that links a business and its suppliers to the market, so its about buying as much as its about selling.

E-commerce is not just about technology. It is about making technology work to achieve the best outcomes for your business. Business Link advise on both the business issues involved in making e-commerce happen, as well as the technical issues such as security basics, Web site design and development.

They also advise on choosing and using computers and information technology (IT) systems and have access to a network of advisers, often based at the Business Link premises.

Managing and improving

Most businesses face decisions about property and premises. Entering inappropriate leasing agreements is an area where many small businesses have come unstuck. Business Link provide a topic guide on *Property and Premises* including guidance sourced from some of the UK's most authoritative experts. They also offer information on *Supply Chain Management* and all the logistical problems associated with getting products from where you make or assemble them to where the customer wants them.

Business Link offer information on two areas where small businesses can learn from and beat their large organisation counterparts. *Process Improvement*, which is concerned with being efficient at making products or delivering services, and *Quality Improvement*, which is concerned with meeting customer requirements. They also offer information and access to a benchmarking service, which lets small firms compare themselves to the best of their peers and so learn where and how to improve performance.

If you want to go beyond merely improving what you are doing to create something distinctive and innovative, the Business Link also offers information on innovation.

Adhering to regulations and taxation

Regulations and taxation are unwelcome but essential parts of an entrepreneur's business life. Whether you are taking on your first employee, have ideas and intellectual property you want to protect, or want to know about tax and VAT, Business Link offer some practical guidance.

All the regulatory information on their site has been provided by or checked by the relevant government department to provide authoritative material and is linked directly via the Business Link Web site at www.businesslink.org.

- ✔ To read the individual pieces of legislation guidance published by other government departments, visit Direct Access Government (DAG).

- ✔ Information about local trading standards and regulations is available from your local authority. Available Web sites are listed on the UK Online Web site. The network of Local Business Partnerships around the country provides a framework to enable business and Local Authorities to work together and streamline the regulation process.

- ✔ Visit the Inland Revenue Web site to view their 'Starting up in business' guide to cutting through the red tape.

Special Initiatives

At any one time, there is a range of government initiatives that may be able to help your small business. Business Link provide the entry point to all of these. Some, like Smart, are intended to help fund the development of advanced technology. Others are focused on helping specific groups, such as Women in Business and Ethnic Minorities. This topic area maintains signposts and overview documents of government initiatives that are relevant to small business. Current topic areas include:

- ✔ The Small Business Research Initiative, which aims to increase the success of smaller firms in obtaining contracts from government bodies to conduct research and development.

- ✔ Grants, under the Finance and Money topic area, lists and describes all the currently available grants for new and small businesses, together with contact details.

Linking to Local Enterprise Agencies (LEAs)

Some 250 Local Enterprise Agencies (LEAs) in the UK deliver business support services under contract to Business Link – sometimes they're located in the same premises. The key purpose of LEAs is to promote economic regeneration by helping small firms to set up. Local Enterprise Agencies are companies limited by guarantee, typically set up as partnerships between big companies and organisations in the private sector and local authorities, with support from central government depending on their individual circumstances.

LEAs are independent and are controlled by no single group of sponsors. They were created by big businesses, the major banks and accountancy bodies, in response to government pressure. The thinking is that big business has much to gain from a successful small business sector and they have a responsibility to pass the knowledge and experience they have gained on to the next generation of entrepreneurs. The private sector generally retains the largest sponsorship stake, and almost invariably a local businessperson will chair the LEA. LEAs have great, in-depth experience of the local small and medium enterprise (SME) economy, with the ability to draw on a local network of specialist skills, such as accountants, lawyers, and banks.

Typically LEAs directly or indirectly provide advice, information, counselling, and training on a comprehensive range of business issues, as well as very often providing shared workspace with access to some business services. They are involved with all types of SMEs, including pre-starts, start-ups, sole traders, partnerships, co-operatives, and limited companies.

LEAs provide business services like the following:

- ✔ **Business counselling:** As a direct consequence of private sector sponsorship, LEAs are able to offer start-up companies and small business firms free business counselling, delivered by practicing business people.

- ✔ **Business training:** LEAs provide a wide variety of training. All provide training in business planning and other pre-start essentials. In addition, most LEAs offer training for established businesses in topics such as marketing, exporting, management development, financial management, personnel management, and so on.

- ✔ **Consultancy:** Many LEAs assist established businesses with strategy, business planning, and raising finance; total quality and ISO9000; marketing and exporting, and so on. LEAs are partners in Business Link and, if they are unable to help directly, can signpost you to appropriate assistance locally.

- ✔ **Managed workspace:** Nearly half of LEAs operate managed workspace for small firms, offering tenants a sheltered working environment in which the landlord is also the business adviser. Length of tenure can vary, but all offer easy in, easy out terms. This gives agencies a first-hand insight into the critical early years in the life of the start-up small firm.

You can find your nearest Local Enterprise Agency in the phone book or at the National Federation of Enterprise Agencies (NFEA) Web site: www.nfea. com. NFEA maintains a current directory of all its members on its Web site. The NFEA also offers an online version of the range of services provided by the local agencies themselves at www.smallbusinessadvice.org.uk

Choosing Small Business Associations

Whilst the services of government supported help agencies are often free, there is also a growing army of commercial or semi-commercial self-help organisations in the field. Their basic premise is that if small firms can band together either to buy goods, services, or advice, or to influence government policy, they are more likely to be effective than they would be on their own. I cover the more established of these organisations in the following sections.

The Federation of Small Businesses

The Federation of Small Businesses (FSB) (www.fsb.org.uk) is a national organisation with 165,000 members that protects small firms' interests and fights for their rights. The Federation has the resources to take major test cases of importance to small business through the expensive legal process leading to the House of Lords and the European Courts if necessary. They have been particularly effective in dealing with taxation and employment matters.

The Federation maintains Press and Parliamentary Offices at Westminster, in Glasgow, Cardiff, and Belfast; an Administration Office at Blackpool, and Regional Offices elsewhere in the UK. Thirty-one regional committees and over 200 branch committees run by people who themselves operate small businesses and who donate their time to the Federation, complement the professional staffs.

For people thinking of starting their own business they offer legal, environmental, fire, and premises tips, as well as advice on many other issues which the small business person may have to address as they grow. They also provide information on other agencies that might be of use or assistance when starting up.

Membership costs range from £100 per annum, including a one-off registration fee of £30 for a person working on their own, up to £650 for a firm employing more than 101 people. (Prices exclude VAT.)

Amongst the benefits on offer provided by a partner organisation, Abbey Legal Protection Ltd (ALP) is an underwriting service specialising in legal and professional fees insurance. In addition ALP's in-house solicitors, barristers, and tax experts provide legal and taxation advice lines, including litigation and representation services.

Forum of Private Business Ltd

The mission of the Forum of Private Business Ltd (FPB) (www.fpb.co.uk) is to influence laws and policies that affect private businesses and support members to grow profitably. The Forum researches and distributes a referendum a number of times each year and keeps both members and government aware of how small firms feel about key topical issues. Membership fees are based on a sliding scale dependant on the number of referendums you take part in. Membership of the Forum brings the following benefits:

- A direct influence on laws and policies affecting your business, for example employment law, uniform business rates, taxation, red tape, bank services, late payment, and so on.

- Information on tap when you need it with unlimited *free* access to the Member Information Service, on any issue affecting your business.

- User-friendly management tools to help your business stay within the law – as you complete, you comply. For example, FPB Employment Manual (produced with TUC), FPB Health & Safety Audit (produced with TUC), FPB Bank Finance Review (produced with the Institute of Chartered Accountants), FPB Credit Control Audit.

- Free access to VUSME (the Virtual University for Small and Medium-Sized Enterprises), which offers online training resources.

- Grant search, covering all types of business grant, including those funded by the EU.

The British Chambers of Commerce

Though not aimed exclusively at small businesses, the British Chambers of Commerce (www.britishchambers.org.uk) does offer an extensive range of services for business-starters. Their national network of accredited chambers is managed and developed by their business membership and monitored at the national level to ensure that they deliver appropriate products and services to prescribed standards. They are funded by membership subscriptions.

Currently over 135,000 businesses belong to a Chambers in the Accredited Network, from growth-oriented start-ups to local and regional subsidiaries of multinational companies, in all commercial and industrial sectors, and from all over the UK.

British Chambers of Commerce have access to a range of benefits all geared to help businesses big or small succeed and grow. With over 2,500 staff, covering more than 100 locations, their network provides a ready-made management support team for any business anywhere in the UK.

Business training, information resources, networking, and savings on essential overheads, all of which are tailored to individual business needs, are on offer from local Chambers. Increasingly, many of their services are also available online.

Some specific membership benefits include:

- A total vehicle management service providing fleet solutions for business of all sizes and added benefits including free AA cover and accident management
- Unlimited access to free 24-hour, professional advice on commercial and employment law, health and safety, and tax related issues
- Guaranteed discounts on gas and electricity from one of the UK's leading energy suppliers
- A stakeholder pension solution
- A complete, comprehensive package of legal insurance cover which is relevant to the minefield of legal problems a business faces today
- A professional and confidential counselling service for employees, to help support and improve company performance
- A range of healthcare packages to suit every business size at discounted rates

The British Chambers of Commerce are also part of the global network of Chambers of Commerce, and for existing or potential exporters there is simply no better route to the global marketplace.

Their regular surveys, consultations, and reports provide grassroots business opinion and have strong influence on government ministers and officials, MPs, and other decision makers and opinion formers.

Entering an Incubator

Incubators, also known as accelerators, science parks, innovation centres, technology parks, and a whole variety of other names coined over the years, are places where new business can set up in a benign environment, with support services and advice close at hand. The many names try to describe the tasks that accelerators perform.

Tempting though it might be to believe that business accelerators are an Internet phenomena, the first serious attempt at incubation is credited to a near derelict building near New York City in 1959. The name came into common usage more by way of a joke because one of the businesses involved was actually incubating real chicken eggs. Several waves of accelerators followed this inauspicious start and by the 1980s several hundred such facilities were scattered around the US, Canada, Europe and Australia. Later incubator progressions took in the developing economies and the Internet variation, which came into being in the mid 1990s, swept across the US, Europe, India, China, Malaysia, Singapore, The Philippines, and elsewhere, bringing the total by 2003 to some 4,000 facilities world-wide.

Finding the right type of incubator

Varieties of accelerators and incubators now co-exist in the market, with radically different aims and objectives. Some, such as those founded by entrepreneurs, venture capital firms, the 'for profit' variety, only want to get rich by helping entrepreneurs to get rich. That goal at least has the merit of transparency. Some incubators have revenue models that can make the incubator rich without necessarily benefiting anyone else that much. Governments and local governments are more concerned with job creation than wealth, and universities, another major player, want jobs for the students and funding for faculty research, rather than riches themselves. Big corporate firms run private incubators to encourage firms who might buy their products or services or create career opportunities for their more entrepreneurial and potentially less fickle employees.

These incubators are havens for entrepreneurs with innovative or technology-based business ideas that need more help than most to be brought to fruition. Such ventures usually have more potential than other business starters, but they are also more risky. No one knows how many entrepreneurs graduate from these incubators each year but it's a reasonable supposition that each of the estimated 4,000 incubators has two or three graduates each year. So 10,000 or so 'eggs' are hatched in a safe environment each year. That's not a big number in terms of business start-ups. Across Europe and the US somewhere between 3 and 4 million new businesses get going in most years. But for the entrepreneurs, some of them at any rate, who get into an incubator, their chances of success are better than if they went it alone.

Getting into an accelerator

There is almost invariably an application process to getting into any business incubator. All that does vary is the process itself. Some incubators positively invite and encourage the informal approach, some are highly structured, some have their own models and techniques that they believe can sort the wheat from the chaff. All the application processes take time and if they didn't you would have cause for concern. After all, if an incubator takes in anyone without any serious consideration as to what they can do to help their businesses, that particular incubation process is unlikely to be of much value. Most application processes require some sort of a business plan. It may be little more than an executive summary to be done online with your application. Or it may be a more comprehensive written document setting out your latest thinking on what is so special about you and your big idea. Then comes the interview and after that the decision.

Most accelerators have details of their application process on their Web sites, as well as case examples of successful clients. Some have business plan application templates to help in the process. You can expect it to take anything from a couple of weeks to a couple of months to get through the process.

How much will incubation cost? If you are just paying rent and for services as you use them, as say in the Cranfield or St John's Innovation Centres, then the cost of being in an incubator is transparent. Such not-for-profit incubators are usually aimed at non-business-educated people who have good ideas to create traditional small businesses, usually with little technology involved. These incubators are frequently government funded, often in underdeveloped cities, and provide mentoring, business development, and office space. The typical equity stake required ranges from none to nominal (some require CEOs to give back to the community).

But if giving an incubator an equity stake in your business is involved, as it surely will be in any for-profit incubator, then the cost can run the scale from a few per cent of the business to being an outrageously expensive 30 to 50 per cent. It's not always clear that the more you pay the more value you get. It depends on your business needs and the scale of the opportunity you want to exploit.

Contact either UK Business Incubation (www.ukbi.co.uk) or United Kingdom Science Park Association (UKSPA) (www.ukspa.org.uk) to find out all you need to know about incubators or innovation centres that might help you achieve your ambitious goals.

Helping Young Entrepreneurs

Under 25s are a fast-growing segment of the business start-up market. Even if you are not in that age group the two organisations in this section can help get your son or daughter off to a flying start.

Attracting Livewire

Livewire (www.shell-livewire.org) is a national programme supported by Shell, the oil multinational, to help young entrepreneurs start their own business.

Gaming his way to fame

David Darling, a schoolboy entrepreneur, created a multi-million-pound company from modest beginnings – his first venture operated from his grandparents' garden shed. As a teenager growing up in the early 1980s, he developed his first digital game and placed an advert in a specialist magazine. The exercise was a success. Darling, 34, is now head of Codemasters, a group that employs more than 380 people and in 2001 made profits of £22m.

Darling and his brother, Richard, were fascinated by the new technology of computer games. They were avid readers of *Popular Computing Weekly*, a specialist magazine for Atari, Commodore, and Sinclair users. One section of the publication was devoted to programming, featuring the computer codes for popular games as well as tuition and advice. The technology was primitive and with the help of the magazine, the two brothers were able to copy simple codes for games such as Space Invaders. Next they started to develop games, initially for themselves.

Thus they decided to test the market and saved up the money for a half-page advertisement in *Popular Computing Weekly*. The price was £70, which they raised by missing school dinners for weeks.

They created their own advert and logo – a Superman-type character – with the help of a friend whose father ran an advertising design company. Under the name Galactic Software, they offered '14 great games from America' for £10. Whilst they had merely hoped to make enough money to cover the cost of the advert, in the event, 40 readers replied, generating £400 of sales. Encouraged by their success the brothers ran a second and third advert in consecutive issues. After the third, some 500 orders came in, which was more work than two people could manage, especially with exams approaching. In response Darling employed the services of a music duplication business in Bridgwater, Somerset. It made copies of tapes for local bands and he struck a deal paying the company to copy the 14 games at the rate of 50p per tape.

The first company vehicle was a very second-hand Honda moped bought for £60 to collect the tapes, while he used his grandparents' garden shed as a warehouse.

After the Darling brothers sat their exams, they went into business full time.

A part of the Shell UK community investment programme, Shell Livewire helps young people (aged 16–30) set up in business with information, advice and support, including how to write a business plan and how to carry out market research.

There are free downloadable booklets on how to carry out market research and how to write a business plan on the Web site. They are useful, if a little dated in terms of useful links, as the booklets were last updated in 1996.

There are also annual Young Business Start-Up Awards, where the winner of the UK final wins $10,000.

Trusting the Prince's Trust

The Princes Trust (www.princes-trust.org.uk) helps 14–30 year olds to develop confidence, learn new skills, and get into work. It offers opportunities when no one else will. So if you've got an idea for a business but no one will give you the money to get it off the ground, it can offer you finance and advice. The Prince's Trust can offer:

- A low interest loan of up to £5,000

- Test marketing grants of up to £250

- Grants of up to £1,500 in special circumstances

- Advice from a volunteer 'Business Mentor' during your first three years of trading

- Extra support, including discounted exhibition space and specialist advice

In 2003 the Prince's Trust helped more than 4,800 young people to set up in business. Over 71 per cent of all start-up applications to The Prince's Trust were converted into new ventures – creating almost 18,000 businesses in just five years. One in ten of those businesses had a turnover in excess of £1 million.

The top 50 Prince's Trust businesses turn over £148 million and employ over 1,600 people and since the Trust was established it has helped 43,000 young people to set up in business to 2002.

Chapter 8

Finding the Money

· ·

In This Chapter

▶ Working out how much outside money you need

▶ Looking at the different types of money available to you

▶ Choosing the best source of money for you

▶ Finding money to work with

· ·

Setting up a business requires money – there is no getting away from that. You have bills such as rent to pay, materials and equipment to purchase, and all before any income is received. Starting a business on the road to success involves ensuring that you have sufficient money to survive until the point where income continually exceeds expenditure.

Raising this initial money and the subsequent financial management of the business is therefore vital, and great care should be taken over it. Unfortunately, more businesses fail due to lack of sufficient day-to-day cash and financial management than for any other reason. This chapter helps you avoid common pitfalls and helps you find the right type of money for your business.

Assessing How Much Money You Need

You should work out from the outset how much money you will need to get your business off the ground. If your proposed venture needs more cash than you feel comfortable either putting up yourself or raising from others, then the sooner you know the better. Then you can start to revise your plans. The steps that lead to an accurate estimate of your financial needs start with the sales forecast, which you do as part of feasibility testing, which I cover in Chapter 5, along with advice on estimating costs for initial expenditures such as retail or production space, equipment, staff, and so on.

Forecasting cash flow is the most reliable way to estimate the amount of money a business needs on a day-to-day basis.

Do's and don'ts for making a cash flow forecast:

- ✔ Do ensure your projections are believable. This means you need to show how your sales will be achieved.

- ✔ Do base projections on facts not conjecture.

- ✔ Do describe the main assumptions that underpin your projections.

- ✔ Do explain what the effect of these assumptions not happening to plan could be. For example, if your projections are based on recruiting three sales people by month three, what would happen if you could only find two suitable people by that date?

- ✔ Don't use data to support projections without saying where it came from.

- ✔ Don't forget to allow for seasonal factors. At certain times of the year most business are influenced by regular events. Sales of ice-cream are lower in winter than in summer, sales of toys peak in the lead up to Christmas and business-to-business sales dip in the summer and Christmas holiday periods. So rather than taking your projected annual sales figure and dividing by twelve to get a monthly figure, you need to consider what effect seasonal factors might have.

- ✔ Don't ignore economic factors such as an expanding (or shrinking) economy, rising (or falling) interest rates and an unemployment rate that is so low that it may influence your ability to recruit at the wage rate you would like to pay.

- ✔ Don't make projections without showing the specific actions that will get those results.

- ✔ Don't forget to get someone else to check your figures out – you may be blind to your own mistakes but someone else is more likely to spot the mistakes/flaws in your projections.

Projecting receipts

Receipts from sales come in different ways, depending on the range of products and services on offer. And aside from money coming in from paying customers, the business owner may, and in many cases almost certainly will, put in cash of their own. However not all the money will necessarily go in at the outset; you could budget so that £10,000 goes in at the start, followed by sums of £5,000 in months four, seven, and ten respectively.

There could be other sources of outside finance, say from a bank or investor, but these are best left out at this stage. In fact the point of the cash flow projection, as well as showing how much money the business needs, is to reveal the likely shortfall after the owner has put in what they can to the business and the customers have paid up.

You should total up the projected receipts for each month and for the year as a whole. You would be well advised to carry out this process using a spreadsheet program, which will save you the problems caused by faulty maths.

A sale made in one month may not result in any cash coming into the business bank account until the following month, if you are reasonably lucky, or much later if you are not.

Estimating expenses

Some expenses, such as rent, rates, and vehicle and equipment leases, you pay monthly. Others bills such as telephone, utilities, and bank charges come in quarterly.

If you haven't yet had to pay utilities, for example, you put in your best guesstimate of how much you'll spend and when. Marketing, promotion, travel, subsistence, and stationery are good examples of expenses you may have to estimate. You know you will have costs in these areas, but they may not be all that accurate as projections.

After you've been trading for a while, you can get a much better handle on the true costs likely to be incurred.

Total up the payments for each month and for the year as a whole.

Working out the closing cash balances

This is crunch time, when the real sums reveal the amount of money your great new business needs to get it off the ground. Working through the cash flow projections allows you to see exactly how much cash you have in hand, or in the bank, at the end of each month, or how much cash you need to raise. This is the closing cash balance for the month. It is also the opening cash balance for the following month as that is the position you are carrying forward.

The accounting convention is to show payments out and negative sums in brackets, rather than with minus signs in front.

Testing your assumptions

There is little that disturbs a financier more than a firm that has to go back cap-in-hand for more finance too soon after raising money, especially if the reason should have been seen and allowed for at the outset.

So in making projections you have to be ready for likely pitfalls and be prepared for the unexpected events that will knock your cash flow off target. Forecasts and projections rarely go to plan, but the most common pitfalls can be anticipated and to some extent allowed for.

You can't really protect yourself against freak disasters or unforeseen delays, which can hit large and small businesses alike. But some events are more likely than others to affect your cash flow, and it is against these that you need to guard by careful planning. Not all of the events listed here may be relevant to your business, but some, perhaps many, will at some stage be factors that could push you off course.

Getting the numbers wrong

It's called estimating for a reason. You can't know ahead of time how the future will pan out, so you have to guess, and sometimes you guess wrong. Some of the wrong guesses you can make about stock and costs are:

- ✔ **A flawed estimate:** There is no doubt that forecasting sales is difficult. The numbers of things that can and will go awry are many and varied. In the first place the entire premise on which the forecast is based may be flawed. Estimating the number of people who may come into a restaurant as passing trade, who will order from a catalogue mailing, or what proportion of Internet site hits will turn into paying customers, depends on performance ratios. For example a direct mail shot to a well-targeted list could produce anything from 0.5–3 per cent response. If you build your sales forecast using the higher figure and actually achieve the lower figure then your sales income could be barely a sixth of the figure in your cash flow projection. You can't avoid this problem, but you can allow for it by testing to destruction (see elsewhere in this checklist).

- ✔ **Carrying too much stock:** If your sales projections are too high, you will experience the double whammy of having less cash coming in and more going out than shown in your forecast. That is because in all probability you will have bought in supplies to meet anticipated demand. Your suppliers offering discounts for bulk purchases may have exacerbated the situation if you took up their offers.

✔ **Missed or wrong cost:** You may underestimate or completely leave out certain costs due to your inexperience. Business insurance and legal expenses are two often missed items. Even where a cost is not missed altogether it may be understated. So, for example, if you are including the cost of taking out a patent in your financing plan, it is safer to take it from the supplier's Web site rather than from a friend who took out a patent a few years ago.

✔ **Testing to destruction:** Even events that have not been anticipated can be allowed for when estimating financing needs. 'What if' analysis using a cash flow spreadsheet will allow you to identify worst-case scenarios that could knock you off-course. After this you will end up with a realistic estimate of the financing requirements of the business or project.

✔ **Late deliveries:** If your suppliers deliver late, you may in turn find you have nothing to sell. Apart from causing ill will with your customers, you may have to wait weeks or months for another opportunity to supply. This problem can be minimised using online order tracking systems, if your suppliers have them, but some late deliveries will occur. Increasing your stocks is one way to insure against deficiencies in the supply chain, but that strategy too has an adverse impact on cash flow.

Settling on sales

Sales may be slow, pricing may be high – just two of the ways sales can make your projections look silly. More ways follow:

✔ **Slower than expected sales:** Even if your forecasting premise is right, or nearly so, customers may take longer to make up their minds than you expect. A forecast may include an assumption that people will order within two weeks of receiving your mail-order catalogue. But until you start trading you will not know how accurate that assumption is likely to be. Even if you have been in business for years, buying patterns may change.

✔ **Not being able to sell at list price:** Selling price is an important factor in estimating the amount of cash coming into a business and hence the amount of finance needed.

Often the only way a new or small business can win certain customers is by matching a competitor's price. This may not be the price in your list, but it is the one you have to sell at.

Also the mix of products or services you actually sell may be very different from your projection and this can affect average prices. For example a restaurant owner has to forecast what wines his or her customers will buy. If the house wine is too good, then more customers might go for that rather than the more expensive and more profitable wines on the list.

✔ **Suppliers won't give credit:** Few suppliers are keen to give small and particularly new businesses any credit. So before you build in 30, 60, or even 90 days' credit into your financial projections, you need to confirm that normal terms of trade will apply to what a supplier may view as an abnormal customer.

You need to remember that whilst taking extended credit may help your cash flow in the short term, it could sour relationships in the long term. So in circumstances where a product is in short supply poor payers will be last on the list to get deliveries and the problems identified above may be further exacerbated.

Miscounting customers

Customers can confound your most well-thought-out projections. They pay late, they may rip you off, and they may not buy your goods as quickly as you'd like. Some of the ways customers can be to blame for throwing your estimates off are:

✔ **Paying slowly:** Whilst you set the terms and conditions under which you plan to do business, customers are a law unto themselves. If they can take extra credit they will. Unless you are in a cash-only business, you can expect a proportion of your customers to be late payers. Whilst with good systems you will keep this to an acceptable figure, you will never get every bill paid on time. You need to allow for this lag in your cash flow projections.

✔ **Bad debts:** Unfortunately late payers are not the only problem. Some customers never pay. Businesses fail each year and individuals go bankrupt, each leaving behind a trail of unpaid bills. You can take some steps to minimise this risk, but you can't eliminate the risk. You can try to get a feel for the rate of non-payment in your sector and allow for it in your plans. For example, the building and restaurant industries have a relatively high incidence of bad debts, whilst business services have a lower rate.

✔ **Fraud and theft:** Retailers claim they could knock 5 per cent off everything they sell if they could eliminate theft. But despite their best endeavours with security guards and cameras, theft continues.

✔ **Repeat orders take longer to come in than expected:** It is hard to know exactly what a customer's demand for your product or service is. The initial order may last them months, weeks, or days. For strategic reasons they may want to divide up their business between a number of suppliers. If, for example, they have three suppliers and they order a month's worth at a time, it may be some time before they order from you again. If your customer sales are sluggish or seasonal, then that timeframe could extend further still. So even delighted customers may not come back for quite some time.

Reviewing Your Financing Options

Knowing how much money you need to get your business successfully started is an important first step, but it is only that: a first step. There are many sources of funds available to small firms. However not all are equally appropriate to all firms at all times. These different sources of finance carry very different obligations, responsibilities, and opportunities. The differences have to be understood to allow an informed choice.

Most small firms confine their financial strategy to long-term or short-term bank loans, viewing other financing methods as either too complex or too risky. In many respects the reverse is true. Almost every finance source other than banks shares some of the risks of doing business with you to a greater or lesser extent.

The great attraction of borrowing from a bank lies in the speed of the transaction. Most small businesses operate without a business plan so most events that require additional funds, such as sudden expansion or contraction, come as a surprise, either welcome or unwelcome, and with a sense of urgency. Basing financing choices on the fact that you need the money quickly may lead to more difficulties in the long run.

Deciding between debt capital and equity capital

At one end of the financing spectrum lie shareholders – either individual *business angels* who put their own money into a business, or corporate organisations such as *venture capital providers* – who provide equity capital which is used to buy a stake in a business. These investors share all the risks and vagaries of the business alongside you and expect a proportionate share in the rewards if things go well. They are less concerned with a stream of dividends, which is just as well as few small companies ever pay them, and instead hope for a radical increase in the value of their investment. They expect to realise this value from other investors who want to take their places for the next stage in the firm's growth cycle, rather than from any repayment by the founder. Investors in new or small businesses don't look for the security of buildings or other assets to underpin their investment. Rather they look to the founder's vision and the core management team's ability to deliver results.

At the other end of the financing spectrum are debt financiers – banks that try hard to take no risk and expect some return on their money irrespective of your business's performance. They want interest payments on money lent, usually from day one. Whilst they too hope the management is competent, they are more interested in making sure either you or the business has some type of asset such as a house that they can grab if things go wrong. At the end of the day, and that day can be sooner than the borrower expects, a bank wants all its money back, with interest. Think of bankers as people who help you turn part of an illiquid asset such as property into a more liquid asset such as cash – for a price.

Understanding the differences between lenders, who provide debt capital, and investors, who provide equity, or share, capital is central to a sound grasp of financial management.

In between the extremes of shareholders and the banks lie a myriad of other financing vehicles, which have a mixture of lending or investing criteria. You need to keep your business finances under constant review, choosing the most appropriate mix of funds for the risks you plan to take and the economic climate ahead. The more risky and volatile the road ahead, the more likely it is that taking a higher proportion of equity capital will be appropriate. In times of stability and low interest, higher borrowings may be more acceptable.

As a rule of thumb debt and equity should be used in equal amounts to finance a business. If the road ahead looks more risky than usual go for £2 of equity to every £1 of debt. Table 8-1 illustrates some of the differences between risk-averse lenders and risk-taking investors.

Table 8-1	Comparing Benefits of Lenders and Investors	
Category	*Lenders*	*Investors*
Interest	Paid on outstanding loan	None, though dividends sometimes paid if profits warrant it
Capital	Repaid at end of term or sooner if lender has concerns	Returned with substantial growth through new shareholders
Security	Either from assets or personal guarantees	From belief in founders and their business vision

If your business sector is generally viewed as very risky, and perhaps the most reliable measure of that risk is the proportion of firms that go bust, then financing the business almost exclusively with borrowings is tantamount to gambling.

Debt has to be serviced whatever your business performance, so it follows that, in any risky, volatile marketplace, you stand a good chance of being caught out one day.

If your business risks are low, the chances are that profits are relatively low too. High profits and low risks always attract a flood of competitors, reducing your profits to levels that ultimately reflect the riskiness of your business sector. As venture capitalists and shareholders generally are looking for much better returns than they could get by lending the money, it follows they will be disappointed in their investment on low-risk, low-return business. So if they are wise they will not get involved in the first place, or if they do they will not put any more money in later.

Examining your own finances

Obviously the first place to start looking for money to finance your business is in your own pockets. Whilst you may not have much in ready cash you may have assets that can be turned into cash or used to support borrowing.

Start by totalling your assets and liabilities. The chances are that your most valuable assets are your house, your car, and any life assurance or pension policies you may have. Your liabilities are the debts you owe. The difference between your assets and liabilities, assuming you have more of the former than the latter, is your 'net worth'. That in effect is the maximum security you can offer anyone outside the business that you want to raise money from.

Now the big questions are: what is your appetite for risk and how certain are you your business will be successful? The more of your own money you can put into your business at the outset, the more you will be truly running your own business in your own way. The more outside money you have to raise, the more power and perhaps value you have to share with others.

Now you have a simple piece of arithmetic to do. How much money do you need to finance your business start-up, as shown in your worst-case scenario cash flow forecast? How much of your own money are you willing and able to put into your business? The difference is the sum you are looking to outside financiers to back you with.

If that sum is more than your net worth, then you will be looking for investors. If it is less then bankers may be the right people to approach.

If you do have free cash or assets that you could but won't put into your business, then you should ask yourself if the proposition is worth pursuing. You can be absolutely certain that any outsider you approach for money will ask you to put up or shut up.

Another factor to consider in reviewing your own finances is your ongoing expenses. You have to live whilst getting your business up and running. So food, heat, and a roof over your head are essential expenses. But perhaps a two-week long-haul summer holiday, the second car, and membership of a health club are not essentials. Great whilst you were a hired hand and had a pay cheque each month, but an expendable luxury once you are working for yourself.

Determining the Best Source of Finance for You

Choosing which external source of finance to use is to some extent a matter of personal preference. One of your tasks in managing your business's financial affairs is to keep good lines of communication open with as many sources as possible.

The other key task is to consider which is the most appropriate source for your particular requirement at any one time. The main issues you need to consider are explored in the following sections.

Considering the costs

Clearly if a large proportion of the funds you need to start your business are going to be consumed in actually raising the money itself, then your set-up costs are going to be very high. Raising capital, especially if the amounts are relatively small (under £500,000) is generally quite expensive. You have to pay your lawyers and accountants, and those of your investor or lender, to prepare the agreements and to conduct the due diligence examination (the business appraisal). It is not unusual to spend between 10 and 15 per cent of the first £500,000 you raise on set-up costs.

An overdraft or factoring agreement is relatively cheap to set up, usually a couple of per cent or so. However, long-term loans, leasing, and hire-purchase agreements could involve some legal costs.

Sharing ownership and control

The source of your money helps determine how much ownership and control you have to give up in return. Venture capitalists generally want a large share of stock and often a large say in how the business is run. At the other end of the spectrum are providers of long-term loans who generally leave you alone so long as you service the interest and repay the capital as agreed. You have to strike the balance that works best for you and your business.

If you do not want to share the ownership of your business with outsiders then clearly raising equity capital is not a good idea. Even if you recognise that owning 100 per cent of a small venture is not as attractive as owning 40 per cent of a business ten times as large it may not be the right moment to sell any of your shares. Particularly if, in common with many business founders, long-term capital gain is one of your principal goals. If you can hold onto your shares until profits are reasonably high you will realise more gain for every share sold than if you sell out in the early years or whilst profits are low.

Parting with shares inevitably involves some loss of control. Letting 5 per cent go may just be a mild irritation from time to time. However once 25 per cent has gone, outsiders could have a fair amount of say in how things are run. At that point, even relatively small groups of shareholders could find it easy to call an Extraordinary General Meeting and put it to a vote to remove you from the board. Nevertheless, whilst you have over 51 per cent you are in control, if only just. Once past the 51 per cent things could get a little dangerous. Theoretically you could be out voted at any stage.

Some capital providers take a hands-on approach and will have a view on how you should run the business.

Beating the clock

Overdrafts can be arranged in days, raising venture capital can take months. Very different amounts of scarce management time are needed, dependent on the financing route taken. So if speed matters, your funding options may be limited.

Venture capital providers (also called Venture Capitalists or VCs) have been known to string out negotiations long enough to see if the bullish forecasts made in the business plan come to pass. After all, venture capital is there to help businesses to grow faster than they might otherwise do not just to keep them afloat. Don't expect a decision from a venture capital firm in under three months whatever their brochure says. Four to six months is a more realistic timescale and nine months is not too unusual.

Business Angels can usually make investment decisions much more quickly than VCs, after all it's their money they are risking. Weeks rather than months, is the timescale here.

Banks finance is usually a fairly speedy process. Even large loans of £100,000 and upwards can be arranged in a few weeks. But the speed depends more on how much collateral you have to give the bank manager comfort that his money is safe.

Staying flexible

As your plans change, the amount of money you actually need may alter during negotiations. Some sources of funds such as leasing, hire-purchase agreements, and long-term loans dictate the amount that has to be agreed at the outset. If you're selling shares in the company, you have some fluidity during negotiations, and if you're arranging overdrafts it is possible to draw down only what you need at any one time, with the upper limit negotiated usually each year.

Once you have investigated and used a source of funds you may want to be able to use that source again as your plans unfold. Loans and hire purchase/ leasing agreements are for a specific sum and it can be difficult and expensive going back to the same source for more. Many venture capitalists, for example, already have a full weighting of investments in your business sector and so may not be anxious to invest more, however successful your firm. So that might mean starting all over again with another venture capital firm.

It may pay to make sure that at least some of your financing comes from a source such as factoring, which gives you total flexibility to change the amount of money drawn down to mirror the amount needed at any one time – both upwards and downwards.

Adding value to the business

With some sources of finance you can get useful expertise as well as money. For example, with factoring you could get expertise in managing your home and overseas credit, which could result in better credit control, fewer bad debts, and less capital tied up in debtors. You could even close or reduce your credit control department. With new share capital you may get a director with relevant experience in the industry. While the director's principal task is to ensure the capital provides interest, you also get the benefit of his or her knowledge.

Gaining security and certainty

For most sources of money, if you comply with the agreed-upon terms, the future is reasonably predictable – in so far as that money is concerned. The exception to this rule is an overdraft. An overdraft is technically, and often actually, repayable on demand. Overdrafts are sometimes called in at the moment you need them most.

Limiting personal liability

As a general rule most providers of long-term loans and overdrafts look to you and other owners to provide additional security if the business assets are in any way inadequate. You may be asked to provide a personal guarantee – an asset such as your house. Only when you raise new share capital, by selling more stock in your company, do you escape increasing your personal liability. Even with the new share capital you may be asked to provide warranties to assure new investors that everything in the company's past history has been declared.

Going for Debt

You can explore borrowing from a number of possible sources in your search for outside finance. It is worth giving them all the once over, but it has to be said that most people start and stop at a bank. The other major first source of money is family and friends, but many business starters feel nervous about putting family money at risk and in any event would rather deal with professional financiers. *Credit Unions* and *mezzanine finance* are relatively unusual sources of finance for a start-up, but finding any money to start a business is a tough task, so no source should be completely overlooked. (These terms are explained later in this chapter.)

Borrowing from banks

Banks are the principal, and frequently the only, source of finance for nine out of every ten new and small businesses.

Banks are usually a good starting point for almost any type of debt financing. They are also able to provide many other cash flow and asset backed financing products, although they are often not the only or the most appropriate provider. As well as the main clearing banks, a number of the former building societies and smaller regional banks are competing hard for small firm lending.

TECHNICAL STUFF

Seeing the five Cs

Bankers like to speak of the five Cs of credit analysis, factors they look at when they evaluate a loan request. When applying to a bank for a loan, be prepared to address the following points:

✔ **Character:** Bankers lend money to borrowers who appear honest and who have a good credit history. Before you apply for a loan, it makes sense to obtain a copy of your credit report and clean up any problems.

✔ **Capacity:** This is a prediction of the borrower's ability to repay the loan. For a new business, bankers look at the business plan. For an existing business, bankers consider financial statements and industry trends.

✔ **Collateral:** Bankers generally want a borrower to pledge an asset that can be sold to pay off the loan if the borrower lacks funds.

✔ **Capital:** Bankers scrutinise a borrower's net worth, the amount by which assets exceed debts.

✔ **Conditions**: Whether bankers give a loan can be influenced by the current economic climate as well as by the amount requested.

Banks also use CAMPARI, which stand for: Character, Ability, Means, Amount, Repayment, Interest and Insurance. You can find out more about this alternate system on the banking liaison group Web site: www.bankexperts.co.uk/campari.htm.

Keeping the money men happy

Most owner-managers don't give much thought to how to deal with their bank, factoring company, or venture capitalist. They just jump right into their business and don't think about how they should treat these people, what their bankers can do for them, and what their bankers in turn are looking for in a client. With a little thought and effort, you can ensure that you get the most from your banking relationships.

Your banker, or any other source of finance, has the ability to radically influence the success of your business. It is very important that you develop long-term, personal relationships with them – if you do that, when you hit the inevitable bumps in the road they'll be there to help you.

Keep in mind when you meet your banker for the first time that you want to develop a long-term relationship with this person. The meeting should be a two-way interview. You should ask yourself: 'Is this person genuinely interested in me? Is he or she trying to understand my business? Does he or she understand my objectives?' If the answer to any of these is no, then find another banker.

While you often hire your lawyer and accountant by the hour or job, your banker is another matter – he or she makes money off the fees that your business generates. Your banker is usually very happy to help you, and can therefore be a great source of free consulting, though you do need to be a little more careful today as bankers are beginning to get wise to the idea of charging out services.

Abbey National, for example, set out in 2002 to recruit around 600 staff across the UK as part of a push to snatch market share from its rivals in the business banking market, in a drive to challenge the 'big four' clearing banks in the business banking and finance markets. The move came hot on the heels of an aggressive push by rival HBOS the merged Halifax and Bank of Scotland into the small business banking market. Both groups have announced plans to offer a current account, which is money the bank can recall at any moment, for small businesses paying interest of 2 per cent.

All the major clearing banks offer telephone banking and Internet services to their small business customers or are in the process of doing so. Branch location seems less likely to be a significant factor to bank customers in the future, so you no longer have to confine your search for a bank to those with a branch nearby.

Bankers, and indeed any other sources of debt capital, are looking for property, land, insurance policies, or any other investments you may have to back their loan and the near certainty of getting their money back. They also charge an interest rate that reflects current market conditions and their view of the risk level of the proposal.

Winter
Break?

Get travel insurance before you go!

Whether it's for a winter break, a summer holiday, a weekend away or cover for all your travels this year, visit **www.churchill.com/amazon** for a great deal on travel insurance.

	Without winter sports	With winter sports
Single trip cover from	**£12.50**	**£16**
Annual cover cover from	**£55**	**£60.50**

Trust us to take care of you

We have comprehensive cover – we even cover false teeth! Take a look at a few of our benefits:

- Earn up to **10% renewal** discount on annual policies
- **24 hour** medical assistance helpline
- Cover for up to **£5,000,000 medical expenses**
- Cover against **cancellation up to £5,000**
- You can choose to **add on winter sports**
- **UK and Ireland** only call centres

So, choose Churchill and give yourself a break when it comes to travel insurance.

Call us today on
0800 916 7139

Quote ref **Amazon** or buy online at
www.churchill.com/amazon

An offer brought to you in conjunction with
amazon.co.uk®
and you're done.™

churchill™ *surprisingly passionate about insurance*™

If you import raw materials, the bank can provide you with Letters of Credit, which guarantees your suppliers payment from the bank when they present proof of satisfactory delivery. If you have a number of overseas suppliers who prefer settlement in their own currency for which you will need foreign currency, cheque facilities or buying forward, banks can make the necessary arrangements.

Running an overdraft

The principal form of short-term bank funding is an *overdraft*. An overdraft is permission for you to use some of the bank's money when you don't have enough of your own. The permission is usually agreed annually, but can be withdrawn at anytime. A little over a quarter of all bank finance for small firms is in the form of an overdraft. The overdraft was originally designed to cover the time between having to pay for raw materials to manufacture finished goods and selling those goods. The size of an overdraft will usually be limited to a modest proportion of the amount of money owed to you by your customers and the value of your finished goods stock. The bank will see those items as assets, which in the last resort can be used to get their money back.

Starting out in a cleaning business, for example, you need sufficient funds initially to buy the mop and bucket. Three months into the contract they will have been paid for and so there is no point in getting a five-year bank loan to cover this, as within a year you will have cash in the bank.

However if your overdraft does not get out of the red at any stage during the year then you need to re-examine your financing. All too often companies utilise an overdraft to acquire long-term assets, and that overdraft never seems to disappear, eventually constraining the business.

The attraction of overdrafts is that they are very easy to arrange and take little time to set up. That is also their inherent weakness. The keywords in the arrangement document are 'repayable on demand', which leaves the bank free to make and change the rules as they see fit. (This term is under review and some banks may remove this term from the arrangement.) With other forms of borrowing, as long as you stick to the terms and conditions, the loan is yours for the duration. Not so with overdrafts.

Taking on a term loan

If you are starting up a manufacturing business, you will be buying machinery to last probably five years, designing your logo and buying stationery, paying the deposit on leasehold premises, buying a vehicle, and investing funds in winning a long-term contract. As the profits on this are expected to flow over a number of years, then they need to be financed over a similarly long period of time, either through a bank loan or inviting someone to invest in shares in the company – in other words a long-term commitment.

Term loans, as these long-term borrowings are generally known, are funds provided by a bank for a number of years. The interest can be either variable – changing with general interest rates – or it can be fixed for a number of years ahead. In some cases it may be possible to move between having a fixed interest rate and a variable one at certain intervals. It may even be possible to have a moratorium on interest payments for a short period, to give the business some breathing space. Provided the conditions of the loan are met in such matters as repayment, interest and security cover, the money is available for the period of the loan. Unlike having an overdraft, the bank cannot pull the rug from under you if their circumstances (or the local manager) change.

Going with a loan guarantee

These are operated by banks at the instigation of governments in the UK, and in Australia, the US, and elsewhere. These schemes guarantee loans from banks and other financial institutions for small businesses with viable business proposals, which have tried and failed to obtain a conventional loan because of a lack of security.

Loans are available for periods of between two and ten years on sums from £5,000 to £250,000 .The government guarantees 70–90 per cent of the loan. In return for the guarantee the borrower pays a premium of 1–2 per cent per year on the outstanding amount of the loan. The commercial aspects of the loan are matters between the borrower and the lender.

Uniting with a credit union

If you don't like the terms on offer from the *high street banks,* as the major banks are often known, you may consider forming your own bank. It's not as crazy an idea as it sounds. Credit unions formed by groups of small business people, both in business and aspiring to start up, have been around for decades in the US, UK, and elsewhere. They have been an attractive option for people on low incomes, providing a cheap and convenient alternative to banks. Some self-employed people such as taxi drivers have also formed credit unions. They can then apply for loans to meet unexpected capital expenditure either for repairs, refurbishments, or technical upgrading.

Established credit unions will usually require you to be in a particular trade, have paid money in for a number of months or perhaps years and have a maximum loan amount limited to the types of assets people in their trade are most likely to need.

Certainly, few could argue about the attractiveness of an annual interest rate 30 per cent below that of the high-street lenders, which is what credit unions aim for. Members have to save regularly to qualify for a loan, though there is no minimum deposit and, after ten weeks, members with a good track record can borrow up to five times their savings, though they must continue to save while repaying the loan. There is no set interest rate, but dividends are distributed to members from any surplus, usually about 5 per cent a year. This too compares favourably with bank interest on deposit accounts.

Borrowing from family and friends

Those close to you are often willing to lend you money or invest in your business. This helps you avoid the problem of pleading your case to outsiders and enduring extra paperwork and bureaucratic delays. Help from friends, relatives, and business associates can be especially valuable if you've been through bankruptcy or had other credit problems that make borrowing from a commercial lender difficult or impossible.

Involving friends and family in your business brings a range of extra potential benefits, costs, and risks that are not a feature of most other types of finance. You need to decide if these are acceptable.

Some advantages of borrowing money from people you know well are that you may be charged a lower interest rate, may be able to delay paying back money until you're more established, and may be given more flexibility if you get into a jam. But once the loan terms are agreed to, you have the same legal obligations as you would with a bank or any other source of finance.

Borrowing money from relatives and friends can have a major disadvantage. If your business does poorly and those close to you end up losing money, you may well damage your personal relationships. So in dealing with friends, relatives, and business associates be extra careful not only to establish clearly the terms of the deal and put them in writing but also to make an extra effort to explain the risks. In short, it's your job to make sure your helpful friend or relative won't suffer true hardship if you're unable to meet your financial commitments.

Many types of business have loyal and devoted followers, people who care as much about the business as the owners do. A health food restaurant, a specialist bookstore, or an art gallery, for example, may attract people who are enthusiastic about lending money to, or investing in, the business because it fits in with their lifestyle or philosophy. Their decision to participate is driven to some extent by their feelings and is not strictly a business proposition. The rules for borrowing from friends and relatives apply here as well. Put repayment terms in writing, and don't accept money from people who can't afford to risk it.

When raising money from family and friends, follow these guidelines.

1. Do agree proper terms for the loan or investment.

2. Do put the agreement in writing and if it involves a limited partnership, share transaction, or guarantee have a legal agreement drawn up.

3. Do make an extra effort to explain the risks of the business and the possible downside implications to their money.

4. Do make sure when raising money from parents that other siblings are compensated in some way, perhaps via a will.

5. Do make sure you want to run a family business before raising money from them. It will not be the same as running your own business.

6. Don't borrow from people on fixed incomes.

7. Don't borrow from people who can't afford to lose their investment.

8. Don't make the possible rewards sound more attractive than you would say to a bank.

9. Don't offer jobs in your business to anyone providing money unless they are the best person for the job.

10. Don't change the normal pattern of social contact with family and friends after they have put up the money.

Managing mezzanine money

Mezzanine finance (also known as subordinated debt) is a form of debt where the lender takes on more risk than a bank would normally be up for. Mezzanine finance providers accept the fact that they will only get their money back after bank overdraft and loans and the like have been paid back. But in return they expect a higher rate of interest and they may ask for an option to convert some of that debt into shares in the company at a certain point. By doing that they can get a slice of the upside if your business is a roaring success.

The benefit of mezzanine finance is that it often bridges the gap between the funds provided by a bank and the high-risk investment by you, a venture capitalist, and business angels.

Mezzanine finance can now also be considered a stand-alone funding solution, often as an alternative to more expensive equity finance. Mezzanine is now commonly used to provide acquisition finance, development capital, and replacement capital, as well as finance for the more traditional management buy-out, buy-in scenarios.

Sources of mezzanine finance include many of the clearing banks and insurance companies, as well as specialist finance boutiques. With larger transactions it is possible to access the capital markets using an investment bank to achieve public offerings of high yield or 'junk' bonds. These are typically sold to institutional investors such as insurance companies and pension funds.

The amount and cost of funds under a mezzanine arrangement will depend on many factors including industry sector, historic performance, credit ratings, seasonality, and predictability of revenues and forecasts for future cash flow and profitability, as well as the strength of management, the nature of a company's financial backers and the structure of the overall financing package.

It is usual for mezzanine finance to be provided on an interest-only basis until some or all of general bank debt has been repaid, typically after four to five years, with typical loan terms ranging up to ten years. Loans are usually secured with a second charge on a company's assets such as property, plant, and equipment.

Sharing Out the Spoils

If your business is particularly risky, requires a lot of up-front finance, or involves new technology, then you usually have to consider selling a portion of your business's shares to outside investors.

However, if your business plan does not show profit returns in excess of 30 per cent compound (see Chapter 12 for more on profit ratios) and you are not prepared to part with upwards of 15 per cent of your business, then equity finance is probably not for you.

A number of different types of investor could be prepared to put up the funds if the returns are mouth-watering enough. I talk about each type in the following sections.

Going for venture capital

Venture capital is a means of financing the start-up, development, expansion, or the purchase of a company. The venture capitalist acquires a share of the company in return for providing the requisite funding. Venture capital firms often work in conjunction with other providers of finance in putting together a total funding package for a business.

Venture capital providers (*VCs*) invest other people's money, often from pension funds. They are likely to be interested in investing a large sum of money for a large stake in the company.

Venture capital is a medium- to long-term investment, of not just money, but of time and effort. The venture capital firm's aim is to enable growth companies to develop into the major businesses of tomorrow. Before investing, a venture capital provider goes through *due diligence*, a process that involves a thorough examination of both the business and its owners. Accountants and lawyers subject you and your business plan to detailed scrutiny. You and your directors are required to warrant that you have provided *all* relevant information, under pain of financial penalties.

In general VCs expect their investment to pay off within seven years. But they are hardened realists. Two in every ten investments they make are total write offs, and six perform averagely well at best. So the one star in every ten investments they make has to cover a lot of duds. VCs have a target rate of return of 30 per cent plus, to cover this poor success rate.

Raising venture capital is not a cheap option. The arrangement costs will almost always run to six figures. The cost of the due diligence process is borne by the firm raising the money, but will be paid out of the money raised, if that's any consolation. Raising venture capital is not quick either. Six months is not unusual and over a year has been known. Every VC has a deal done in six weeks in their portfolio, but that truly is the exception.

Venture capital providers want to exit from their investment at some stage. Their preferred route is via a public offering, taking your company onto the stock market, but a trade sale to another, usually larger business in a related line of work, is more usual.

New venture capital funds are coming on stream all the time and they too are looking for a gap in the market.

The British Venture Capital Association (www.bvca.co.uk) and the European Venture Capital Association (www.evca.com) both have online directories giving details of hundreds of venture capital providers.

Benefiting by business angels

One source of equity or risk capital is a private individual, with their own funds, and perhaps some knowledge of your type of business, who is willing to invest in your company in return for a share in the business.

Such investors have been christened *business angels,* a term first coined to describe private wealthy individuals who backed theatrical productions, usually a play on Broadway or in London's West End.

By their very nature such investments are highly speculative in nature. The angel typically has a personal interest in the venture and may want to play some role in the company – often an angel is determined upon some involvement beyond merely signing a cheque.

Business angels are informal suppliers of risk capital to new and growing businesses, often taking a hand at the stage when no one else will take the chance; a sort of investor of last resort. But whilst they often lose their shirts, they sometimes make serious money. One angel who backed Sage with £10,000 in their first round of £250,000 financing, saw his stake rise to £40 million.

These angels often have their own agenda and frequently operate through managed networks. Angel networks operate throughout the world, in some cases on the Internet. In the UK and the US there are hundreds of networks with tens of thousands of business angels prepared to put up several billion pounds each year into new or small businesses.

One estimate is that the UK has approximately 18,000 business angels and that they annually invest in the region of £500 million.

Business Direct in Association with *The Daily Telegraph* (www.business-direct.uk.com), Business Link for London (www.bl4london.com), and National Business Angels Network (www.bestmatch.co.uk) all have online directories of business angels.

Research has unravelled these sketchy facts about business angels as a breed. Knowing them may help you find the right one for your business.

- Business angels are generally self-made, high net-worth individuals, with entrepreneurial backgrounds. Most are in the 45–65 year age group; 19 per cent are millionaires; and only 1 per cent are women.

- Fifty per cent of angels conduct minimal or no research on the business in question, meet their entrepreneur an average of 5.4 times before investing (compared with venture capitalists who meet on average 9.5 times), and 54 per cent neglected to take up independent personal references compared to only 6 per cent of venture capitalists. Angels fundamentally back people rather than propositions and venture capitalists do the reverse.

- Typically business angels invest 5–15 per cent of their investment portfolio in start-up business ventures and their motivation is, first and foremost, financial gain through capital appreciation, with the fun and enjoyment of being involved with an entrepreneurial business an important secondary motive. A minority are motivated in part by altruistic considerations, such as helping the next generation of entrepreneurs to get started, and supporting their country or state.

✔ Business angels invest in only a very small proportion of investments that they see: typically at least seven out of eight opportunities are rejected. More than 90 per cent of investment opportunities are rejected at the initial screening stage.

✔ Around 30 per cent of investments by business angels are in technology-based businesses. Most will tell you that they vigorously avoid investing in industries they know nothing about.

✔ The majority of business angels invest in businesses located in close proximity to where they live – two-thirds of investments are made in businesses located within 100 miles of their home or office. They are, however, prepared to look further afield if they have specific sector-related investment preferences or if they are technology investors.

✔ Ninety-two per cent of angels had worked in a small firm compared, for example, with only 52 per cent of venture capitalists who had similar experience.

✔ On average, business angels sell their shareholding in the most successful investments after four years (and 75 per cent after seven years). Conversely, half of the investments in which business angels lost money had failed within two years of the investment being made.

✔ Business angels are up to five times more likely to invest in start-ups and early stage investments than venture capital providers in general.

Looking to corporate venturing

Alongside the venture capital firms are 200 or so other businesses who have a hand in the risk capital business, without it necessarily being their main line of business. For the most part these are firms with an interest in the Internet or high technology that want an inside track to new developments. Their own research and development operations have slowed down and become less and less entrepreneurial as they have gotten bigger. So they need to look outside for new inspiration.

Even successful firms invest hundreds of millions of dollars each year in scores of other small businesses. Sometimes, if the company looks a particularly good fit, they buy the whole business.

Apple, for example, whilst keeping its management team focused on the core business, has a $12 million stake in Akamai Technologies, the firm whose software tries to keep the Web running smoothly even under unusual traffic demands.

It's not only high-tech firms that go in for corporate venturing. Any firm whose arteries are hardening a bit is on the look out for new blood. McDonald's, for example, hardly a business in the forefront of the technological revolution, has stakes in over a dozen ventures including a 35 per cent stake in Prêt-à-Manger. Table 8-2 lists the top corporate venturers.

Table 8-2	The World's Top Corporate Venturers
Company	*$ millions*
Electronic Data Systems	1,500
Accenture Consulting	1,000
PriceWaterhouseCoopers	500
Time Warner Inc	500
Intel Corporation	450
Cisco Systems	450
Microsoft	450
Softbank	350
News Corporation	300
Comcast Corporation	250
Unilever	200
Sun Microsystems	200
Novell Inc	170

Finding Free Money

Sometimes, if you're very lucky or very smart – or both – you can get at least some of the money you need for free. The following sections tell you how to cash in on government grants and how winning a contest can earn you lots of lovely loot.

Getting help from the government

Unlike debt, which has to be repaid, or equity, which has to earn a return for the investors, grants and awards from the government or the European Union are often not refundable. So, although they are frequently hard to get, they can be particularly valuable.

Almost every country has incentives to encourage entrepreneurs to invest in particular locations or industries. The US, for example, has an allowance of Green Cards (work and residence permits) for up to several hundred immigrants each year prepared to put up sufficient funds to start-up in a substantial business in the country.

In the UK, if you are involved in the development of a new technology then you may be eligible for a grant for Research and Development that is now available. Under the new grant scheme, 60 per cent of eligible project costs up to a maximum grant of £75,000 can be claimed on research projects (previously called 'feasibility studies'); 35 per cent of costs up to £200,000 on development projects; 35 per cent of costs up to £500,000 on exceptional development projects; and 50 per cent of costs up to a maximum grant of £20,000 on micro projects. Business Links can give full details of the new grants.

Support for business comes in a very wide variety of forms. The most obvious is the direct (cash) grant but other forms of assistance are also numerous. The main types of grant also include *soft loans* – money lent on terms more advantageous than would usually be available from a bank – additional share capital, free or subsidised consultancy, which could help you with market research, staff development or identifying business opportunities, or with access to valuable resources such as research facilities.

Though several grant schemes operate across the whole of the UK and are available to all businesses that satisfy the outline criteria, there are a myriad of schemes that are administered locally. Thus the location of your business can be absolutely crucial, and funding may be strongly dependent on the area into which you intend to grow or develop. Additionally, there may well be additional grants available to a business investing in or into an area of social deprivation, particularly if it involves sustainable job creation.

The assistance provided for enterprise is limited so you will be competing for grants against other applicants. You can enhance your chances of success by following these seven rules:

1. **Keep yourself informed about which grants are available.**

   Grants are constantly being introduced (and withdrawn), but there is no system that lets you know automatically. You have to keep yourself informed.

   Business Link (www.businesslink.org), the Department of Trade and Industry (www.dti.gov.uk), Funders online (www.fundersonline.org), and Grants On-line (www.co-financing.co.uk) are all Web sites that can help you find out about grants.

2. **Do not start the project for which you want a grant before you make the application.**

   The awarding body will almost certainly take the view that if you can start the project without a grant you must have sufficient funds to complete it without assistance. Much better to show that your project is dependent on the grant being made.

3. **Talk to the awarding body before you apply.**

   Make contact with an individual responsible for administering the scheme. You will be given advice on whether it is worthwhile your applying before you start spending time and effort on making the application; you may get some help and advice on completing the application form; you may get an insight into how you should shape your application.

4. **Make sure your application is in respect of a project.**

   Usually, grants are given for specific projects, not for the normal organic growth of a business. If, for example, you need new equipment to launch a product, make sure your application emphasises the project, not the equipment. State the advantages of the project's success (for example, it will safeguard or create jobs) and explain that the purchase of the equipment is a prerequisite for that success.

5. **Get your application in early.**

   The chances of a successful application are always highest just after a scheme is launched. That is when there is the most money in the pot, and it's also the time when those administering the scheme are keenest to get applications in and grants awarded. Competition is likely to be less fierce.

6. **Make your application match the awarding body's objectives.**

   The benefits of your project should fit in with the objectives of the awarding body and the grant scheme itself. So if the grant is intended to help the country in the form of potential exports, for example, make sure your application details your exports.

   Most grant applications require the submission of a business plan, so make sure you have an up to date one.

7. **Make sure you have matching funds available.**

   It is unusual for a grant to finance 100 per cent of the costs of any project. Typically nowadays a grant will contribute 15–50 per cent of the total finance required. Those making the decision about the grant are spending public money. They have a duty to ensure it is spent wisely and they will need to be absolutely convinced that you have, or can raise from other sources, the balance required.

Winning money

If you enjoy publicity and like a challenge then you could look out for a business competition to enter. Like government grants, business competitions are ubiquitous and, like national lotteries, they are something of a hit or miss affair. But one thing is certain. If you don't enter you can't win.

There are more than 100 annual awards in the UK alone, aimed at new or small businesses. For the most part, these are sponsored by banks, the major accountancy bodies, chambers of commerce, local or national newspapers, business magazines, and the trade press. Government departments may also have their own competitions as a means of promoting their initiatives for exporting, innovation, job creation, and so forth.

The nature and the amount of the awards change from year to year, as do the sponsors. But looking out in the national and local press, particularly the small business sections of *The Times*, *Daily Telegraph*, *Daily Mail*, and *The Guardian*, should put you in touch with a competition organiser quickly, as will an Internet search. Money awards constitute 40 per cent of the main competition prizes. For the most part, these cash sums are less than £5,000. However, a few do exceed £10,000 and one UK award is for £50,000. Other awards are for equally valuable goods and services, such as consultancy or accountancy advice, training, and computer hardware and software.

Part II
Managing the Business

"I'm getting worried about the boss."

In this part . . .

Running your own business means constantly juggling resources. You need to focus on a product or service that you can provide better or differently to those already in the market. This part will help you decide on the best way to develop and communicate your marketing strategy, set a selling price, decide on a place to operate from, and how and where to advertise.

Having customers means you have to produce product or deliver your service, which in turn means operating effectively. If you don't do everything yourself the next resource you have to consider is people, either those you employ directly, or through outsourcing. You'll need to set clear goals for yourself and anyone working with you.

Chapter 9

Considering Your Mission

- -

- -

To be successful in the marketplace, you need to have a clear picture of exactly what you want to do and who you're doing it for. In other words, you need a vision and a mission.

Say you want to start your own airline. Those ideas in themselves don't make a business. What destinations will you fly to, what type of planes will you use, how will you sell your tickets, and to whom will you sell them, are all burning questions which set what are known as the parameters of your business. You can think of this as a process that narrows down the big universe that, say, starting your own airline begins with, until you focus down on flying tourists to and from New York, which is where Virgin began.

Defining the parameters of your vision involves getting to know more about your future customers and more about what you plan to do to woo and win them. Every business needs a winning concept, a clear mission, an inspirational vision, and achievable objectives and goals. No rocket science in that.

In this chapter, I tell you how to refine your vision and compose a mission statement you can adjust to suit your goals throughout the life of your business.

Developing Your Concept

Once you know the basic concept of what you are selling and to whom, you should refine that by examining the features of the product (or service) and the benefits that customers will get when they purchase. Features are what a product has or is, and benefits are what the product (or service) does for the customer. For example, cameras and even film or tapes are not the end product that customers want; they are looking for good photos. Finally, include proof that these benefits can be delivered.

Reading Amazon.com

Jeff Bezos, Amazon.com's founder, came up with the idea for selling books online while he was working as a senior vice president of D E Shaw, a New York-based investment management firm. Bezos was assigned to come up with profitable ideas for selling over the Internet and he concluded that online bookselling would be a good business because two of the US's largest book distributors already had electronic lists.

The distributors who carried thousands of titles acted as the warehouse for most stores, particularly smaller booksellers. When customers asked a store for a book it did not have in stock, they filled the customer's order through one of the two largest distributors – Ingram or Baker & Taylor. These companies' inventory lists were digitised in the late 1980s. The online inventory lists would enable Bezos to offer books online through the company he envisioned creating.

Bezos' firm was not willing to invest in the idea. So as Bezos and his wife drove across country to Seattle to start the company he typed the business plan on his laptop while his wife drove. Bezos used the plan to raise the first $1 million of seed capital from 15 wealthy individual investors and built a prototype of the Amazon.com website in a converted garage of a rented home in Bellevue, Washington.

The naming of Amazon.com was based on the importance of its relative size. Bezos reasoned that the Amazon River was ten times as large as the next largest river, which was the Mississippi, in terms of volume of water and Amazon.com had six times as many titles as the world's largest physical bookstore.

Amazon.com was launched in July 1995, and every week, the revenues went up. By the second or third week, Amazon.com was generating revenues of $6,000 or $10,000 per week. By the end of early September 1995, revenues were $20,000 a week.

The reason for locating in Seattle was not just to be near a technology hub; it was to be near one of the distribution facilities of Ingram, Amazon.com's largest book supplier. Bezos recognised that this proximity to distribution facilities would allow for quicker turnaround on deliveries.

Bezos also focused on ways to enhance Amazon.com customers' experiences. He altered the Web site to make it easier to understand, streamlining the ordering process and responding immediately to each customer's questions.

You need to decide your business concept, and you really need to get a good handle on it before you can go much further with your business plans.

Composing Your Mission Statement

A *mission statement* explains in clear concise terms what the business does. To devise a worthy mission statement, focus your attention on your strengths and the value you give your customers.

Your mission should be narrow enough to give direction and guidance to everyone in the business. This concentration is the key to business success because it is only by focusing on specific needs that a small business can differentiate itself from its larger competitors. Nothing kills off a business faster than trying to do too many different things too soon. Also, your mission should address a large enough market to allow your business to grow and realise its potential.

Thinking through your mission

Mission statements must not become too bland or too general. Anyone reading the statement should be able to tell what business your company is in, what it aims to achieve in the next three years, and how it aims to do so.

Your mission statement should explain what business you are in or plan to enter. It should include some or all of the following:

- ✔ Market/customer needs: who are we satisfying/delighting?

- ✔ What product/service are we offering that meets those needs?

- ✔ What are our capabilities, both particular skills and knowledge, and resources?

- ✔ What market opportunities are there for our product or service, and what threats are there from competitors (and others)?

- ✔ What do we want to achieve both now and in the future?

Above all, mission statements should be realistic, achievable, and brief. You certainly don't need to take a long weekend in a country hotel with key staff and management consultants poring over flip charts to develop your mission statement. If you can't distill the essence of what you plan to do in a simple, direct sentence or two, then you had better hold back on the launch party and definitely don't order champagne and balloons.

Run through the following checklist periodically to make sure that your mission statement is still on track:

- ✔ Write down your company's mission statement from memory. Have your oldest employee and your newest employee do the same, then compare the three. Use the differences to refine either the mission statement or employee training.

- ✔ How long ago did you write your mission statement? A mission written before you have carried out lots of market research or sold anything much may need to be looked at again to see if it is still valid.

- ✔ Does it still accurately reflect what you do?

✔ Would this mission statement stand out in a crowd?

✔ Could a 14-year old understand it?

✔ Does your mission statement provide a clear guide to action?

✔ Does it tell you what businesses you are not in?

Ultimately, your mission statement reflects the unique quality of your business that makes people want to buy from you. That uniqueness may be contained in the product or service, but it is more likely to be woven into the fabric of the way you do business. Try telephoning any three car hire firms, or walking into three restaurants. The chances are that it will not be their products, but their people and systems that make them stand out.

Missing a mission

So what happens if you don't have a mission? Does nothing get done? Worse than nothing, everything gets done, including a whole lot of things neither you nor the backers wanted or expected.

Following a visit to a very busy company that was losing money hand-over-fist, it became clear to the consultant that no-one had any idea what the business was supposed to be doing. As fast as one team took on business another were turning the same type of business away because they thought the firm was 'not in that business'. In the consultant's report he used this quote, which he said was representative of most of the 26 face-to-face interviews he had conducted with the management team: 'We have lost our way. That is if we ever knew it.'

The best imagery to describe what is going on in rudderless firms with no clear mission is of three people pulling against each other on a rope joined in the centre. Everyone is pulling hard, but in different directions and no one is getting anywhere. Substitute departments or individual employees for the three pullers and the same happens to a company without a mission statement. Try telling anyone in this organisation that they are not working hard enough and they will laugh at you. The staff is launching new services, upgrading processes, and offering clients customised services by the dozen. Everyone is working hard, but nothing much is really happening because everyone is pulling in different directions.

What the mission statement does is get everyone pulling hard in the same direction. The direction may change slightly, but everyone will still be pulling the same way and the company will move forward, rather than stand still or decline.

Seeing the Vision Thing

Vision is not the same as mission. Missions can be thought of as providing direction for the medium term along a line that most people can follow. Vision is about stretching the organisation's reach beyond its grasp. Generally few people concerned with the company can now see how the vision is to be achieved, but all concerned agree that it would be great if it could be. Once your vision becomes reality it may be time for a new challenge, or perhaps even a new business.

Microsoft founder Bill Gates had a vision of a computer in every home at a time when few offices had one. As a mission statement 15 years ago it might have raised a wry smile. After all, only a few decades before IBM estimated the entire world demand for its computers as seven! Now, Mr Gates's vision has nearly been reached.

You need to work up the vision with the people who work with you in order to be sure of their wholehearted commitment. You won't get that commitment if the only people who buy into the vision are you, your partner and the management consultant who sold it to you.

As with the mission, only when everyone knows and shares the business's vision is it likely to be achieved. All parts of the organisation are so connected to each other, to the market, and to the customer in such a complex series of relationships that the management team can't hope to achieve anything much without everyone's input. Rather in the way that markets work better with perfect information, businesses work better when everyone knows and believes in the goal.

Answering the questions and doing the exercises in the following list can help you determine how clear your vision is.

✔ Write down your vision statement.

✔ How did you arrive at the vision statement?

✔ Get your team (or partner or spouse) to draw – yes draw – their idea of the vision of the company (one company founder received a picture of a flock of geese on the wing; the message was that the company should ultimately comprise of individuals who knew the common goals, took turns in leading, and adjusted their structure to the task in hand. Geese fly in a wedge, for instance, but land in waves).

✔ How big is the gap between where you are now and where your vision is taking you? If you are already close to achieving your vision, say in the next few weeks and months, perhaps it is not challenging enough to stretch you. The gap, after all, is the task you have set yourself to at least start achieving in your business plan.

✔ What are the major milestones between now and achieving your vision?

✔ How can you ensure your vision and values are shared more effectively by everyone in the company? This is best achieved by explaining the compelling business reasons for having them and arguing the case convincingly.

✔ What internal factors look like working against you in terms of achieving your vision, and how could you overcome them? The main factor that could hold you back are people who don't share your ideas on what the vision should be. In that case you are back in the selling game. Other limiting factors could be resources such as money or premises, or the skill and knowledge level of your staff.

✔ What external factors look like working against you in terms of achieving your vision, and how could you overcome them? These will include the economic environment, which may be unfavourable, or the strength of competitors. Prudence and patience may be the best policies if the economy is working against you. Build up resources and wait for better times. Beating the competition is what your marketing strategy is designed to achieve. But you can't expect the competition to take your punches lying down. They will fight back and you will have to find new strategies.

✔ What factors are working in your favour in terms of achieving your vision and how can you use them more effectively?

✔ Now re-write your vision statement in the light of your answers to the questions above and prepare a statement of company values. Values are the attitudes and behaviour that you want to be the norm in your business. You would expect anyone working for you to be honest and have integrity in all their dealings with customers, suppliers and others in the business. Sometimes employees can get the wrong idea and believe that short-term gain is all that matters. So if a customer is overcharged they bank the extra money and congratulate themselves on doing better, when in value terms they have done badly. They will also have done badly over the longer term when that customer, or another like them, finds out and switches supplier.

Setting Objectives and Goals

Missions and visions are vital, but they aren't much good without clear objectives, which are the major measurable tasks for the business and operating goals for individuals. For example you need some idea of how big you want the business to be – in other words, what your share of the market will be.

It certainly is not easy to forecast sales, especially before you have even started trading, but if you do not set a goal at the start and instead just wait to see how things develop, then one of two problems is likely to occur. Either you will not sell enough to cover your fixed costs and so lose money and perhaps go out of business, or you will sell too much and run out of cash whilst you wait for your customers to pay up, in other words, over-trade.

Obviously, before you can set a market share and sales objective you need to know the size of your market. (See Chapter 5 for information on how to research the market.)

The size you want your business to be is more a matter of judgement than forecast. You make a judgement tempered by the resources you have available to achieve those objectives and by some idea of what is reasonable and achievable and what is not. The amount of money you can persuade outsiders to pump into your business will also limit your ambition.

Set near-term objectives covering the next 18 months or so, and longer-term objectives covering up to five or so years further on.

You can set objectives in any number of areas, but the most vital areas are: *Profits*, the money you have left after everyone has been paid, *Margins*, the profit made per item sold, *Return on Capital Employed*, the profit made for every pound invested and *Value Added per Employee*, the profit made per person employed, which are looked at in Chapters 13 and 15; and *Sales Volume and Value in Pounds* and your *Percentage Share of the Market* which we looked at in Chapter 6.

You also need to ensure any objectives set meet these criteria:

- ✔ **Measurable.** There is an old saying, what gets measured gets done. It is certainly true that if you can't measure a thing it's pointless setting goals in that area.

- ✔ **Challenging.** Objectives need to stretch but not break.

- ✔ **Achievable.** If a goal is way beyond any reasonable chance of being achieved it will de-motivate all concerned, yourself included, when you fail to get there.

- ✔ **Accepted.** This means that whoever is set a goal must commit to the task. Silence is not a sufficient response. So, for example, sales staff should sign off acceptance of targets and production staff confirm they accept output goals.

- ✔ **Allocated.** No objective should be left hanging, without some named person or persons being assigned the task of achieving all or part of the task in question.

- ✔ **Time-scaled.** Not great English, but an objective without a date by which it is to be achieved is meaningless. Saying you must get sales of £100,000 a month might be challenging if it is your first month in business, but altogether too laid back for year five.

Chapter 10

Marketing Your Wares

*E*ntering the market involves deciding on what mix of marketing ingredients to use. In cooking, the same ingredients used in different ways can result in very different products and the same is true in business. In business, the 'ingredients' are product (or service), price, place and promotion. A change in the way these elements are put together can produce an offering tailored to meet the needs of a specific market. For example, a hardback book is barely more expensive to produce than a paperback. However with a bit of clever publicity, bringing them out a few weeks before the paperback edition and a hefty price hike, an air of exclusivity can be created which satisfies a particular group of customers.

Making Up the Marketing Mix

The key to successful promotion lies in knowing exactly what you want people to do. A few elements can make or break the successful marketing of your business. The elements you need to consider in the marketing mix are:

✔ The *product or service* is what people use, but what they buy are the underlying benefits it confers on them. For example, cameras, SLR or digital, lens, even film are not the end products that customers want; they are looking for good pictures.

✔ *Pricing* strategies can range from charging what the market will bear, right through to *marginal cost* (just enough to cover direct costs and a small contribution to overheads). While it is important to know your costs, this is only one element in the pricing decision. You also have to take account of the marketplace, your competition, and your product position (for example, if you offer a luxury item, your place in the market is different than someone who sells necessities).

✔ Place is a general title to cover everything from where you locate to how you get your product or service to market. Poor distribution often explains sluggish sales growth. If your type of product gets to market through several channels but you only use one of them, then no amount of price changes or extra promotion will make much difference.

Defining Your Product Parameters

To be successful in the marketplace, you need to have a clear picture of exactly what you want to do and for whom you're doing it. In other words, you need a vision and a mission. (Chapter 9 offers advice on developing your mission statement.)

To effectively market your product, you have to make decisions about factors such as product range and depth before you are ready to enter the market. Having decided to open a corner shop, for example, you still have to decide if you will focus on food only, or will you carry household items and perhaps newspapers and flowers too. You will also need to decide if you will carry more than one brand and size of each product.

If the key advantages of your corner shop are its location, opening hours, delivery service and friendly staff, all at competitive prices, then perhaps you don't need a wide or deep product range.

Using Advertising to Tell Your Story

The skill of advertising lies in reducing the global population to your target audience and reaching as many of them as you can at an economic cost. You first analyse the benefits or virtues of your product, isolate the features, and translate these into customer benefits. Who has a need for your product? Discover who your potential customers are.

Question all the time. Then set objectives for your campaign, decide on a budget, design the message, and pick the medium to reach your target audience, and determine how you're going to evaluate the success of your advertising.

When you understand the basics, which I go through in the following sections, you should be able to analyse advertisements better, to break them down, and avoid the all too common mistakes that are made every day.

Advertising by itself does not sell. It will not shift a bad product (more than once) or create new markets. Sales literature, order forms, a sales force, stocks, distributors, and a strategy must back it up.

Considering the customer's point of view

It is important to recognise that people buy a product or service for what it will do for them. Customers look for the benefits. As the seller, your mission is to answer the question 'What's in it for me?' from your potential customer's point of view.

Every time you compose a sales letter, write an advertisement, or plan a trade show, you must get to the heart of the matter. Why should customers purchase your wares? What benefit will it bring them?

All your marketing efforts need to be viewed from the prospect's point of view and not just your own. Once you know what you are selling and to whom, you can match the features of the product (or service) to the benefits the customer will get when they purchase. A *feature* is what a product has or is, and *benefits* are what the product does for the customer. Finally, include proof that these benefits can be delivered. Table 10-1 shows an analysis of features, benefits, and proofs.

Table 10-1	Listing Features and Benefits	
Feature	*Benefit*	*Proof*
We use a unique hardening process for our machine.	Our tools last longer and that saves you money.	We have a patent on the process; independent tests carried out by the Cambridge Institute of Technology show our product lasts longest.
Our shops stay open later than others in the area.	You get more choice when to shop.	Come and see.
Our computer system is fault tolerant using parallel processing.	You have no down-time for either defects or system expansion.	Our written specification guarantees this; come and talk to satisfied customers operating in your field.

You can use this format to examine the features, benefits, and proofs for your own products or services and use the information to devise your ads. Remember, the customer pays for the benefits and the seller for the features. So the benefit will provide the copy for most of your future advertising and promotional efforts.

Try this out for your business idea. Keep at it until you really have a good handle on what makes your customers tick. To make the process work you will need to talk to some real prospective customers in your target market.

Setting advertising objectives

There is no point in advertising your product or service unless it leads to the opportunity for a sale in a significant number of instances. Ask yourself what potential customers have to do to enable you to make these sales. Do you want them to visit your showroom, phone you, write to your office, return a card, or send an order in the post? Do you expect them to order now, or to remember you at some future date when they have a need for your services?

The more specifically you identify the response you want, the better you can tailor your promotional effort to achieve your objective, and the more clearly you can assess the effectiveness of your promotion.

The more general your advertising objective is – for example, to 'improve your image' or 'to keep your name in front of the public' – the more likely it is to be an ineffective way of spending your money.

Deciding the budget

Two methods are commonly used to calculate advertising budget numbers:

- ✔ **What can we afford?** This approach accepts that cash is usually a scarce commodity and advertising has to take its place alongside a range of competing demands.

- ✔ **Cost/benefit:** This approach comes into its own when you have clear and specific promotional goals. If you have spare capacity in your factory or want to sell more out of your shop, you can work out how much it will cost you to increase your production and sales, and how much you could benefit from those extra sales. You then figure out how much advertising money it takes to get you the extra business.

Suppose a £1,000 advertisement is expected to generate 100 enquiries for your product. If your experience tells you that on average 10 per cent of enquiries result in orders, and your profit margin is £200 per product, then you can expect an extra £2,000 profit. That benefit is much greater than the £1,000 cost of the advertisement, so it seems a worthwhile investment.

In practice, you should use all of these methods to decide how much to spend on promoting your products.

Defining the message

To define your message, you must look at your business and its products from the customer's standpoint and be able to answer the question, 'Why should I buy your product?' It is better to consider the answer in two stages:

1. **'Why should I buy your *product?'***

   The answer is provided naturally by looking carefully at buying motives and the benefits customers get from the product.

2. **'Why should I buy *your* product?'**

   The only logical and satisfactory answer is: 'Because it is better and so it is different.'

   The difference can arise in two ways:

   1. You, the seller, are different. To achieve this, you establish a particular niche for your business.

   2. Your product is different. Each product should have a unique selling point, based on fact.

Your promotional message must be built around your product's strengths and must consist of facts about the company and about the product.

The stress here is on the word '*fact*' and although there may be many types of fact surrounding you and your products, your customers are only interested in two: The facts which influence their buying decisions, and the facts of how your business and its products stand out from the competition.

The assumption is that everyone buys for obvious, logical reasons only, but of course innumerable examples show that this is not so. Does a woman buy a new dress only when the old one is worn out? Do bosses have desks that are bigger than their subordinates' because they have more papers to put on them?

Choosing the media

Broadly, your advertising choices are media *above-the-line,* which is jargon for newspapers, TV, radio, and other broadcast media, and *below-the-line* activities such as distributing brochures, stationery letterhead, and the way you answer the phone. The printed word (newspapers and magazines) will probably take most of your above-the-line advertising budget. It is the accepted medium to reach the majority of customers. Most people read the newspaper, especially on Sunday, and there are magazines to cater for every imaginable interest from the parish magazine to the Sunday supplements.

You must advertise where your buyers and consumers are likely to see the message. Your market research (which I talk about in Chapter 5) tells you where your likely prospects lie. Before making your decision about which paper or journal to advertise in, you need to get readership and circulation numbers and the reader profile.

You can get this information directly from the journal or paper or from *BRAD* (British Rate and Data), www.brad.co.uk, which has a monthly classified directory of all UK and Republic of Ireland media. You should be able to access this through your local business library.

The approach to take when considering below-the-line advertising is to identify what business gurus call *moments of truth* – contact points between you, your product or service, and your customer. Those moments offer you a chance to shine and make a great impression. You can spot the difference at once when you get a really helpful person on the phone or serving you in a shop. The same is true of product literature that is actually helpful, a fairly rare event in itself.

Some of the most effective promotional ideas are the simplest, for example a business card with a map on the reverse side showing how to find you, or 'thank you cards', instead of letters, on which you can show your company's recently completed designs.

Choosing the frequency

The copy dates of some monthlies are two months before publication. This poses problems if you are waiting on a shipment or uncertain about a product change. Dailies or weeklies allow much prompter changes. The ultimate is probably radio, where messages can be slotted in on the same day. Yearbooks, diaries, and phone directories require long forward notice.

Providing opportunities to see

One claimed benefit of breakfast television is that it can get your message out before the shops open. Trade buyers are deluged with calendars, diaries, pen sets, and message pads in the hope that when the buyer is making a decision, the promotional materials are still close at hand and have an influence on the buyer's decision.

The more opportunities you give potential customers to see your name or your product, the greater the chance that they'll remember you. This is why direct mail letters usually involve more than one piece of literature. The theory is that each piece is looked at before being discarded. It may only be a brief scan but it gives the seller another chance to hook a customer. So rather than using different advertising messages, try getting the same or a similar message to one customer group several times.

Figuring your bang-for-the-buck ratio

Advertising should only be undertaken where the results can realistically be measured. Everything else is self-indulgent. The formula to keep in mind is:

Effectiveness = Total cost of the advertising activity concerned ÷ by the Results (in measurable units such as customers, new orders, or enquiries).

A glance at the advertising analysis below will show how one organisation tackled the problem.

Table 10-2 shows the advertising results for a small business course run in London. At first glance the Sunday paper produced the most enquiries. Although it cost the most, £340, the cost per enquiry was only slightly more than the other media used. But the objective of this advertising was not simply to create interest; it was intended to sell places on the course. In fact, only ten of the 75 enquiries were converted into orders – an advertising of £34 per head. On this basis the Sunday paper was between 2.5 and 3.5 times more expensive than any other medium.

Table 10-2		**Measuring Advertising Effect**			
Media used	*Enquiries*	*Cost of advertising*	*Cost per enquiry*	*No. of customers*	*Advertising cost per customer*
Sunday paper	75	£340	£4.50	10	£34
Daily paper	55	£234	£4.25	17	£14
Posters	30	£125	£4.20	10	£12
Local weekly paper	10	£40	£4.00	4	£10
Personal recommendation	20	N/A	N/A	19	N/A

Getting in the News

The surest way to get in the news is to write a press release. Better still write lots of them. To be successful, a press release needs to get attention immediately and be quick and easy to digest. Studying and copying the style of the particular journals (or other media) you want your press release to appear in can make publication more likely.

The introduction is the most vital part. You should ask yourself, 'Will it make the reader want to read on?' Avoid detail and sidetracks. The paragraphs should have bite and flow. Keep the sentences reasonably short. State the main point of the story early on. Follow these suggestions for a successful press release:

- ✔ Type the release on a sheet of A4 paper headed up 'Press Release' or 'Press Information'. Address it to the News Editor, News Desk, or a named journalist.

- ✔ Use double spacing and wide margins to allow for editorial changes and printing instructions, respectively. Use one side of the paper only.

- ✔ Date the release and put a headline on to identify it.

- ✔ Tell your story in three paragraphs. The substance should come in the first one. The first paragraph must say who, what, why, when, and where, and succeeding paragraphs can fill in the detail. If space is short then the sub-editor will delete from the bottom and papers are always looking for fillers – short items that can be dropped into gaps. Even if the bulk of the story is cut, at least the main facts will get printed.

- ✔ Include at least one direct quotation or comment, always from a named individual and ideally from someone of standing or relevance.

- ✔ Keep it simple and write for the readership. The general public prefers images or descriptions to technical facts. For example a new car lock could be described as being able to keep out a professional thief for 30 minutes for a story in the general press. For the trade press the same story would be better supported by facts about the number of levers, codes, and so forth that are involved in beefing up the lock's security system.

- ✔ Finish with a contact for more information. Give phone numbers for work and home, as well as your e-mail and Web site addresses. This will help a journalist looking for more detail and by being available your story will be more attractive if a gap occurs suddenly.

- ✔ Submit the release before the paper or journal's deadline. All the media work to strict deadlines. Many local papers sold on a Friday are printed on a Tuesday or Wednesday morning. A release that fails to make it by then will probably be ignored. The national dailies, of course, have more flexibility and often have several editions. At the other end of the scale, many colour supplements and monthly journals have a cut-off date six weeks in advance.

- ✔ Steer away from selling your firm and product, and write news. Anything else is advertising and will be discarded. You are not writing an advertisement, you are telling a story to interest the readers.

- ✔ A good picture, they say, is worth a thousand words. Certainly from a journalist's point of view it's worth half a page of text they don't have to write themselves.

Deciding who to contact

Remember that the target audience for your press release is the professional editor; it is he or she who decides to print. With UK editors receiving an average of 80–90 press releases per week, make sure that you are making your latest newsworthy item public, but make sure it is free of jargon.

Do your research to find not only the right newspapers or journals, but also the right journalists. Read their columns, or listen to or watch their programmes and become familiar with their style and approach to news stories. Hollis (www.hollis-pr.com) publish the details of all news contacts, listed by business area. Your goal is to write a press release that is so close to their own style that they have almost no additional work to do to make your news usable.

Following through

You will get better results by following up your press release with a quick phone call. Journalists get bogged down and distracted like everyone else, so don't be too surprised if your masterpiece sinks to the bottom of a pile of prospective stories before the day is out. That phone call, or even an e-mail if you can't get through, is often enough to keep up interest and get your story through the first sifting.

Once you start getting results you will want to keep it going. But even if you are not successful at first, don't be disappointed or disheartened. Keep plugging away. Try to find a story regularly for the local press and get to know your local journalists and editors. Always be truthful, helpful, and available. If they ring you and you are at a meeting, make sure you always ring back.

Some companies always seem to get a piece in the paper every week. The stories published are not always earth-shattering news, but the continuous drip of press coverage eventually makes an impact. For example, Virgin Air has been virtually created by successful press coverage. Few of the millions of words of copy written about Branson or Virgin have been paid for.

Selling and Salesmanship

Selling is at the heart of every business. Whatever kind of selling your business involves, from moving goods over a counter to negotiating complex contracts, you need to understand the whole selling process and be involved with every aspect of it.

Telling the difference between selling and marketing

Marketing involves the whole process of deciding what to sell, who to sell it to, and how. The theory is that a brilliant marketing strategy should all but eliminate the need for selling. After all, selling is mostly concerned with shoe-horning customers into products that they don't really want, isn't it? Absolutely not! Whilst it is true that the more effort you put into targeting the right product or service to the right market, the less arduous the selling process is, you still have a selling job to do.

The primary job of the sales operation is to act as a bridge or conduit between the product and the customer. Across that gulf flows information as well as products and services. Customers need to be told about your great new ideas and how your product or service will perform better than anything they have seen to date.

Most businesses need selling and marketing activities in equal measure to get their message across effectively and get goods and services into their markets.

Selling yourself

One of the most important operational issues to address is your personal selling style. If you've sold products or services before, you may have developed a successful selling style already. If not, you need to develop one that is appropriate for your customers and comfortable for you. Regardless of your experience, assessing your selling style will help define and reinforce your business goals.

Check you and your salespeople always see things from the customer's point of view. Review the sales style of your salespeople to see how they can be improved.

Consider if your selling style is consultative, where you win the customer over to your point of view, or hard, where you try forcing them to take your product or service.

In assessing your selling style, consider the following:

✔ Always have a specific objective for any selling activity, together with a fall back position. For example your aim may be to get an order but you would settle for the chance to tender for their business. If you don't have objectives there is a danger that much of your sales activity will be wasted on courtesy calls that never reach the asking-for-an-order stage.

- The right person to sell to is the one who makes the buying decision. You may have to start further down the chain, but you should always know whom you finally have to convince.

- Set up the situation so you can listen to the customer. You can best do this by asking open questions. When they have revealed what their needs really are, confirm them back to them.

- Explain your product or service in terms of the customer's needs and requirements.

- Deal with objections without hostility or irritation. Objections are a sign that the customer is interested enough in what you have to say to at least discuss your proposition. Once you have overcome their objections and established a broad body of agreement you can try to close the deal.

- Your approach to closing can be one of a number of ways. The *assumptive close* takes the tack that as you and the customer are so much in agreement an order is the next logical step. If the position is less clear you can go for the *balance sheet close,* which involves going through the pros and cons, arriving at a larger number of pros. So once again the most logical way forward is for the customer to order. If circumstance allow, you can use the *special situation* closing technique. This might be appropriate if a product is in scarce supply or on special offer for a limited period.

- If you are unsuccessful, start the selling process again using your fall back objective as the goal.

Outsourcing selling

Few small start-up firms can afford to hire their own sales force at the outset as it costs over £40,000 a year to keep a good salesperson on the road, including commission and expenses. Inevitably there is a period where no sales are coming in yet salary and expenses are being paid out. Plus, you run the very real risk of employing the wrong person.

A lower-cost and perhaps less risky sales route is via agents. Good agents should have existing contacts in your field, know buyers personally, and have detailed knowledge of your product's market. Unlike someone you recruit, a hired agent should be off to a flying start from day one.

The big thing is that agents are paid purely on commission: if they don't sell they don't earn. The commission amount varies but is rarely less than 7 per cent and 25 per cent is not unknown.

You can find an agent by advertising in your specialist trade press or the *Daily Telegraph,* and *Exchange and Mart.* You can also find agents' associations listed in trade directories. However the most reliable method is to approach outlets where you wish to sell. They know the honest, competent, and regular agents who call on them. Draw up a shortlist and invite those agents to apply.

When interviewing a potential sales agent, you should find out:

- ✔ What other companies and products they already sell. You want them to sell related but not competing products.
- ✔ What is their knowledge of the trade and geographical area covered? Sound them out for specific knowledge of your target market.
- ✔ Who are their contacts?
- ✔ What is their proven selling record? Find out who their biggest customers are and talk to them directly.
- ✔ Do they appear honest, reliable, and a fit person to represent your business? Take up references and talk to their customers.

It is a challenge to find professional representation so your product has to be first-class, growth prospects good, with plenty of promotional material and back-up support.

When you do find a person to represent your product, draw up an agreement to cover the main points including geographic area, commission rates, when payable, customers you will continue dealing with yourself, training and support given, prohibiting competing agencies, and periods of notice required to terminate. Also build in an initial trial period after which both parties can agree to part amicably.

Measuring results

Sales results can take time to appear. In the meantime you need to make sure you're doing the things that will eventually lead to successful sales. You should measure the following:

Activities

- ✔ Sales appointments made
- ✔ Sales calls made per day, per week, per month. Monitor trends, as last quarter's sales calls will give you a good feel for this quarter's sales results.
- ✔ Quotations given

Results

- ✔ New accounts opened
- ✔ Old accounts lost
- ✔ Average order size

Pricing for Profit

Pricing is the biggest decision you have to make about your business and the one that has the biggest impact on company profitability. You need to keep pricing constantly under review.

To get a better appreciation of the factors that could have an influence on what you should charge, every business should keep these factors in mind.

Caring about business conditions

Obviously, the overall condition in the marketplace has a bearing on your pricing policy. In boom conditions, where products are so popular that they're virtually being rationed, the overall level of prices for some products could be expected to rise disproportionately. Conditions can vary so much from place to place as to have a major impact on pricing. For example, one business starter produced her beauty treatment price list based on prices near to her home in Surrey. However she planned to move to Cornwall to start her business, where prices were 50 per cent lower, reflecting lower rates of pay in the county. So whilst she got a boost by selling her Surrey home for much more than she paid for a house in Cornwall, that gain was offset by having to charge much lower prices for her services.

Seasonal factors can also contribute to changes in the general level of prices. A turkey, for example, costs less on the afternoon of Christmas Eve than it does at the start of Christmas week.

Working to your capacity

Your capacity to produce your product or service, bearing in mind market conditions, influences the price you set. Typically, a new venture has limited capacity at the start. A valid entry could be to price so high as to just fill your capacity, rather than so low as to swamp you.

A housewife started a home ironing service at £2.50 per hour's ironing, in line with competition, but as she only had 20 hours a week to sell she rapidly ran out of time. It took six months to get her price up to £5 an hour and her demand down to 20 hours per week. Then she was able to recruit some assistance and had a high enough margin to pay some outworkers and make a margin herself.

Understanding consumer perceptions

A major consideration when setting your prices is the perception of the value of your product or service to the customers. Their opinion of value may have little or no relation to the cost, and they may be ignorant of the price charged by the competition, especially if your product or service is a new one.

Skimming versus Penetrating

The overall image that you want to portray in the marketplace influences the prices you charge. A high-quality image calls for higher pricing, naturally. However, within that pricing policy is the option of either a high price which will just *skim* the market by only being attractive to the small population of wealthier customers; or to go for a low price to *penetrate* the market, appealing to the mass of customers.

Skim pricing is often adopted with new products with little or no competition that are aimed at affluent buyers who are willing to pay more to be the trend-setters for a new product. Once the innovators have been creamed off the market, the price can be dropped to penetrate to lower layers of demand.

The danger with this strategy is that high prices attract the interest of new competitors. If you have a product that's easy to copy and impossible to patent, you may be better off setting the price low to discourage competitors and to spread your product throughout the market quickly.

Avoiding setting prices too low

The most frequent mistake made when setting a selling price for the first time is to pitch it too low. Either through failing to understand all the costs associated with making and marketing your product, or through yielding to the temptation to undercut the competition at the outset, you set your price so low that you risk killing your company.

Pondering Place and Distribution

Place makes you review exactly how you get your products or service to your customers.

If you are a retailer, restaurateur, or garage proprietor, for example, then your customers come to you. Your physical location probably is the key to success. If your business is in the manufacturing field, you're more likely to go out and find customers. In this case, your channels of distribution are the vital link.

Pricing in real time

The stock market works by gathering information on supply and demand. If more people want to buy a share than to sell it the price goes up until supply and demand are matched. If the information is perfect, that is every buyer and seller knows what is going on, the price is optimised. For most businesses this is not a practical proposition. Their customers expect the same price every time for the same product or service. And in any case, they have no accurate idea what the demand is at any given moment in time.

But for companies trading on the Internet it is possible to see how much consumer demand exists for a given product at any time. Anyone with a point-of-sale till could do the same, but the reports may come in weeks later. So online companies could change their price hundreds of times each day, in certain circumstances, in some markets, and so improve profits dramatically.

Easyjet.com, a budget airline operating out of Luton (just north of London) does just this. They price to fill their planes, and you could pay anything from £30 to £200 for the same trip depending on the demand for that flight.

Even if you are already in business and plan to stay in the same location, it would do no harm to take this opportunity to review that decision. If you are looking for additional funds to expand your business, your location will undoubtedly be an area prospective financiers will want to explore.

Choosing a location

From your market research data you should be able to come up with a list of criteria that are important to your choice of location. Some of the factors you need to weigh up when deciding where to locate are:

- ✔ If you need skilled or specialist labour, is it readily available?
- ✔ Are the necessary back-up services, such as computer support, equipment repairs and maintenance, available?
- ✔ How readily available are raw materials, components, and other supplies?
- ✔ How does the cost of premises, rates, and utilities compare with other areas?
- ✔ How accessible is the site by road, rail, and air?
- ✔ Are there any changes in the pipeline, which might adversely affect trade? Examples include a new motorway by-passing the town, changes in transport services, and closure of a large factory.
- ✔ Are there competing businesses in the immediate neighbourhood? Will these have a beneficial or detrimental effect?

✔ Is the location conducive to the creation of a favourable market image? For instance, a high fashion designer may lack credibility trading from an area famous for its heavy industry and infamous for its dirt and pollution.

✔ Is the area generally regarded as low or high growth? Is the area pro-business?

✔ Can you and your key employees get to the area easily and quickly?

You may even have spotted a role model – a successful competitor, perhaps in another town, who appears to have got the location spot on. You can use their location criteria as a guide to developing your own.

Using these criteria you can quickly screen out most unsuitable areas. You may have to visit other locations several times, at different hours of the day and on different days of the week, before screening them out.

Selecting a distribution channel

Selecting a distribution channel involves researching methods and deciding on the best way to get your product to your customers. Distribution methods have their own language and customs. This section familiarises you with them.

Moving a product through a distribution channel calls for two sorts of selling activity. *Push* is the name given to selling your product in, for example, a shop. *Pull* is the effort that you carry out on the shop's behalf to help them sell your product out of that shop. Your advertising strategy or a merchandising activity may cause that pull. You need to know how much push and pull are needed for the channel you are considering. If you are not geared up to help the retailers to sell out your product, and they need that help, then this could be a poor channel.

The way in which you have to move your product to your end customers is an important factor to weigh up when choosing a channel. As well as such factors as the cost of carriage, you also have to decide about packaging materials. As a rough rule, the more stages in the distribution channel the more robust and expensive your packaging has to be.

Not all channels of distribution settle their bills promptly. Mail-order customers, for example, pay in advance, but retailers can take up to 90 days or more. You need to take account of this settlement period in your cash flow forecast.

If your customers don't come to you, then you have the following options in getting your product or service to them. Your business plan should explain which you have chosen and why.

✔ **Retail stores:** This general name covers the great range of outlets from the corner shop to Harrods. Some offer speciality goods such as hi-fi equipment, where the customer expects professional help from the staff. Others are mostly self-service, with customers making up their own minds on choice of product.

✔ **Wholesalers:** These organisations typically buy in bulk, store in ware-houses and sell on in smaller quantities to retailers. The pattern of wholesalers' distribution has changed out of all recognition over the past two decades. It is still an extremely important channel where physical distribution, stock holding, finance, and breaking bulk are still profitable functions.

✔ **Cash & carry:** This slightly confusing route has replaced the traditional wholesaler as a source of supply for smaller retailers. In return for paying cash and picking up the goods yourself, the wholesaler shares part of their profit margin with you. The attraction for the wholesaler is improved cash flow and for the retailer a bigger margin and a wide product range. Hypermarkets and discount stores also fit somewhere between the manufacturer and the marketplace.

✔ **Internet and mail order:** This specialised technique provides a direct channel to the customer, and is an increasingly popular route for new small businesses.

✔ **Door-to-door selling:** Traditionally used by vacuum cleaner distributors and encyclopaedia companies, this is now used by insurance companies, cavity wall insulation firms, double-glazing firms, and others. Many use hard-sell techniques, giving door-to-door selling a bad name. However, Avon Cosmetics have managed to sell successfully door-to-door without attracting the stigma of unethical selling practices.

✔ **Party plan selling:** A variation on door-to-door selling, which is on the increase with new party plan ideas arriving from the USA. Agents enrolled by the company invite their friends to a get-together where the products are demonstrated and orders are invited. The agent gets a commission. Party plan has worked very well for Tupperware and other firms who sell this way.

✔ **Telephone selling:** This too can be a way of moving goods in one single step from maker to consumer. Few products can be sold easily in this way; however, repeat business is often secured via the telephone.

Consider these factors when choosing channels of distribution for your particular business:

✔ *Does it meet your customers' needs?* You have to find out how your customers expect their product or service to be delivered to them and if they need that particular route.

✔ *Will the product itself survive?* Fresh vegetables, for example, need to be moved quickly from where they are grown to where they are consumed.

✔ *Can you sell enough this way?* 'Enough' is how much you want to sell.

✔ *Is it compatible with your image?* If you are selling a luxury product, then door-to-door selling may spoil the impression you are trying to create in the rest of your marketing effort.

✔ *How do your competitors distribute?* If they have been around for a while and are obviously successful it is well worth looking at how your competitors distribute and using that knowledge to your advantage.

✔ *Is the channel cost-effective?* A small manufacturer may not find it cost-effective to supply retailers miles away because the direct 'drop' size, that is the load per order, is too small to be worthwhile.

✔ *Is the mark-up enough?* If your product cannot bear at least a 100 per cent mark-up, then it is unlikely that you will be able to sell it through department stores. Your distribution channel has to be able to make a profit from selling your product too.

Working from home

If you plan to work from home, have you checked that you are not prohibited from doing so by the house deeds, or whether your type of activity is likely to irritate the neighbours? This route into business is much in favour with sources of debt finance as it is seen to lower the risks during the vulnerable start-up period. Venture capitalists, on the other hand, would probably see it as a sign of 'thinking too small' and steer clear of the proposition. Nevertheless, working from home can make sound sense.

You will also have to consider if working from home suits you and your partner's domestic arrangements. For instance, if you have young children it may be difficult to explain to them that you are really at work, when everything looks much the same all the time.

If you are the type of person who needs the physical separation of work and home to give a structure to their lives, then working from home may not be right for you.

Looking at Legal Issues in Marketing

Nothing in business escapes the legal eye of the law and marketing is no exception. If anything, marketing is likely to produce more grey areas from a legal point of view than most others. You have patent and copyright issues to consider.

There are a number of vitally important aspects of your business that distinguish it from other similar firms operating in or near to your area of operations.

Having invested time, energy, and money in acquiring some distinction you need to take steps to preserve any benefits accruing from those distinctions. Intellectual property, often known as IP, is the generic title that covers the area of law that allows people to own their creativity and innovation in the same way that they can own physical property. The owner of IP can control and be rewarded for its use, and this encourages further innovation and creativity.

The following three organisations can help direct you to most sources of help and advice across the entire intellectual property field. They also have helpful literature and explanatory leaflets and guidance notes on applying for intellectual property protection:

- UK Patent Office (www.patent.gov.uk)
- European Patent Office (www.european-patent-office.org)
- US Patent and Trade Mark Office (www.uspto.gov)

I cover the most common types of intellectual property in the following sections.

Naming your business

You are reasonably free to use your last name for the name of your business. The main consideration in choosing a business name, however, is its commercial usefulness. You will want one that will let people know as much as possible about what you do. It is therefore important to choose a name that will convey the right image and message.

Whichever business name you choose, it will have to be legally acceptable and abide by the rules of the Business Names Act 1985. Detailed information on this subject is available from the Business Names section at the Companies House website. Go to www.companieshouse.gov.uk and click on 'Guidance Booklets & FAQ' and then 'Business Names'.

Looking at logos

It is not mandatory to have a logo for your business, but it can build greater customer awareness. A logo could be a word, typeface, colour, or a shape. The McDonald's name is a logo because of its distinct and stylistic writing. Choose your logo carefully. It should be one that is easily recognisable, fairly simple in design and one that can be reproduced on everything associated with your business. As far as the law is concerned a logo is a form of trademark.

Registering a domain name

A domain name is your own Web address, which you register so that your business will have the exclusive right to use. It identifies your business or organisation on the Internet, and it enables people to find you by directly entering your name into their browser address box. You can check whether your choice of name is available by using a free domain search service available at Web sites that register domain names such as www.yourname.com.

If your company name is registered as a trademark (see below), you may (as current case law develops) be able to prevent another business from using it as a domain name. Once you have decided on a selection of domain names, you can choose several different registration options:

✔ Use Nominet UK (www.nic.uk), which is the Registry for UK Internet domain names. Just as Companies House holds authoritative records for company names, Nominet maintains the database of UK registered Internet names. They charge £80 plus VAT for two years' registration.

✔ Most countries have a central registry to store these unique domain names. Two sites that maintain world directories of Internet domain registries are www.internic.net and www.norid.no/domreg.html, who between them cover pretty well every registration authority in the world.

In order to be eligible to register direct you must provide the Internet Protocol addresses of two named servers that are permanently connected to the Internet.

✔ Use Internet service providers (ISPs), which act as agents for their customers and will submit a domain name application for registration.

✔ Register online. Hundreds of Web sites now offer domain-name registration online; it's a good idea to search the Internet for these sites, as they often sell domain names as loss-leaders. Most of these providers also offer a search facility so you can see if your selected name has already been registered.

✔ Obtain free domain names along with free Web space by registering with an Internet community. These organisations offer you Web pages within their community space as well as a free domain name, but most communities only offer free domain names that have their own community domain tagged on the end – this can make your domain name rather long and hard to remember.

Once your domain name has been registered and paid for, you will receive a registration certificate, either directly or through your ISP. This is an important document as it confirms you as the legal registrant of a domain name. If any amendments need to be made at any point during the registration period, the registry and your ISP must be informed.

Protecting patents

The patent system in its current form was introduced over 100 years ago; although some type of protection has been around for about 350 years, as an incentive to get inventors to disclose their ideas to the general public and so promote technical advancement in general.

A patent can be regarded as a contract between an inventor and the state. The state agrees with the inventor that if she or he is prepared to publish details of their invention in a set form and if it appears that they have made a real advance, the state will then grant them a monopoly on their invention for 20 years: 'protection in return for disclosure'. The inventor uses the monopoly period to manufacture and sell the innovation; competitors can read the published specifications and glean ideas for their research, or they can approach the inventor and offer to help to develop the idea under licence.

The granting of a patent doesn't mean the proprietor is automatically free to make, use, or sell the invention themselves since to do so might involve infringing an earlier patent which has not yet expired. A patent really only allows the inventor to stop another person using the particular device which forms the subject of the patent. The state does not guarantee validity of a patent either, so it is not uncommon for patents to be challenged through the courts.

If you want to apply for a patent it is essential not to disclose your idea in non-confidential circumstances. If you do, your invention is already 'published' in the eyes of the law, and this could well invalidate your application. Ideally, the confidentiality of the disclosure you make should be written down in a confidentiality agreement and signed by the person to whom you are making the disclosure. This is particularly important if you are talking to a commercial contact or potential business colleague. The other way is to get your patent application on file before you start talking to anyone about your idea. You can talk to a Chartered Patent Agent in complete confidence as they work under strict rules of confidentiality.

There are two distinct stages in the patenting process:

- From filing an application up to publication of the patent
- From publication to grant of the patent

Two fees are payable for the first part of the process and a further fee for the second part. The Patent Office Search and Advisory Service will give some estimate of the costs associated with a specific investigation. They suggest, for example, that subject matter searches will cost upwards of £500, validity searches from £1000, and infringement searches from £1,500. And these are just the costs for the very start of the procedure.

The whole process takes some two and a half years. Relevant forms and details of how to patent are available free of charge from the Patent Office at www.patent.gov.uk. You can also write to them: The Patent Office, Concept House, Cardiff Road, Newport NP10 8QQ.

Registering a trademark

A *trademark* is the symbol by which the goods of a particular manufacturer or trader can be identified. It can be a word, a signature, a monogram, a picture, a logo, or a combination of these.

To qualify for registration the trademark must be distinctive, must not be deceptive and must not be capable of confusion with marks already registered. Excluded are national flags, royal crests, and insignia of the armed forces. A trademark can only apply to tangible goods, not services (although pressure is mounting for this to be changed).

The Trade Mark Act 1994 offers protection of great commercial value since, unlike other forms of protection, your sole rights to use the trademark continue indefinitely.

To register a trademark you or your agent should first conduct preliminary searches at the Trade Marks Branch of the Patent Office to check there are no conflicting marks already in existence. You then apply for registration on the official trademark form and pay a fee (currently £200). Your application is then advertised in the weekly *Trade Marks Journal* to allow any objections to be raised. If there are none, your trademark will be officially registered and you pay a further fee (currently £200).

Registration is initially for ten years. After this, it can be renewed for further periods of ten years at a time, with no upper time limit. It is mandatory to register a trademark.

If an unregistered trademark has been used for some time and could be construed as closely associated with the product by customers, it will have acquired a 'reputation' which will give it some protection legally, but registration makes it much simpler for the owner to have recourse against any person who infringes the mark.

Detailing your design

You can register the shape, design, or decorative features of a commercial product if it is new, original, never published before or – if already known – never before applied to the product you have in mind. Protection is intended to apply to industrial articles to be produced in quantities of more than 50. The Design Registry can be accessed at the Patent Office website www.patent.gov.uk.

Design registration only applies to features that appeal to the eye – not to the way the article functions.

To register a design, you should apply to the Design Registry and send a specimen or photograph of the design plus a registration fee (currently about £100).

There is no such thing as an all-embracing international registration for designs. If you want protection of your design outside the UK, you generally have to make separate applications for registration in each country in which you want protection.

You can handle the design registration yourself but it might be preferable to let a specialist do it for you.

Controlling a copyright

Copyright gives protection against the unlicensed copying of original artistic and creative works – articles, books, paintings, films, plays, songs, music, engineering drawings. To claim copyright the item in question should carry this symbol © with the author's name and date.

No other action is required to take out copyright. The Copyright service is accessed through the Patent Office website (www.patent.gov.uk).

Copyright does not last forever. The duration is dependant on the type of copyright involved and can be anything from 25 to 70 years after the creator's death.

Setting terms of trade

All business is governed by terms of trade, which are in turn affected by *contractual* relationships. Almost everything done in business, whether it is the supply of raw materials, the sale of goods and services, or the hire of a fax machine is executed under contract law. This is true whether the contract is in writing or whether it is verbal – or even merely implied.

Only contracts for the sale of land, hire-purchase, and some insurance contracts have to be in writing to be enforceable.

To make life even more complicated, a contract can be part written and part oral. So statements made at the time of signing a written contract can legally form part of that contract. For a contract to exist three events must take place:

- There must be an offer.
- There must be an acceptance.
- There must be a consideration – some form of payment.

When selling via the Internet or mail order the contract starts when the supplier 'posts' an acceptance letter, a confirmation, or the goods themselves – whichever comes first.

Under the Distance Selling Regulations brought into effect in October 2001, customers have seven working days after they have received the goods to change their minds and return them. They do not need a reason and can get a full refund.

Consumers must also be given:

- ✔ Information about the company they are dealing with, such as the business name, registered and trading addresses and directors.

- ✔ Written confirmation of the order – by fax, letter, or e-mail.

- ✔ A full refund if their goods do not arrive by the date agreed in the original order; if no date was agreed they must be delivered within 30 days.

- ✔ Information about cancellation rights.

- ✔ Protection against credit card fraud.

Certain standards have to be met by law for the supply of goods and services. Over and above these you need your own terms and conditions if you are not to enter into 'contracts' you did not intend. You will need help to devise these terms. The following four basic propositions will govern your conditions:

- ✔ The conditions must be brought to the other party's attention before he or she makes the contract.

- ✔ The last terms and conditions specified before acceptance of an offer apply.

- ✔ If there is any ambiguity or uncertainty in the contract terms they will be interpreted against the person who inserted them.

- ✔ The terms may be interpreted as unreasonably unenforceable being in breach of various Acts of Parliament.

The Office of Fair Trading (www.oft.gov.uk) and the Trading Standards Institute (www.tsi.org.uk) and Trading Standards Service (www.trading-standards.gov.uk) can provide useful information on most aspects of trading relationships.

Describing your goods

You can't make any claim you like for the performance of your goods or services. If you state or imply a certain standard of performance for what you are selling, your customers have a legally enforceable right to expect that to happen. So if you state your new slimming method will not only make people lose weight, but make them happier, richer, and more successful, then you had better deliver on all those promises.

The Trades Descriptions Acts and related legislation make it an offence for a trader to describe their goods falsely. The Acts cover everything from the declared mileage of second-hand cars to the country of manufacture of a pair of jeans.

The Trading Standards Service is operated at county level throughout the country to ensure trading laws are met. Contact your council by phone or via their website (www.tradingstandards.gov.uk).

Abiding by fair business rules

The whole way in which businesses and markets operate is the subject of keen government interest. It is not a good idea, for example, to gang up with others in your market to create a *cartel*, in which you all agree not to lower your prices, or to compete with each other too vigorously.

Any such action may be brought to the attention of the Office of Fair Trading (OFT). The OFT's (www.oft.gov.uk) job is to make markets work well for consumers. Markets work well when businesses are in open, fair, and vigorous competition with each other for the consumer's custom. As an independent organisation, the OFT have three main operational areas which make up three divisions – Competition Enforcement, Consumer Regulation Enforcement, Markets and Policies Initiatives.

The OFT's Consumer Regulation Enforcement department

- ✔ Ensures that consumer legislation and regulations are properly enforced
- ✔ Takes action against unfair traders
- ✔ Encourages codes of practice and standards
- ✔ Offers a range of information to help consumers understand their rights and make good choices
- ✔ Liaises closely with other regulatory bodies that also have enforcement powers

Dealing with payment problems

Getting paid is not always as simple a process as sending out a bill and waiting for the cheque. Customers may dispute the bill, fairly or unfairly.

A businessperson can use the Small Claims Court to collect bills, to obtain a judgement for breach of contract, or to seek money for minor property damage claims – for example, suing someone who broke a fence around your property or parking area. The Small Claims Court offers you an opportunity to collect money that would otherwise be lost as it would be too expensive to sue in regular court. True, for very small cases, it's not always cost-effective, and occasionally you'll have problems collecting your judgement. But the Small Claims Court should still be part of the collection strategies of your business.

The Small Claims Court aims to provide a speedy, inexpensive resolution of disputes that involve relatively small amounts of money. The advantage of the Small Claims Court is that if you cannot afford a solicitor and you are not entitled to Legal Aid you can still bring your case to the court yourself. Even if you can afford a solicitor, their fees may be more than the amount you are claiming. If you do not manage to get your opponent to pay your costs then you will not be any better off.

The *jurisdictional limits* (the amount for which you can sue) in these courts are rising fairly quickly. In the UK if the amount of money claimed is under £5,000, it is likely to come under the jurisdiction of the Small Claims Court. However, if your claim is for personal injury it will only be heard in the Small Claims Court if the claim for the injury itself is not more than £1,000.

Before you start legal proceedings, investigate alternatives. If your case involves a written contract, check to see if the contract requires mediation or arbitration of disputes. If so, this may limit or cut off your right to go to any court, including the Small Claims Court. Second, consider other cost-effective options, such as free or low-cost publicly operated mediation programmes. If you're in a dispute with a customer, or perhaps another business, and you still have hopes of preserving some aspect of the relationship, mediation – even if not provided for in a contract – is often a better alternative than going to court. Any litigation tends to sour people's feelings.

Since January 2002 anyone claiming up to £100,000 can sue through the Internet at any time, day or night. If the claim is undefended, the money can be recovered without anyone having to go to court. The service, called Money Claim Online, can be reached at www.courtservice.gov.uk.

Chapter 11

Employing People

. . . .

In This Chapter

▶ Finding the best employees for your business

▶ Finding motivations and rewards

▶ Keeping on the right side of employment law

. . . .

*U*nless you intend working on your own, you will be involved in employing and motivating others to do what you want them to do. Even if you don't employ people full-time, or if you outsource some portion of your work to others, you will have to choose who to give those tasks too, how to get the best out of them and how to reward their achievements.

Profiling Great Employees

Firstly you may need to change your attitude to the whole hiring process. Most entrepreneurs dislike hiring employees and do it as little as possible and fit it around their other 'more important' tasks.

Finding good staff is *the* number one job for the boss. You need good people to delegate to. The current team needs a stream of new people who do not need to be carried and who can bring fresh and innovative ideas with them to stimulate everyone on to greater things.

Recruitment has to become a routine task, like selling or monitoring cash flow, that you do every day. Furthermore you need a budget to carry out the recruitment and selection task, just as you need a budget for equipment and rent. If you don't have a recruitment budget, you shouldn't be surprised if a task for which no money is budgeted goes wrong.

Deciding on full- or part-timers

One important decision you need to make before you can start your search for staff is whether you need to hire a full-time person. There are some very good reasons why you may not. If, for example, the demand for your products is highly seasonal and has major peaks and troughs it may make no sense to keep people on during slack periods. This could be the case if you were selling heating oil, where you might expect to peak in the autumn and tail off in the late spring because of variations in the weather. Other examples of seasonal fluctuations are increased sales of garden furniture and barbeques in summer and toys and luxury items before Christmas.

Using part-timers can open up whole new markets of job applicants, sometimes of a higher quality than you might expect on the general job market. Highly skilled and experienced retired workers, or mothers who have given up successful careers to have a family, can be tempted back into temporary or part-time work. It can sometimes make sense to have two part-time staff sharing the one job, each working part-time. This tactic can also be used to retain key staff that want to leave full-time employment. This makes for continuity in the work, allows people to fit in work around their personal circumstances, and brings to the business talents that might have been lost if full-time work had been insisted upon.

Part-time work is more prevalent than many people think. Up to a third of all those in employment in some countries are working part-time and most of those are working in small firms whose flexibility in this area can often be a key strength over larger firms when it comes to recruiting and retaining employees.

You can find part-time staff using the same methods as for full-time employees, which I discuss in the next sections. If you are looking for people to work anti-social hours, or to do just a few hours' work at short notice to meet sudden peaks, then the chances are you will have to recruit close to your work. In such a situation you may get the best results by circulating a leaflet that sets out your requirements. Target housing estates close to your premises or on good transport routes that operate at the times you want people to start and finish work. Make your leaflet stand out as lots of junk mail goes through most people's doors today. Have a key benefit that will grab people's attention, then give the basic details of the work, hours, pay, and who to contact.

Recruiting and selecting

To make sure that you get great people into your business, follow the tips in these sections.

Review your business goals

The starting point for any recruitment activity is a review of your short- and medium-term business goals. If you have recently updated your business plan, then your goals will be fresh in your mind. If not, then you need to do so. For example if you plan to sell, service, and dispatch software via your Web site, then the people needed will be quite different from those required if you plan dispatching physical products.

Define the job

You need to set out the scope and responsibilities of the job before you start recruiting. The job description should include the measurable outcomes that you expect, as well as a description of the tasks. So for a salesperson you need to spell out what the sales target is, how many calls should be made, what the customer retention target is, and so on.

Too many small firms don't get round to preparing the job description until the person is in place, or worse still they don't have job descriptions at all. The argument advanced is that, as jobs in the small business world have a short shelf-life because the company is growing and changing all the time, why bother?

Profile the person

Flesh out your idea of the sort of person who could do the job well. If you are looking for a salesperson, then communication skills and appearance are important factors to consider, as might their personal circumstance, which may have to allow them to stay away from home frequently.

As well as qualifications and experience, keep in mind their team skills and that all too rare attribute, business savvy.

Advertise the job

You can fill positions from inside your company or outside it. Don't overlook your existing staff. You may be able to promote from within, even if you have to provide some additional training. Also your staff, suppliers, or other business contacts may know of someone in their network who might be suitable.

Press advertising is still a popular external source of new staff. The Internet is now exploding onto the recruitment market. But despite the hype only a few percentage of jobs are actually filled from advertisements on the Internet.

The type of vacancy will determine the medium. The Internet might be right for design engineers, but a leaflet drop on a housing estate would be better when looking for shift workers.

Advertising for recruitment is subject to legal restrictions that vary from country to country. The laws most likely to apply are those of libel, and those relating to discrimination on the grounds of gender, race, or age. Avoid sexist language and the words 'he' or 'she' and select your words carefully to avoid stipulating characteristics that exclude potential applicants of a specific sex or race or in a particular age range. If in doubt consult your Advertising

Standards Authority or take legal advice. Most restrictions apply to newspapers, magazines, radio, and television; however, you would be wise to include the Internet on that list.

Advertising is intended to give you a reasonable choice of applicants. If you get it right you should end up with enough applicants to have a choice to make.

Make your selection

Firstly screen out the people who don't meet your specifications. Phone them if you need to clarify something, for example to establish whether they have experience of a particular software package. Then interview your shortlist perhaps using a test where possible. There are many self-administered tests, custom-designed for different types of work – I talk about tests in the upcoming 'Testing to find the best' section.

Let the applicants meet others in the business. This will give them a better feel for the company and you can get a second opinion on them. When Apple was developing the Macintosh the entire Mac team was involved in every new appointment. Applicants spent a day with the team, and only when the team decided a person was suitable did they let them in on the project.

Ideally, you end up with at least three people who you would be happy to appoint. Offer the job to the best candidate, keeping the others in reserve. You must have a reserve in case your first choice lets you down, accepts but then changes their mind, or quits or is fired after a week or two.

Always take up references, preferably on the phone. Don't take 'testimonials' at face value.

Make the new employee welcome

Having got the right people to join you, make sure they become productive quickly and stay for a long time. The best way to do this is to have a comprehensive induction process showing them where everything is and the way things are done in your business. Keep them posted of developments, put them on the memo/e-mail list. Set them short-term objectives and monitor performance weekly, perhaps even daily at first, giving praise or help as required. Invite them to social events as appropriate.

Testing to find the best

What are known as the classic trio of selection methods, application forms, interviews and references, can be supplemented by other tools which can improve your chances of getting the right candidate for most of the jobs you may want to fill. These tools are often clustered under the general heading of psychometric tests, although most of the tests themselves have less to do with psychology than with basic aptitude.

Plumbing the depths of employees

Sam had worked for a large national firm of builders' merchants for ten years before he branched out on his own. He had trained as a plumber so he was confident that he would have no difficulty in finding work, and he was right. Soon Sam was working a 60-hour week, returning home exhausted late in the evening to do his paperwork and plan for the next day's work. Within four months of starting up Sam desperately needed more staff. An acquaintance recommended an out-of-work plumber who could work for Sam almost immediately. Sam reckoned that anyone was better than no one as at least some of the backlog of work could be tackled. He took the man on and sent his new employee to work on a small task for a customer. The task should have taken three days and Sam planned to try and get out to see how he was getting on during the first day. Unfortunately, Sam couldn't get out to that job until the afternoon of the second day. He arrived to find his new workman had failed to show up for work that day and had produced such a low standard of work that everything had to be done again. Sam ended up losing a valued client, wasting valuable materials, and still had the job to do at a later date.

Tests are particularly useful for those in small firms as they can provide a much needed and valuable external view on candidates, which big firms have already in their human resources departments. Tests can also be applied quickly and without using many scarce internal resources.

Used correctly and fairly and in the right situations, tests can objectively measure skills (such as word processing or software proficiency), assess acquired knowledge and qualifications, and determine aptitude for certain jobs. But although tests are popular and becoming more reliable, they are neither certain to get selection decisions right nor are they risk-free.

There are dozens of commercial test publishers producing over 3,000 different tests. You can locate the appropriate test for your business through the British Psychological Society (www.bps.org.uk) or the Chartered Institute of Personnel and Development (www.cipd.co.uk).

Exploring Sources

You don't have to do everything involved in recruiting employees yourself. You can find a recruitment consultant or use a government Job Centre to do much of the hard work for you. In fact they may even be better at this than you will be, as they recruit and select every day of the week. Research suggests that Recruitment Consultants, for example, are twice as successful at filling vacancies than are entrepreneurs on their own.

You could consider taking the job in question out of your business and pay someone else to do it. See the section 'Outsourcing jobs' for more on this.

Outsourcing jobs

Almost every part of the work you do can probably be bought in. Web sites can be designed and hosted, and technology can be rented. There are e-wholesalers and packers and Internet-only delivery groups. Customer services can be handled by third-party call centres, and online banks compete with traditional banks to offer online payment processing. Almost every other aspect of business from accounting and recruitment, to payroll and human resource services can be outsourced, often via the Internet itself.

So you need to be very sure that you need to do everything yourself or with your own employees all the time. Clearly, if you can buy something in cheaper than you can do it yourself then it makes sense to do so. You might also consider outsourcing in areas that may not be cheaper but could save scarce cash or unnecessary upheaval. For example if your premises will fit six people and no more, it may make sense to outsource packaging and despatch to a fulfilment house and use the space saved to fit in more salespeople, or any other high skilled high value-adding job. The alternative of moving to larger premises will mean disruption and a higher fixed cost, which you may not feel ready for yet.

Using agencies

There may well be occasions when you feel that either you are unable or unwilling to do the job of recruiting yourself. In such circumstances you may find it useful to use a recruitment agency. Their costs may sound high, but when you reckon up the internal costs you may find they are not that expensive. Doing the recruiting yourself could take several days of your time and that of others in your firm. If you are working on your own or with just one or two others, this may be too great a distraction from other key tasks.

Costs that are deferred or reduced by the use of an outside recruitment agency include:

 ✔ The salaries and benefits of those involved in the recruitment process in your firm, including your own.

 ✔ The cost of advertisements, trade shows, phone time and so on incurred via alternative methods.

 ✔ The cost of the work that is not getting done while those doing the recruitment are busy on the search.

✔ Associated costs of staff due to travel, food, lodging, and entertainment expenses.

✔ Costs associated with developing sources to look for prospective employees.

✔ Office expenses such as telephone time and expenses, mailings, and postage.

✔ The time/effort involved in keeping track of applicants, reviewing CVs, checking references, dealing with unqualified applicants, interviewing qualified ones.

✔ The cost of revealing your hiring needs and strategies to competitors.

✔ The cost of getting it wrong. On average recruitment consultants are more likely to succeed than you are. After all, they recruit people every day; they are more likely to find a suitable candidate and one who stays in the job.

Choosing a recruitment consultant

Fundamentally there are two types of recruitment agency, contingency agencies and retained agencies, and they charge you in different ways.

A contingency agency charges a fee only when they find a suitable candidate for the position, whereas a retained agency asks for payment of their fees upfront, and will not provide a refund even if they fail to fill the position. For this reason, retained agencies are normally only used to find very skilled individuals within higher salary bands (perhaps £40,000 or more), whereas a contingency agency will find candidates for a range of positions – analysts, bookkeepers, consultants. You could use several contingency agencies at a time to find a candidate, because there is no risk of losing money.

All finding fees are based on the first year's annual salary, which consists of the income guaranteed to the applicant by the employer, including shift allowances and bonuses. It is hard to say precisely what commission rate you will be charged by a recruitment agency, because this information is related to the position you wish to fill. For example, the finding fee for a software engineer is likely to be higher than the one for a secretary. Specialist qualifications such as a degree, number of years of experience, and language skills, for example, are also taken into consideration.

Finding fees are generally 18–20 per cent of the first year's annual salary, although in some sectors this is significantly higher.

Fees are always open to discussion as this is a highly competitive marketplace, so you should try and negotiate the percentage you want to pay for a candidate.

Using Job Centre Plus

Job Centre Plus is the government-run employment services, which have pro-fessionally run offices with a growing number of SME (Small and Medium Enterprises) specialist staff. Typically these employment services are run out of 1,000 Job Centres based in towns where job-seekers are likely to live. At any one time they have 400,000 job-seekers on their database.

Their services are particularly helpful to small firms with little experience of recruiting as they offer a wide range of free help and advice on most mat-ters concerned with employing people as well as signposting to other related services.

The Job Centre Plus range of services includes everything you would expect of a recruitment consultant. But unlike other recruitment agencies, many of their services are free and in any event will cost less than using any other external recruiter.

Screening over the Internet

The fastest growing route to new job applicants is via the Internet itself. The number of websites offering employment opportunities has exploded in recent years. The advantages of Internet recruitment to both candidates and clients are obvious. Internet recruitment offers fast, immediate, and cheap service compared to more traditional methods of recruitment. However, a number of Internet recruitment sites have established formidable reputations in Europe and the US. These include:

- *Futurestep* (www.futurestep.com), which covers all job functions and industry sectors.

- *LeadersOnline* (www.leadersonline.com) is becoming one of the lead-ing Internet recruitment sites, aided by the fact that is focused towards technology professionals and handles recruitment between a salary range of £50,000 to £100,000.

- *monster.co.uk* (www.monster.co.uk) attracts approximately 100,000 visits per month and contains over one million CVs. Vacancies cover every industry sector and regional area.

Another option is to have a job-listing section on your own Web site. This is absolutely free, however you are certain to be trawling in a very small pool. This may not matter if the right sort of people are already visiting your site. At least they will know something about your products and services before they apply.

Motivating and Rewarding Employees

Management is the art and science of getting people to do what you want them to do, because *they* want to do it. This is easier said than done.

Most entrepreneurs believe that their employees work for money and their key staff work for more money. Pay them enough and they'll jump through any hoop. This view is not borne out by most of the research, which ranks pay as third or even fourth in the reasons why people come to work.

If it isn't necessarily money, why do people work where they do? I help provide some of the answers in the following sections.

The practice of management

In this section, I give you some practical tools you can use to get the very best out of your employees.

The starting point in getting people to give of their best is to assess them as individuals and to recognise their specific needs and motivations. These differences are in part influenced by age, gender, or job. They are also affected by an individual's personality. You need to tailor your actions to each person to get the best results.

My best advice is: Get to know everyone. This may sound insane in a small firm and after all you almost certainly recruited them all in the first place. By observing and listening to your employees you can build a picture of them that will help you motivate them by making them feel special.

✔ Show an interest in people's work. This is nothing to do with monitoring performance and more to do with managing by walking about, and seeing everyone, and talking with them as often as possible.

If you employ less than five people you need to spend some time with each of them every day, up to ten people every week. After that, you should have managers doing much the same thing, but you still need to get around as often as possible.

There is a famous management story, known as the Hawthorne Experiment, which demonstrates the power of this approach as a motivator. A manager was trying to improve output in a manufacturing unit so he called in some consultants to see what could be done. First they tried altering the lighting to make it easier for employees to see what they were doing. Output rose immediately. Then they gave them control of the speed of the production line and output rose again. Next they rearranged the flow of work, after discussions with the work team, and output improved again. The consultants, despite much deliberation, could see no logical link between their actions and the employees' improved work output. In the end they concluded that what really made the difference was that for the first time in years someone showed an interest in what they were doing and how they could improve their lot.

✔ Promote from within when you can. Too often people look outside for every new appointment. That is more or less saying that people you currently employ are not up to the task. There will be occasions where you have to bring someone in with new skills and special abilities. But if you can promote from within everyone can be a winner. When one employee gets a promotion others see career prospects perhaps they hadn't seen before, and you have someone you know and trust in a key job. Your newly promoted employee can help train someone up to take his or her former job, thereby saving you training time, also.

✔ Give title promotions in lieu of job promotions. A worker you don't want to lose may crave a certain position that you know he or she would fail in. Make the employee's benefits and status the same as for the desired position and add a new title to show that you value the employee and his or her work.

A likely situation is with a great salesperson. If they are ambitious as well as a brilliant salesperson they will want to become sales manager, which is an important step on their career ladder and demonstrates to their spouse, partner, and peers, as well as to themselves that they are doing a good job. Unfortunately most great salespeople make lousy managers. If you promote them the chances are you'll lose a good salesperson and have to fire them for being a useless manager in a few months' time. So keep them motivated by giving them the same package you would a sales manager, the same level of car, salary and other employment conditions, and promote them to a new title, sales executive or key account manager, for example. After all if they are selling so much they must be making good money for the business. They have the status and the cash and you keep a great salesperson doing what they do best, selling.

This can be a strategy in a small firm to create career progression for more people than might otherwise be possible.

✔ Give praise as often as you can. The rule is simple: Minimise your reaction to bad results and maximise your appreciation of good results. Autocratic employers continually criticise and complain, finding only poor performance wherever they look. Criticism reinforces poor behaviour. Everyone wants to be recognised and strangely enough people often prefer to be shouted at than ignored. So if doing things wrong is the only way to get noticed that's what may well happen.

You can always leaven out criticism with some favourable comment. For example if an employee is making some progress, but is short of being satisfactory, saying something like, 'This is certainly an improvement, but we still have a way to go. Let's spend a little time together and I'll see if we can't get to the bottom of what is holding you back', might produce a better level of motivation than just shouting out your criticism.

✔ Create a no-blame culture. Everything in business is a risk. If it were not there would be no chance of making a profit. It's the uncertainty around all business processes that creates that opportunity to make money. Not many bookmakers would be prepared to take a bet on a horse race after it had happened and the winner had been announced.

To a greater or lesser extent, you delegate some of the responsibility for taking risks on to your employees. But how should you react when the inevitable happens and things go wrong, as they will in some cases. If you jump up and down with rage, then no one will ever take a risk again. They'll leave all the decisions to you and you'll become even more over-worked. Good people will get highly de-motivated and leave. If you take a sympathetic and constructive attitude to failure you will motivate and encourage employees to try again.

You need to make clear that tolerance of mistakes has its limits and repetition of the same mistake will not receive an equally tolerant reaction.

✔ Reduce de-motivation. In fact, very often the problem is not so much that of motivating people, but of avoiding de-motivating them! If you can keep off the backs of employees, it is quite possible that they will motivate themselves. After all, most of us want the same things: a sense of achievement or challenge, recognition of our efforts, an interesting and varied job, opportunities for responsibility, advancement, and job growth. But in a small firm the potential for de-motivation is high. Workloads invariably peak and there is never any slack in the systems of a small firm. Inevitably some employees will feel overloaded, neglected, or just plain hard done by. It may not reach the stage where people will complain, or start taking time off sick, but having de-motivated people around can create an unhealthy climate for everyone else.

So you need to look out for any negative behaviour and find out the cause. A 'couldn't care less attitude', lack of enthusiasm, or any signs of aggression can be useful indicators that all is not well. You need to counter de-motivators with a burst of motivators such as recognition and advancement, which cause satisfaction.

✔ Motivate off-site employees. Part-time workers, telecommuters, and key subcontractors, who either do much of their work off-site or who are not around all of the time, have to be built into your motivational plans too.

Dealing with difficult or de-motivated employees

Difficult or de-motivated people need prompt and effective managing. Dissatisfaction can spread quickly and lower motivation levels in others. The first step is to identify the causes of the problem. The causes may be to do with the employee or with the job itself. The problem may be brought about by illness, stress, or a personality clash between people working together.

Whatever the cause, the initiative for re-motivating them has to come from you. However the only reason for going through this effort is because either that employee has delivered satisfactory results in the past or you believe they have the potential to do so, if you can just find the key.

A good starting point is to recognise some basic truths about difficult or de-motivated people.

✔ Difficult people are not always out to take advantage of you or others. It is possible to pull them into a partnership if you can find the right shared goals. These have to be exciting, realistic, attainable, and important to them as well as the business.

✔ Difficult people can change. Dramatic changes in behaviour are possible and even the most intransigent employee can be won over. Very often it's just the approach taken to the problem that limits a difficult person's desire to change. If, for example, an employee consistently comes in late, you could start by warning them, then shouting at them, and finally you could threaten them with disciplinary action. It may even have to come to that. But how would events turn out if you started by giving the business reasons why turning up on time is important, with some examples of how being late affects their performance and ultimately limits their options for advancement.

✔ Difficult people can't be ignored. Unfortunately employees who set their own standards of behaviour well below the standard you expect of others do have a bad influence, especially on new employees. You can hardly demand punctuality of some people and not of others. Nor can you adopt the philosophy that if you leave them long enough they will really step out of line and then you can fire them. As the boss you have to manage all those who you employ and motivate them to perform.

Keeping motivation all in the family

Over 80 per cent of small businesses are family businesses in which one or more family members work in the organisation. Family businesses have both strengths and weaknesses when it comes to motivation. By being aware of them you can exploit the former to do your best to overcome the latter to give your business a better chance of prospering.

The factors that motivate or de-motivate family members can be different than those affecting non-family members.

The overwhelming strength of the family business is the different atmosphere and feel that a family concern has. A sense of belonging and common purpose more often than not leads to good motivation and performance. Another advantage is that the family firm has greater flexibility, since the unity of management and shareholders provides the opportunity to make quick decisions and to implement rapid change if necessary. On the downside, there are several weaknesses. Although these are not unique to family businesses, family firms are particularly prone to them. These are the main ones:

- ✔ Unwillingness to change has been identified as the single most common cause of low motivation in family firms. Family firms often do things the way they've always done them just because that's the way they've always done them. This can lead to stagnation in the marketplace and failing confidence in investors. Resistance to change is exacerbated by diminishing vitality, as founders grow old.

- ✔ Family goals and commercial goals come into conflict. Unlike other businesses, family firms have additional objectives to their financial performance targets, for example: building family reputation and status in the community; providing employment for the family; protecting family wealth; ensuring independence; a dynastic wish to pass on a position, in addition to wealth, to the next generation. However, superimposing these family values on the business can lead to difficulties. For example nepotism may lead to employment of family members beyond their competence, or a salary above their worth. This can lead to discontent and be de-motivational for non-family members.

- ✔ Facing conflict between growth and ownership. Families prefer majority ownership of a small company to minority holdings in a big company where they are answerable to outside shareholders. Basically a dilemma that all family managers face is one of either growing the company, keeping purely commercial goals in mind at whatever risk to family control, or to subordinating the firm's welfare to family constraints. This affects all areas of the business, from recruitment through to management.

- ✔ Impact of and career prospects of non-family employees may be limited. At management level family pride will sometimes not allow a situation where its members are subordinate to an outsider – even if the outsider is a better person for the job. Also, reliance on family management to the exclusion of input from outsiders may starve a growing firm of new ideas. A family firm may become inward looking, insensitive to the message of the marketplace, unreceptive to outside ideas, and unwilling to recruit competent outside managers. None of these are factors likely to be motivational to others in the business.

These are problems a family firm must address if all the effort put into motivating employees is not to be seen as a cynical deception. It would certainly be helpful to have a clear statement of family policy on the employment of family members, succession, and on ownership. Then non-family members can either buy in or not join in the first place.

Rewarding achievements

Whilst people often come to work for a set number of hours each week, it is what they do during that time that matters most to the organisation. Different types of work have different measurable outcomes. Those outcomes have to be identified and a scale arrived at showing the base rate of pay and payment above that base for achieving objectives. Different types of 'payment by results' schemes are in common use in different types of firm and the conditions that most favour these types of pay need to be carefully examined to make sure you pick the right mix of goals and rewards.

Ground rules in matching pay to performance:

✔ Make the rules clear so everyone knows how the reward system will work.

✔ Make the goals specific and if possible quantifiable.

✔ Make the reward visible so everyone knows what each person or team gets.

✔ Make it matter. The reward has to be worthwhile and commensurate with the effort involved.

✔ Make it fair, so people believe their reward is correctly calculated.

✔ Make it realistic because if the target is set too high no one will try to achieve it.

✔ Make it happen quickly.

The following sections address specific reward systems.

Paying a commission

This is perhaps the easiest reward system, but it really only works for those directly involved in selling. A *commission* is a payment based in some way on the value of sales secured by the individual or team concerned.

You have to make sure that the order is actually delivered or executed before any commission is paid and you may even want to make sure the customer has paid up. However, as with all rewards, you must keep the time-scale between doing the work and getting the reward as short as practicably possible, otherwise people will have forgotten what the money is for.

It makes sense to base the commission on your gross profit rather than sales turnover; otherwise you could end up rewarding salespeople for generating unprofitable business.

Awarding bonuses

A *bonus* is a reward for successful performance, usually paid in a lump sum related as closely as possible to the results obtained by an individual, team, or the business as a whole. In general, bonuses are tied to results so that it's less obvious how an individual contributed directly to the result achieved. For example a company bonus may be paid out if the firm achieves a certain level of output. Keeping everyone informed as to how the firm is performing towards achieving that goal may well be motivational, but the exact role say a cleaner or office-worker has in helping attain that goal is not easy to assess – not as easy as it is to calculate a salesperson's commission, say.

Bonuses can be paid out periodically or as a one-off payment for a specific achievement.

Sharing profits

Profit sharing involves giving a specific share of the company's profit to the firm's employees. The share of the profits can be different for different jobs, length of service, or seniority.

This type of reward has the great merit of focusing everyone's attention on the firm's primary economic goal – to make money. It is quite possible that one or more employees can be performing well, but others drag down the overall performance. The theory is that the performing staff puts pressure on the others to come up to the mark.

If profits go up, people get more; but it can go the other way too, which can be less attractive. Also, profit targets can be missed for reasons outside of the employees' direct control. If you are dependent on customers or supplies from overseas, for example, and the exchange rate moves against you, profits, and hence profit-related pay, can dip sharply. However unfair this may seem to a receptionist who has been hoping for extra cash to pay for a holiday, this is the hard reality of business. If you think your employees are adult enough to take that fact on board, then this can be a useful way to reward staff.

Sharing ownership

Share option schemes give employees the chance to share in the increase in value of a company's shares as it grows and prospers.

The attraction of turning employees into shareholders is that it gives them a long-term stake in the business and hopefully will make them look beyond short-term issues and ensure their long-term loyalty. Of course, there can be unwelcome side effects if the value of the business goes down rather than up.

Giving skill and competence awards

You can give a skill or competence award when an employee reaches a certain level of ability. These awards are not directly tied to an output such as improved performance, but you must believe that raising the skill or competence in question will ultimately lead to better business results.

The award itself could be cash, gift certificates, extra days of holiday, a trip to a show or sports event, or whatever else your employees might appreciate. Bottles of wine always seem to be well received!

Compensating Your Employees

Finding and motivating employees is one part of the employment equation. The other is recompensing them for their efforts and achievements either by way of pay, or by some other benefit that is at least as appealing to each individual employee.

Setting payment levels

It's certainly true that people don't come to work just for money. But they certainly won't come if you don't pay them and they won't stay and be motivated to give of their best if you don't give them the right pay. But how much is the right amount? Get it too low and your ability to attract and retain productive and reliable people capable of growing as your business grows is impaired. But pay too much and your overheads rise so much you become uncompetitive. That is a real danger for small firms where the wages bill often represents the largest single business expense.

These ground rules are not very complicated but they are important:

- ✔ Only pay what you can afford. There is no point in sinking the company with a wage bill that it can't meet.

- ✔ Make sure pay is fair and equitable and is seen as such by everyone.

- ✔ Make sure people know how pay scales are arrived at.

- ✔ See that pay scales for different jobs reflect the relative importance of the job and the skills required.

- ✔ Ensure your pay scales are in line with the law on minimum wage requirements. Since April 1999 a *statutory minimum wage* is in effect in the UK. The amount is governed by the age of the employee and whether an employee is undergoing training. The hourly rate changes over time, so you need to keep abreast of the latest rates. (`www.jobcentreplus.gov.uk` has information on current rules in this area.)

- ✔ Ensure your pay scales are competitive with those of other employers in your region or industry.

Big companies go in for a process known as 'job evaluation'. This involves looking at each job and evaluating it against a range of factors such as complexity, qualifications, skills, experience required, any dangers or hazards involved, and the value of the contribution to your business. Creating and maintaining a structure like this is a full-time job in itself. It is certainly not something a small business should undertake lightly.

You can get most of the advantages of having a job evaluation system by finding out the going rate for key jobs in other people's businesses. The going rate is the pay rate that normally applies to a particular job in a particular geographic area. Inevitably not all jobs are identical and certain aspects involve differences in employment conditions that inevitably affect the going rate. For example, working hours, employment conditions, security of tenure, pension rights, and so forth vary from firm to firm. You need to have a procedure in place to routinely monitor local going rates and a system to correct for variations in employment conditions between your firm and other similar firms.

The consequence of being too far out of line with the going rate is that staff turnover will rise. As long as the businesses you look at are reasonably similar and the jobs much the same you will end up with a defendable, credible, and acceptable pay structure, which should only take you a couple of hours' work twice or at most three times a year.

Ways to find out the going rate for a job include:

- Read articles on pay, job advertisements on the Internet, in the local papers and the relevant trade journals. You may have to correct some pay rates to allow for variations. For example, pay rates for similar jobs are often much higher in or near major cities than they are in rural areas.

- Talk to your Chamber of Commerce or Trade Association, some of whom publish salary surveys, and to other local employers and business owners in your network.

- Contact employment agencies including those run by government agencies. They are usually a bit ahead of the rest of the market in terms of pay information. Other employers only know what they are paying their present staff. Recruitment agencies know what you will have to pay to get your next employee.

Deciding arbitrarily the pay rates of people who work for you may appear to be one of the perks of working for yourself. But inconsistent pay rates will quickly upset people and staff will jump ship at the first opportunity.

Creating a menu of benefits

A *benefit* is defined as any form of compensation that is not part of an employee's basic pay and that isn't tied directly to their performance in those jobs. These non-salary benefits such as pension, working conditions, and company policy can also play a part in keeping people on side.

A wide range of other perks ranging from being allowed to wear casual dress (almost essential) to onsite childcare is on offer to employees in organisations. Personal development training, company product discounts, flexible hours, telecommuting, and fitness facilities are all benefits that people can expect in certain jobs today.

Some benefits have become pretty well obligatory. For example, since October 2001, small firms in the UK that employ more than five people are obliged to provide their employees with a pension. These companies have to contend with choosing an appropriate scheme, setting up the logistics for collecting contributions, and communicating their decisions to their employees.

Interestingly enough, the approach recommended by the UK government to how small firms should handle pensions may form the model to inspire them to introduce a wide range of other benefits.

Staying on the Right Side of the Law

A business operates within a legal framework, the elements of which the owner-manager must be aware. The areas I cover in the following sections summarise only a few of the key legal issues. Different types of business may have to pay regard to different legal issues and employment law itself is dynamic and subject to revision and change.

The Advisory, Conciliation and Arbitration Service (ACAS) (www.acas.org.uk) and The British Safety Council (www.britishsafetycouncil.org) are useful organisations who can help with aspects of employment issues, and Emplaw (www.emplaw.co.uk) is a Web site covering basic British employment law information and will direct you to a lawyer in your area who specialises in the aspect of employment law you are concerned with.

Keeping employment records

You need to keep records about employees both individually and collectively. When you only employ one or two people this may seem like a bureaucratic chore. You may even feel that you can remember all the important details about your employees without keeping copious records. However, the particulars on even a few employees are too much data to carry in your head, especially alongside all the other things you have to remember. The record system can be a manual one, it can be computerised or, as is the case in most small firms, a mix of the two. The great strength of computerised records lies in the ease with which collective data on employees past and present can be produced. This can throw up trends, which may help in recognising problems and setting them in proper context. For example the collective employee data will show average absenteeism and lateness statistics, which you can then use as a comparison during an individual's appraisal.

Some of the data you need to keep is a legal requirement, such as information on accidents. Some of the information will be invaluable in any dispute with an employee, for example in a case of unfair dismissal. All of the information makes the process of employing people run more smoothly.

Individual employee information should include:

- ✔ The application form
- ✔ Interview record and the results of any selection tests used
- ✔ Job history, including details of promotions and assignments
- ✔ Current and past job descriptions
- ✔ Current pay and bonus details and a record of the amount and date of any changes
- ✔ Details of skills and competences
- ✔ Education and training records with details of courses attended
- ✔ Details of performance assessments and appraisals
- ✔ Absence, lateness, accident, medical and disciplinary records, together with details of any formal warnings and suspensions
- ✔ Holiday entitlement
- ✔ Pension contribution data
- ✔ Termination record giving date, details of exit interview, and suitability for re-engagement
- ✔ Copies of any correspondence between you and the employee

Collective information should include:

- ✔ Numbers, grades, and job titles
- ✔ Absenteeism, staff turnover, and lateness statistics
- ✔ Accident rates
- ✔ Age and length of service records
- ✔ Wage and salary structures

- Employee costs
- Overtime statistics showing hours worked and costs
- Records of grievances and disputes
- Training records showing how many person days have been devoted to training and how much that has cost
- Gender, ethnic, and disability profiles

Employees have three basic rights over the information an employer keeps in their employment records:

- To be able to obtain access to one's own personal data
- To be able to claim damages for losses caused by the use of inaccurate data or the unauthorised use of data, or by the loss or destruction of data
- To apply to the courts if necessary for rectification or erasure of inaccurate data

This means that an employee is entitled to gain access to his or her personal data at reasonable intervals and without undue delay or expense. It is a legal requirement that this request be put in writing, although you may choose not to insist on this and you must provide the information within 40 days of the request.

Preparing contracts of employment

Employees have to be given a written statement of a defined list of terms and conditions of their employment within two months of starting working for you.

The list of terms which go into a job description include the following:

- The employee's full name
- When the employee started working for you
- How and how much your employee is paid
- Whether pay is weekly or monthly
- The hours you expect them to work
- The number of days holiday they are allowed, including public holidays and how that holiday is accumulated
- The employee's job title or a brief description of his or her work
- Where you expect the employee to work and what conditions will apply if you expect them to work elsewhere

✔ You need to state if you intend the employment to be permanent or, if it is for a fixed term, when it will start and finish

✔ Details of who the employee will be managed by and who they can talk to if they have any dispute with that person

✔ Any terms and conditions relating to sickness or injury, including any provision for sick pay

✔ Any terms and conditions relating to pensions and pension schemes

✔ Any disciplinary rules applicable to the employee

✔ The period of notice required, which increases with length of service; a legal minimum of one week's notice per year of service is required up to a maximum of 12 weeks (this may be overridden by express terms in the contract)

The job description forms the cornerstone of the contract of employment that exists between employer and employee. However, the contract is rarely a single document and may not even be completely documented. A contract comes into existence as soon as someone accepts an offer of paid employment, even if both offer and acceptance are only oral. In practice the most important contractual document may be the letter offering a person the job, together with the salary and other basic employment conditions.

The contract consists of four types of condition:

✔ **Express terms:** Terms specifically agreed to between employer and employee, whether in writing or not.

✔ **Implied terms:** Terms considered to be so obvious that they don't need spelling out. These include such matters as the employee complying with reasonable instructions and taking care of business property and equipment. For the employer these can include taking reasonable care of the employee and paying them for work done.

✔ **Incorporated terms:** Terms from outside sources, most commonly from trade union agreements, that are included in the contract.

✔ **Statutory terms:** These include any work requirements laid down by law – safety regulations, for example.

Working legal hours

Whilst the owner of a business may be content to work all hours, since 1999 the law has strictly governed the amount of time employees can be asked to put in. The Working Time Regulations, as they are known, apply to any staff over the minimum school-leaving age. This includes temporary workers, home workers, and people working for you overseas. The regulations are summarised in the following points:

✔ Staff cannot be forced to work more than 48 hours a week. However, an employee may work over those hours if he or she agrees to it by signing an opt-out agreement.

✔ You cannot force an employee to sign an opt-out agreement from any aspect of the regulations.

✔ Working time includes travelling when it is part of the job, working lunches and job-related training.

✔ For night workers, there is a limit of an average of eight hours' work in 24. They are also entitled to receive a free health assessment.

✔ All workers are entitled to 11 hours rest a day, a day off each week, and an in-work rest break of at least 20 minutes if the working day is longer than six hours.

✔ If a worker misses some rest, he or she is entitled to *compensatory rest,* which is another period of rest the same time as the part of the period of rest missed.

✔ Full-time staff are entitled to four weeks' paid holiday a year after a 13-week qualification period. However, they do not have the right to choose when to take leave. It must be agreed with the employer.

As an employer, you must keep records that show you comply with the working-time limits and that you have given night workers the opportunity for a health assessment.

Granting leave

As an employer, occasions are bound to arise when you will be obliged to give your staff time off work other than their usual holidays or when they are unwell. You may not have to pay them when these occasions occur, but you do have to respect their right to be absent.

Protecting maternity and paternity rights

All pregnant employees have rights in four main areas. These include the right to reasonable time off to have antenatal care; the right not to be unfairly dismissed; the right to maternity leave; and the right to return to work. There are many conditions and exceptions so you need to examine each case carefully to see how to proceed.

Parental leave applies to men and women alike who have been employed for more than one year and have responsibility for a child as a biological, foster, adoptive, or step parent.

The minimum period of parental leave that can be taken in one go is one week (unless the child is entitled to disability living allowance) and the maximum is four weeks.

Recognising emergency leave

Employees have the right to reasonable unpaid leave where their *dependants* – spouses, children, parents, and other people living in an employee's house (except lodgers), and others who might rely on an employee in emergencies, such as elderly neighbours – are affected by:

- ✔ Illness, injury, assault, or childbirth
- ✔ Breakdown in childcare/other care arrangements
- ✔ The consequences of a death
- ✔ A serious incident at school or during school hours

To take this leave, your employee should give notice as soon as reasonably practicable giving the reason for, and likely duration of, absence. 'Reasonable' time off is not defined but, usually, one or two days should suffice.

Avoiding discrimination

By and large business owners can employ whomever they want to employ. However, when setting the criteria for a particular job or promotion it is usually illegal to discriminate on the grounds of sex, race, marital status, or union membership. If you employ more than 15 people, then disabled employees have the right not to be discriminated against in either the recruitment process or when they are employed.

Whether you can impose age limits on job applicants or on your employees is debatable. You may find that by imposing an age limit you are indirectly discriminating against women, for example, who have had time off work to have children.

New regulations designed to prevent part-time employees from being treated less favourably than comparable full-time employees – that is someone doing broadly similar work and with a similar level of skills and qualifications – are coming into force in the UK. Business owners will have to ensure part-time employees receive equal sick pay and maternity pay (on a pro rata basis), equal hourly rates of pay, and equal access to pension schemes. Employers will also be obliged to ensure that part-time employees have equal access to training opportunities and that part-time employees are not treated less favourably than full-timers in a redundancy situation. The Emplaw website (www.emplaw.co.uk) has a free area covering the current regulations on UK Employment Law and also details on how you can find a lawyer in your area who specialises in the aspect of employment law you are concerned with.

Discrimination starts right from when vacancies are advertised – you cannot include such phrases as 'no women' or 'no men', or 'no blacks' or 'no whites'. It extends to the pay, training, and promotion of those who work for you.

It is also illegal to victimise by treating unfairly someone who has complained about being discriminated against. Sexual harassment is also a form of discrimination defined as the 'unwanted conduct of a sexual nature or other conduct based on sex affecting the dignity of men and women at work'. This can include unwelcome physical, verbal, or non-verbal conduct. Finally it is unfair to include in your reason for dismissing an employee that they are a member of a particular minority group protected by law.

To avoid discriminating in your employment you need to ensure that all your policies and procedures meet the following criteria:

✔ They are applied equally to all who work for you irrespective of sex, race, and so forth

✔ They don't limit the proportion of one group who comply compared with another

✔ They don't disadvantage an individual

✔ They can be objectively justified. For example there is no case to argue when being a man or woman is a genuine occupational qualification – for example, for the purpose of a particular photographic modelling assignment or an acting role. The same is true when you have a part-time vacancy so have no need of a full-time employee.

To make sure you are not discriminating at work follow this six-point checklist:

✔ Ensure your business has an equal opportunities policy

✔ Train staff in equal opportunities

✔ Keep records of interviews showing why candidates were rejected

✔ Ensure complaints are taken seriously, fully investigated, and addressed if needed

✔ Conduct staff surveys to help determine where discrimination may exist within your business

✔ Examine the payroll – pay should reflect an employee's job title, not their gender

Keeping the work environment safe

You have to provide a reasonably safe and healthy environment for your employees, visitors, and members of the general public who may be affected by what you do. This applies to both the premises you work from and the work itself. An inspector has the right to enter your premises to examine it and enforce legal requirements if your standards fall short in any way.

Once you have employees you must take some or all of the following measures dependent on the number of people you employ. However a prudent employer should take all these measures whether or not required by law. Doing so sets the standard of behaviour that is common in the very best firms.

✔ Inform the organisation responsible for health and safety at work for your business of where you are and what you do. For most small businesses this is the Environmental Health Department of your local authority (contact details may be found in your local telephone directory). The Health and Safety Executive Web site has a section devoted to Small Firms, covering both regulations and advice on making your work environment safer (their Web site is www.hse.gov.uk).

✔ Get employer's liability insurance to cover you for any physical injury or disease your employees may get as a result of their work. The amount of coverage must be at least £2 million and the insurance certificate must be displayed at all your places of work.

You, as an employer, can in turn expect your employees:

✔ To take reasonable care of their own health, safety at work, and of other persons who may be affected by their acts or omissions.

✔ To co-operate with the employer in ensuring that the requirements imposed by the relevant statutory provisions are complied with.

Chapter 12

Operating Effectively

- -

In This Chapter

▶ Opting to make it yourself or buy from outside

▶ Choosing and using suppliers

▶ Looking at operating risks

▶ Delving into directors

▶ Deciding on key business advisers

- -

A lthough you have decided to go into business, it doesn't necessarily mean that you have to make your own product, or carry out every aspect of a business yourself. It might be the best use of your time to outsource the most time-consuming and least valuable aspect of your business. For example, I bet you can't get a package from Milton Keynes to Penzance in under 24 hours and see change of a twenty pound note! But a delivery service could.

Whether you buy in most of what you sell, or just some components and assemble then yourself, you will have to chose between the dozens if not hundreds of suppliers in the market. Price alone is rarely a good enough guide to which supplier to chose. If they can't deliver on time, price is irrelevant.

You will have to face risks in your business, not all of which you will either want to or be able to shoulder yourself. For these you will have to make choices about insurance types and levels. Even as a director some of those company risks will fall on you and the consequences of getting it wrong can be serious, even catastrophic.

Fortunately you don't have to face all these decisions alone. There are plenty of advisers out there to help. This chapter looks at these risks and decisions and helps you to choose someone to help you through the minefield.

Taking the Make-or-Buy Decision

If your business involves making or constructing products then you should address the issue of whether to make the product yourself, or buy it either ready to sell, or as components for assembly.

Making it yourself, pros and cons

If you decide to make the whole of your product, or at least a major part of it, yourself, you will need to decide exactly what plant and equipment you need and how many pieces you can produce at what rate. Then you need to consider such factors as: What engineering support, if any, will you need? How will you monitor and control quality?

Put down a rough sketch of the layout of your manufacturing unit, showing the overall size of facility needed, the positioning of equipment, and the path of materials and finished goods.

The great advantage of manufacturing your product yourself is that you have control over every aspect of the business and its products. You can, in theory at least, step up production to meet extra demand, make minor modifications to a product to meet a customer's particular needs and have the resources in-house to develop prototypes of new products to respond to changing market conditions.

However, some possible disadvantages of making products yourself in a start-up business are:

- ✔ The large outlay of money needed from day one.

- ✔ The deflection of management time, mostly your own, to looking inwards at processes rather than outwards at the marketplace.

- ✔ Established manufacturers may be better and cheaper than you are at various elements of the production process – after all, they've been at it longer than you and have the benefit of being further up the learning curve and further down the cost curve than any start-up could realistically expect to be.

Outsourcing, the pros and cons

Outsourcing, contracting out the production of your product, has become a buzz-word in our economy. There are thousands of articles and hundreds of books written on it and you can attend countless seminars on the subject. An Internet search on 'outsourcing' will bring up more links than you could ever hope to handle.

One way to set the boundaries for outsourcing is to decide what you are good at then outsource everything else. In other words focus your company on your core competency, and stick to the knitting. That logic is sound in theory, and to a certain degree in practice, but like everything else you can take it too far. The key is to understand your business and its goals and decide how outsourcing can help you attain them.

There are some things that are central to your business that you should probably not outsource at the outset. You need to keep an eye (your eye!) on them until you have them fully under control. These include cash flow management and most aspects of customer relations. Later on you may consider, for example, outsourcing collecting cash from customers to an invoice discounter or factoring service (which I talk about in Chapter 8), who may have better processes in place to handle larger volumes of invoices than you could afford.

Some tasks make sense to outsource initially and bring in-house later. If you plan to offer a product service that you're not expert at, it makes sense to contract out the core function, at least until you gain confidence and expertise. For example, if you plan to start an upmarket soup kitchen but aren't very experienced at making soup, you could turn to an established soup chef to cook for you. The outside expert will charge you a premium, but for that you get significant value: the contractor understands your requirements, produces the product and delivers to your site with little risk to you. If the quality is wrong, send it back. If you need more product, order it. You don't have to wait for your new equipment to arrive before you can step up production. You may find hidden benefits.

Making the most of simple improvements

James Killick runs a company that grew from £2 million turnover per annum to over £4.5 million within 18 months. In order to achieve his meteoric growth, Killick took a detailed look at everything the firm did with a view to increasing the profitability of every hour worked. Each process was examined and made the subject of a brainstorming session. For example, one part of the manufacturing process of their products required several hundred plastic parts to be tipped onto a table. Invariably, 50 or so fell off the table and were either damaged or took valuable seconds to recover. By putting a 3 inch high rim around the table, at a cost of £5, the company saved two hours' production time per week.

Several hundred simple ideas like this reduced the total production time for one key product by nearly 40 per cent. The overall effect was quite staggering. James subcontracted his low value-added production processes to a subcontractor who could actually make them cheaper than he could. The subcontractor took on the commitment to buy raw material and hold stocks, and James used the factory space saved for better things.

Reasons to outsource

Whether you want access to world-class expertise, increased staffing flexibility, a more predictable cost structure, or the ability to focus on your core business, *outsourcing* offers many strategic advantages.

- ✔ **Meeting unexpected deadlines:** It is often difficult and costly to ramp up your staffing to respond quickly to new technologies, or business needs. Sometimes, it's simply impossible – especially when you're trying to balance your resources to cover numerous other conflicting priorities at the same time. Buying in resources allows you to meet deadlines.

- ✔ **Access to expertise:** The rapid obsolescence of technology and skills is an accepted fact of life, in almost every sphere of business. It can be almost impossible for a small firm, especially in the start-up phase, to attract and retain a team with the latest expertise. It is easier for larger established firms to attract and retain a team with the latest expertise and for you to hire that expertise as needed.

- ✔ **Greater scalability:** It just isn't cost-effective to have production resources on hand from the outset to meet possible future demand. By outsourcing to one or more suppliers you can have, in effect, any level of output you want, all at a variable cost, rather than a fixed cost. (See Chapter 5 for more on fixed costs.)

- ✔ **More predictable costs:** While outside suppliers and manufacturers can sometimes provide products and services at a lower cost than doing it yourself, the main financial reason for choosing an outsourcing solution is to make costs more predictable and establish a smoother cash flow.

✔ **Free-up your time:** Turning over non-core functions and self-contained projects that require specific, cutting-edge expertise lets you and your team focus on strategic development and core business functions to ensure that you are contributing real value to your enterprise.

✔ **Economies of scale:** An outsource supplier has multiple clients with similar needs, and can often leverage this to your advantage when negotiating price and service agreements with equipment, software and raw material providers, and so forth. The outsourcer's range of experience often allows for a more efficient use of equipment for added cost savings.

Reasons to hesitate before outsourcing

While there are many benefits to outsourcing, there are inherent risks involved as well. Many of these risks can be reduced via a well-structured contract with clearly defined responsibilities and expectations, but sometimes a function is simply not a good candidate for outsourcing. The following are some considerations to examine before going for outsourcing:

✔ **Rapidly changing requirements:** If you anticipate frequent changes to your products, processes, and volumes, cost and communication issues may make handling the process yourself more efficient, especially if you need to respond quickly to user needs or want to maintain direct control over the problem resolution.

✔ **In-house expertise:** If best-in-class knowledge is required to stay in business, as in for example the bio-technology markets, then it may be essential for you to acquire and retain key operations staff from the outset. Expensive though it will be, this is a market-entry cost. On the positive side these costs also act as a barrier, keeping other new small firms off your patch.

✔ **Confidentiality of data:** This is a fundamental concern for any business, and is an obvious and essential part of your relationship with an outsourcing partner. Basic contractual provisions, including copyright and non-disclosure agreements, should be established to protect corporate secrets, confidential information, and intellectual property. If the activity to be outsourced is such that the confidentiality of your critical data cannot be ensured, the task is probably not a good candidate for outsourcing.

Making the decision

Whether to make it yourself or to buy in from outside is rarely a cut and dried decision that you can make using a spreadsheet. You always have questions. Can I trust them to keep our trade secrets? Will they be as reliable as they claim? Will they put their prices up once they have us in the bag? There are no easy answers to any of these questions, you just have to weigh up the pros and cons yourself.

Setting quality standards

Quality may well be, like beauty, in the eye of the beholder, but you would be wise to set clear standards that you expect every aspect of your end product, or for that matter service, to conform to. This is true whether you make in-house or outsource.

There are a number of well-regarded quality standards that may help you monitor and control your quality. The BS EN ISO 9000 series are perhaps the best-known standards. They can ensure that your operating procedure delivers a consistent and acceptable standard of products or services. If you are supplying to large firms they may insist on your meeting one of these quality standards, or on auditing your premises to satisfy themselves. The British Standards Institute (www.bsi.global.com) can provide details of these standards.

A number of commercial organisations provide user-friendly guidelines and systems to help you reach the necessary standard. Searching the Web using keywords such as 'Quality Standards' or 'Measurement' will bring you some useful sites.

Choosing a Supplier

Selecting the wrong supplier for your business can be a stressful and expensive experience. This section offers some pointers on how to find a supplier and make sure your supplier can meet your business needs. (Chapter 5 talks about similar issues, so you may want to consult that chapter too.)

Look for value in the service a supplier offers rather than just the price you pay. The key questions you should ask about any prospective supplier to your business are:

- Do they offer a guaranteed level of service?
- Do they have a strong business track record and evidence of financial stability? Check out their accounts at Companies House (www.companieshouse.co.uk).
- Do they have clients in your business sector and local area?
- Can they provide you with client references and impartial evidence of their quality? You should check out references to make sure they are reliable and can meet deadlines.
- Can they meet rushed deliveries in case of emergency?
- What level of after-sales support do they provide?

✔ Do they provide you with value for money when compared to competitor services?

✔ Do you think you will enjoy working with them? If so the relationship will be more productive.

Thomas's Register (www.thomasregister.com), Kelly's (www.kelly.co.uk), and Kompass (www.kompass.com) between them have details on over 1.6 million UK companies and hundreds of thousands of US and Canadian manufacturers, covering 23 million key products and 744,000 trade and brand names. If someone makes it, you will find their details in one of these directories.

Some free search facilities are available online and your local business library will have hard copies and may even have Internet access to all the key data you could ever need on suppliers.

Evaluating trading terms

Buying is the mirror image of selling. Remember that as you negotiate with suppliers, who are essentially selling their services. Even if they have no deliberate intention to mislead, you may be left thinking that a supplier will be doing things that they are not committed to in any way. The moral of that story is to get it in writing.

The starting point in establishing trading terms is to make sure the supplier can actually do what you want and what they claim to be able to do. This involves checking them out and taking up references.

The next crunch point is price. As a small business you may feel you are fairly short on buying power. Whilst there is some truth in that, there is always room for negotiation. All suppliers want more customers and there is always a time when they want them badly enough to shift on price.

If you do your research by contacting several suppliers so you have a good idea of the price parameters before you talk seriously to any supplier set yourself a target discount price, and start negotiating 10 per cent or so below that. In any negotiation you may well have to give ground, so if you start at your target price, you will end up paying more.

The supplier's opening claim is likely to be that they never negotiate on price. Don't be deterred. There are lots of ways to get your costs down without changing the headline price. Some examples are:

✔ Allowing a certain percentage of free product, along the line of the free bottle of wine with every half case, can nudge the price down by 15 per cent.

✔ Agreeing to hold stock in their warehouse that will save you renting your own warehouse.

🖢 Extending an extra 30 days' credit eases your cash flow and may be the difference between growing your young business and standing still.

You need to examine all the contract terms, such as delivery, payment terms, risk, and ownership (the point at which title to the goods passes from the maker to you), warranties and guarantees, termination, arbitration rules if you fall out, and the governing law in the case of dealings with overseas suppliers. These issues are the same ones you deal with when you set your own terms of trade, so turn to Chapter 9 for a detailed review.

Building a relationship

To ensure that problems you have with your suppliers are handled effectively, you need to build relationships with them. That means talking to them and keeping them informed of your plans and intentions. If you're planning a sales drive, new price list, or some other similar activity, let the suppliers know so they can anticipate the possible impact on them. Keeping them informed does not commit you to buying extra product, or indeed any product beyond that contracted for, but it does make your suppliers feel part of the value chain between you and your customers. By involving them you are indirectly encouraging them to commit to helping you meet your goals.

Many business people pay too much for the goods or services they purchase, which shows up as lower gross margin and poorer performance than the competition. Many of these people don't raise the issue with their supplier but instead start looking elsewhere for an alternative source. Don't make their mistake. More often than not, your supplier would rather discuss the terms of your arrangement than lose your business. In many cases, you both end up with a better deal than before.

Three other tips for building good long-term relationships:

🖢 Pay your bills on time.

🖢 Ask for favours only when you really need them.

🖢 Treat your supplier's representatives and agents with courtesy and respect; they are the front line and will convey their experiences of dealing with you to their bosses.

The Chartered Institute of Purchasing and Supply (www.cips.org) administers education and qualifications in the field of purchasing and supply chain management.

Buying online

Buying online has a range of important benefits for a small firm. Big companies have buying departments whose job is to find the best suppliers in the world with the most competitive prices and trading terms. A small firm can achieve much the same at a fraction of the cost. By buying online, a small firm can lower costs, save scarce management time, get supplies just in time hence speeding up cash flow and reducing stock space, along with a range of other benefits.

The range of goods and services that can be bought online is vast and getting larger. As well as office supplies you can buy computer equipment, software, motor vehicles, machine tools, vending equipment, insurance, hotel accommodation, airline tickets, business education, building materials, tractors, work clothing, and cleaning equipment online, to name but a few.

You can use several methods to buy business supplies online. I explain the most useful methods in the following sections.

Joining an e-buying group

Various names are given to online buying groups, including trading hubs, e-marketplaces, online communities, aggregators, and cost reducers.

Buying in this way allows you to collect information from potential vendors quickly and easily. These online markets gather multiple suppliers in one place so you can comparison shop without leaving your office or picking up the phone. For example, if you need to buy toner cartridges for your office laser printer, you can go to an online marketplace and search the catalogues of multiple office supplies vendors, buying from the one that offers the best deal. You can also do this for bigger ticket items such as office furniture or photocopiers. No more calling a handful of potential suppliers, sitting through sales presentations, and negotiating prices. You save time for more valuable business activities and get a better rate through comparison shopping.

Going in for auctions

Online auctions are another way to buy supplies online. Their advantage is that you pay only as much as you're willing to pay. The disadvantage is you may have to wait for the right deal to come up.

Auctions are a great way to significantly reduce the funds you need to purchase items on your business *wish list* – items you want now or will need eventually but that aren't a current necessity.

Bartering online

You can avoid using hard cash by taking advantage of online barter exchanges. These e-exchanges let you trade your company's products and services for those of other businesses. You can swap ad space for accounting services, consulting for computers. For start-ups or cash-strapped companies, barter can be an effective way to get products or services you might otherwise be unable to afford.

Minimising Risk and Assessing Liability

As the saying goes, no pain, no gain. Some of the pain is routine and can be allowed for in the normal course of events. Employees come and go, suppliers have to be paid, premises have to be moved in and out of. But some events are less easy to predict and can have serious if not disastrous consequences for your business. What happens if the warehouse burns down or your pizzas send a few customers to hospital?

You can't be expected to know such things will happen ahead of time, but you can be reasonably sure that *something* will happen *sometime.* The laws of probability point to it and the law of averages give you a basis for estimating your chances (see the nearby sidebar for a technical explanation). You have to be prepared to deal with the unexpected, which is what this section helps you do.

Insurance forms a guarantee against loss. You must weigh up to what extent your business assets are exposed to risk and what effect such events could have on the business if they occurred.

One very simple way to assess risk is to get an insurance quote to cover the risk. Insuring against an earthquake in London will be very cheap, but the same cover in Istanbul will be a significant sum.

Insurance is an overhead, producing no benefit until a calamity occurs. It is therefore a commercial decision as to how much to carry, and whilst it is a temptation to minimise cover, you should resist it. You must carry some cover, either by employment law, or as an obligation imposed by a mortgager.

Establish your insurance needs by discussing your business plans with an insurance broker. Make sure you know exactly what insurance you are buying; and, as insurance is a competitive business, get at least three quotations before making up your mind.

The Association of British Insurers (ABI) (www.abi.org.uk) and the British Insurance Brokers' Association (BIBA) (www.biba.org.uk) can put you in touch with a qualified insurance expert.

Protecting your employees

You must carry at least £2 million of liability insurance to meet your legal liabilities for death or bodily injury incurred by an employee during the course of business. In practice, this cover is usually unlimited, with the premiums directly related to your wage bill.

Employer's liability covers only those accidents in which the employer is held to be legally responsible. You may want to extend this cover to any accident to an employee whilst on your business, whosoever is at fault. You may also have to cover your own financial security, particularly if the business depends on your being fit.

Covering yourself when an employee sues

The advent of the no-win, no-fee legal support is encouraging more individuals to feel confident enough to take on companies both big and small, and often in circumstances where their chances of success are not immediately obvious.

The growing burden of employment legislation facing small firms is forcing more and more businesses to take out legal expense insurance as the risk for being prosecuted for breaking the law rises.

But it is not only the risk that is rising. The consequences are spiralling upwards too. The ceiling for unfair dismissal awards has risen from £12,000 to £50,000 as one example of the burden of new employment laws. In 2001 there was a 40 per cent rise in payouts for discrimination claims, for example, and employment tribunals awarded £3.53million for sex, race, and disability claims.

The remedy for the small firm without its own human resources department to keep it operating clearly within legal boundaries and a legal department to fend of any legal threats, is to take out legal expense insurance.

Firms that sign up for this type of insurance can not only expect any fines and awards to be paid, but their costs associated with defending themselves against allegations will also be met. In many cases, whether the employer wins or loses, they will pay their own legal costs, which makes insurance cover especially attractive. For the small employer, who often takes on the task of handling disputes with employees himself, this is a great benefit, saving not only time but lifting the concerns and anxieties that inevitably accompany litigation.

Protecting assets

Obviously, you need to insure your business premises, plant, and equipment. However, you can choose a couple of ways to do that.

- ✓ **Reinstatement** provides for full replacement cost.
- ✓ **Indemnity** meets only the current market value of your asset, which means taking depreciation off first.

You have to consider related costs and coverage, as well. For example, who pays for removing debris? Who pays the architect to design the structure if you have to rebuild? Who reimburses employees for any damaged or destroyed personal effects? And potentially the most expensive of all, who covers the cost of making sure that a replacement building meets current, possibly more stringent and more expensive, standards?

These factors are covered in the small print of your insurance policy, so if they matter to you check them out.

Also from raw materials through to finished goods, stock is as exposed as your buildings and plant in the event of hazards such as fire and theft. Theft from commercial property runs to hundreds of millions of pounds per annum.

Once in business you can expect threats from within and without. A *fidelity guarantee*, the name given to this particular type of insurance, can be taken to protect you from fraud or dishonesty on the part of key employees. Normal theft cover can be taken to protect your business premises and its contents.

Covering loss of profits

Meeting the replacement costs of buildings, plant, equipment, and stock does not compensate you for the loss of business and profit arising out of a fire or other disaster. Your overheads, employees' wages, and so on may have to continue during the period of interruption. You may incur expenses such as getting subcontracted work done. Insurance for *consequential loss,* as this type of insurance is known, is intended to restore your business's finances to the position they were in before the interruption occurred.

Goods in transit

Until your goods reach your customer and he accepts them, they are still at your risk. You may need to protect yourself from loss or damage in transit.

One newly-established business, planning to expand its activities economically, sought and found a specialist supplier of second-hand reconditioned woodworking machinery – lathes, turners, band saws and so on. After inspecting the machinery in Yorkshire they arranged for it to be transported by the vendor under his own goods in transit insurance cover to their factory in the West Country. While a particularly heavy piece was being unloaded, it fell from the transporter on to the ground immediately outside their factory, and was damaged beyond repair. Their own insurance only covered machinery inside their workshop, the vendor's only while the goods were on the transporter. The gap in between was an insurance 'no man's land', where neither party had cover.

Protecting yourself

Anyone who puts a substantial amount of money into your business – the bank or a venture capitalist, for example – may require you to have *key man insurance.* This type of insurance provides a substantial cash cushion in the event of your death or incapacity – you being the key man (even if you're a woman) on whom the business's success depends.

Key man insurance is particularly important in small and new firms where one person is disproportionately vital in the early stages. Partners may also consider this a prudent protection.

Warranting goods and services

As well as your own specifications confirming how your products or service will perform, you may have legal obligations put on you under the *Consumer Protection Act*, which sets out safety rules and prohibits the sale of unsafe goods and the *Sale of Goods Acts* that govern your contractual relationship with your customer. In addition the common law rules of negligence also apply to business dealings.

If you're a principal in a partnership with unlimited liability, it would be quite possible to be personally bankrupted in a lawsuit concerning product liability. Even if the business was carried out through a limited company, although the directors may escape personal bankruptcy, the company would not. If you believe the risks associated with your product are real, then you need to consider taking out product liability insurance.

If your business involves foodstuffs, you must also pay close attention to the stringent hygiene regulations that now encompass all food manufacture, preparation, and handling. The defence of 'due diligence' will only hold water if thorough examination and identification of all the hazard points has taken place. Trading Standards and Environmental Health Officers are there to help and advise in a free consultative capacity.

Obligations are placed on producers or importers of certain types of goods under both the Consumer Protection Act 1987 and the Sale of Goods Act 1979. Importers can be sued for defects, they cannot disclaim liability simply because they have not been involved in manufacture.

Other liabilities you should consider taking insurance cover are:

- ✔ **Public Liability:** Legal liability to pay damages consequent upon bodily injury, illness, or disease contracted by any other person, other than employees, or loss of or damage to their property caused by the insured.

- ✔ **Professional Indemnity:** Professional indemnity provides protection against any action by clients who believe they received bad or negligent services, and incurred a loss as a result. Most professional bodies have professional indemnity cover – in some cases it is compulsory. Anyone who supplies advice or services such as consultancy should consider professional indemnity.

The main points of liability law in the UK are:

- ✔ Do not make claims like 'So simple a child could understand.' You are laying yourself wide open to rebuttal.

- ✔ Instructions should be crystal clear both on the packet and on the article if possible.

- ✔ Textiles must carry fibre content, labelling, and washing instructions.

- ✔ Because the Acts cover the European Union, if you are exporting to another country in the Union you must double-check translations. It is now possible, for example, for a German person to sue you as manufacturer in a German court for goods exported to Germany that have a product defect.

- ✔ You must keep records for ten years and be ready to institute a product recall operation if necessary.

Dissecting Directors

If you decide to trade as a *limited liability company* (see Chapter 4) then you will in all probability have to become a director of the business. You may be the only director, or you may be one of several, but as well as the status you have responsibilities too.

Some of a director's duties, responsibilities, and potential liabilities are:

- ✔ To act in good faith in the interests of the company; this includes carrying out duties diligently and honestly

- ✔ Not to carry on the business of the company with intent to defraud creditors or for any fraudulent purpose

- ✔ Not knowingly to allow the company to trade while insolvent ('wrongful trading'); directors who do so may have to pay for the debts incurred by the company while insolvent

- ✔ Not to deceive shareholders

- ✔ To have a regard for the interests of employees in general

- ✔ To comply with the requirements of the Companies Acts, such as providing what is needed in accounting records or filing accounts

In the UK alone over 1,500 directors are disqualified each year from being directors, so can no longer legally manage and control their own business. The reasons for their disqualification range from fraud to the more innocuous wrongful trading, which means carrying on doing business whilst the business is insolvent. This latter area is more difficult to recognise by a director before the event, but you need to be aware of the danger signs and remedies.

In practice, a director's general responsibilities are much the same as those for a sole trader or partner (outlined in Chapter 4). By forming a company you can separate your own assets from the business assets (in theory at any rate, unless personal guarantees have been extracted). However, a director also has to cope with more technical and detailed requirements; for example, sending in your accounts to Companies House. More onerous than just signing them, a director is expected and required in law to understand the significance of the balance sheet and profit and loss account and the key performance ratios.

Directors' risks can be insured using Directors Insurance, covering negligent performance of duties and breach of the Companies Acts – particularly the Insolvency Act, which can hold directors personally liable to a company's creditors. The cost of the insurance is borne by the company as the directors are acting on its behalf.

The most dangerous areas of a director's responsibilities are ones that could get you disqualified. In summary the areas to avoid at all costs are:

- ✔ Trading whilst insolvent, which occurs when your liabilities exceed your assets. At this point the shareholders' equity in the business has effectively ceased to exist, which puts directors personally at risk. Directors owe a duty of care to creditors – not shareholders. If you find yourself even approaching this area you need the prompt advice of an insolvency practitioner. Directors who act properly will not be penalised, and will live to fight another day.

- ✔ Wrongful trading can apply if, after a company goes into insolvent liquidation, the liquidator believes that the directors ought to have concluded earlier that the company had no realistic chance of survival. In these circumstances the courts can make directors personally liable for the company's debts.

> ✔ Fraudulent trading is rather more serious than wrongful trading. Here the proposition is that the director(s) were knowingly party to fraud on their creditors. The full shelter of Limited Liability can be removed in these circumstances.

Former directors of insolvent companies can be banned from holding office as a company director for periods of up to 15 years. Fraud, fraudulent trading, wrongful trading, or a failure to comply with company law may result in disqualification.

Undischarged bankrupts cannot act as a director or take part, directly or indirectly, in the management of a company unless they obtain the permission of the court.

Breaches of a disqualification order can lead to imprisonment and/or fines. Also you can be made personally liable for the debts and liabilities of any company in which you are involved. If you're disqualified you can't issue your orders through others, having them act as a director in your place. Doing so puts them at personal risk also.

A register of disqualified directors is available for free access on the Companies House Web site (www.companieshouse.co.uk).

Finding and Choosing Business Advisers

You need lots of help to get started in business and even more when you are successful. Here are some tips on dealing with some of the key people you are almost bound to need at some stage. There are dozens of others including: tax consultants, advertising and public relations consultants, technology and IT advisers, and the like. The rules and tips in the following sections should steer you through dealing with most situations involving choosing and using outside advisers.

Tallying up an accountant

Keeping your financial affairs in good order is the key to staying legal and winning any disputes. A good accountant inside or outside the firm can keep you on track. A bad accountant is in the ideal position to defraud you at worst, or derail you through negligence or incompetence. What attributes should you look for and how can you find the right accountant for your business? The key steps to choosing a good accountant are:

✔ Check they are members of one of the recognised accounting bodies such as the Chartered Institute of Management Accountants (www.cima-global.com) or the Institute of Chartered Accountants in England and Wales (www.icaew.co.uk).

✔ Have a clear idea of what services you require. You need to consider how complete your bookkeeping records are likely to be, whether you need the VAT return done, budgets and cash flow forecasts prepared and updated, as well as an audit.

✔ Clarify the charges scale at the outset. It may well make more sense to spend a bit more on bookkeeping, both staff and systems, rather than leaving it all to a much higher charging qualified accountant.

✔ Use personal recommendations from respected fellow businesspeople. There is nothing like hearing from a fellow consumer of a product or service. Pay rather less attention to the recommendation of bankers, government agencies, family and friends, without totally ignoring their advice.

✔ Take references from the accountant's clients as well as from the person who recommended them. It could just be a lucky event that they get on. They may even be related!

✔ Find out what back-up they have for both systems and people. The tax authorities will not be very sympathetic whatever the reason for lateness. It would be doubly annoying to be fined for someone else's tardiness.

✔ See at least three accountants before making your choice, making sure they deal with companies your size and a bit bigger. Not so much bigger as to have no relevant advice and help to offer, but big enough for you to have some room for growth without having to change accountants too quickly.

✔ Find out whom else the accountant acts for. You don't want them to be so busy they can't service your needs properly, or to be working for potential competitors.

✔ Make the appointment for a trial period only, and set a specific task to see how they get on.

✔ Give them the latest accounts of your business and ask them for their comments based on their analysis of the figures. You will quickly see if they have grasped the basics of your financial position.

Investing in a bank

You may wonder why choosing a bank is listed in this section covering choosing business advisers. Well the answer, crazy as it may seem, is that your banker is almost invariably the first person you turn to when the chips are down. It's not so surprising when you think about it. After all most big business problems turn on money and bankers are the people who turn the money on.

Get the wrong bank and you could lose more than your overdraft. You may lose the chance to acquire a free, or at least nearly free, business adviser.

These are the top ten questions to ask before taking on a bank manager:

✔ How quickly can you make decisions about lending? Anything longer than ten days is too long.

✔ What rate of interest will you charge? Two or three per cent above the Bank of England base rate is fairly normal. Above four per cent is on the high side.

✔ What factors do you take into consideration in arriving at that rate? If the bank proposes a high rate of interest, say four per cent above Bank of England base rate or higher, then you need to know why. It may be that all the bank is asking for is some further security for their loan, which you might think worth giving in return for a lower interest rate.

✔ What other charges will there be? For example will you be charged for every transaction in and out of the account and if so how much?

✔ Do you visit your clients and get to know their business? If the bank doesn't visit its hard to see how they will ever get to really understand your business.

✔ Under what circumstances would you want personal guarantees? When the bank is feeling exposed to greater risk than it wants to take it will ask you to shoulder some of that risk personally. Under the terms of a bank's loan to your business they may state that their lending should not exceed a certain sum. You need to be clear what that sum is.

✔ What help and advisory services do you have that could be useful to me? Banks often provide advice on export trade, currency dealing, insurance and a range of other related services.

✔ What is unique about your banking services that would make me want to use your rather than any other bank? This factor rather depends on what you consider to be valuable. A bank that delivers all its service on the Internet may be attractive to one person and anathema and turnoff to another.

✔ How long will it be before my present manager moves on? If managers are routinely moved every few years then it's hard to see any value in forming personal relationships.

✔ Are there any situations when you would ask for repayment of a loan to be made early? A bank may insist that if you break any major condition of the loan, such as the overdraft limit or repayment schedule, the whole loan is repayable. You need to find out if this is so, and what sum will cause this to happen.

Choosing a lawyer

Lawyers or solicitors are people you hope never to have to use and when you do need one you need them yesterday. Even if you don't appoint a company lawyer, you may well need one for basic stuff if you are forming a company or setting up a partnership agreement. Follow the same rules as you would for choosing an accountant (refer to the previous 'Tallying up an accountant' section).

The fact is that, in business, you know that one day you will need a lawyer. The complexity of commercial life means that, sooner or later, you will find yourself either initiating or defending legal action. It may be a contract dispute with a customer or supplier, or perhaps the lease on your premises turns out to give you far fewer rights than you hoped. A former employee might claim you fired them without reason. Or the Health and Safety Inspector finds some aspect of your machinery or working practices less than satisfactory.

The range of possibilities is extensive, and when things do go wrong, the time and money required to put them right can be an unexpected and unwelcome drain on your cash. By doing things right from the start, you can avoid at least some of the most common disputes and cope more easily with catastrophes.

In addition to ensuring that contracts are correctly drawn up, that leases are free from nasty surprises, and that the right health and safety procedures are followed, a solicitor can also advise on choosing the best structure for your company, on protecting your intellectual property, and on how to go about raising money.

Finding a Lawyer For Your Business

Lawyers For Your Business (www.lfyb.law society.org.uk) represents some 1,400 firms of solicitors in England and Wales, which have come together to help ensure that all businesses, and especially the smaller owner-managed ones, get access to sound legal advice whenever they need it. LFYB is administered by the Law Society, and backed by Business in the Community, the Federation of Small Business, and the Forum of Private Business.

To remove the risk of incurring unexpectedly high legal costs, all Lawyers For Your Business members offer a free consultation, lasting at least half-an-hour, to diagnose your legal problem and any need for action, with full information, in advance, on the likely costs of proceeding.

The Law Society (www.lawsociety.org.uk) will send you a list of Lawyers For Your Business members in your area, and a voucher for a free consultation.

Simply choose one of the firms in the list and arrange an appointment, mentioning Lawyers For Your Business and the voucher.

It makes sense to either see your solicitor before your problems arise, and find out what they can do for you or, at the very least, make yourself conversant with the relevant laws. Taking timely action on legal issues may help you gain an advantage over competitors and will almost certainly save you money in the long run.

If you are going to see a lawyer, it is always best to be well prepared. Have all the facts to hand and know what you want help with.

Considering management consultants

If you are facing a new major problem you have no expertise in, particularly a problem you don't expect to experience again, then hiring a consultant is an option worth considering. For example if you are moving premises, changing your computer or accounting system, starting to do business overseas, or designing an employee share ownership scheme, it may well make sense to get the help of someone who has covered that area several times before and who is an expert in the field.

The time taken for a consultant to carry out most tasks a small business might require is likely to be between a fortnight and three months. Anything much longer will be too expensive for most small firms and anything much shorter is unlikely to have much of an impact on the business. That's not to say they will be working continuously on your project for that time. After an initial meeting a consultant may do much of the work off site and in chunks of time. Costs vary dependant on both the skill of the consultant and the topic covered. A tax consultant, for example can cost upwards of £450 an hour, whilst a training consultant might cost the same sum for a day.

Take on a consultant using much the same procedures as you would a key employee (see Chapter 11). Take time to brief them thoroughly. Don't expect to just dump the problem on their doorstep and walk away. Set the consultant a small measurable part of the task first and see how they perform. Never give them a long-term contract or an open book commitment.

Remember you can't delegate decision-making, you can only delegate the analysis of problems and the presentation of options. In the end you have to choose which way to go. Don't let consultants implement decisions on their own. The line responsibility between yourself and your staff needs to be preserved. If they see someone else giving orders it will undermine the chain of command. If the consultant's solution is so complex it needs their expertise to implement, you have the wrong solution.

The Institute of Management Consultants (www.imc.co.uk) list the 10 golden rules for choosing a consultant. You will also find that your local Business Link will have a national register of approved (and insured) specialist consultants for most business needs.

Chapter 13

Keeping Track of Finances

*E*very business needs reliable financial information for both decision-making and accountability. No one will be keen to pump money into your venture if you can't demonstrate that you know what will happen to it. Reliable information does not necessarily call for complex bookkeeping and accounting systems: simple is often best. As the business grows, and perhaps takes on outside investors, more sophisticated information will be required. That is when using a computer and some of the relevant software packages may be the best way forward. But even with a computer, errors can occur, so you will have to know how to recognise when financial information goes wrong and how it can be corrected.

You have a legal obligation in business to keep accounting records, which will become acute if and when your business runs into serious problems. If as a director or owner of a business you can't see when you are heading for a financial reef, you could find yourself in deep trouble, if not actually heading for jail and definitely not collecting £200 on the way.

Keeping the Books

To survive and prosper in business you need to know how much cash you have, and what your profit or loss on sales is. These facts are needed on at least a monthly, weekly, or occasionally even a daily basis to survive, let alone grow.

Recording financial information

While bad luck plays a part in some business failures, a lack of reliable financial information plays a part in most. However all the information needed to manage well is close at hand. Among the bills to be paid, invoices raised, petty cash slips, and bank statements you have enough to give you a true picture of your business's performance.

All you need to do is record and organise that information so that the financial picture becomes clear. The way financial information is recorded is known as *bookkeeping*.

But it is not only the owner who needs these financial facts. Bankers, shareholders, and tax inspectors will be unsympathetic audiences to anyone without well-documented facts to back them up. If, for example, a tax authority presents a business with a tax demand, the onus then lies with the businessperson, using their records, either to agree or dispute the sum claimed. If you are unable to adequately explain a bank deposit, the tax authority may treat it as taxable income. A bank manager, faced with a request for an increased overdraft facility to help a small business grow, needs financial facts to work with. Without them the bank will generally have to say no, as they are responsible for other people's money.

Keeping even the simplest of records, perhaps as little as writing down the source of the deposit on the slip or in your chequebook, and recording the event in a book or ledger, will make your relations with tax inspectors and bankers go much more smoothly.

In any event if you plan to trade as a limited company (see Chapter 4), you are required under the Company Act 1985 'to keep adequate records sufficient to show and explain the company's transactions'.

Reasons for keeping proper records:

- ✔ To know the cash position of your business precisely and accurately
- ✔ To discover how profitable your business really is
- ✔ To learn which of your activities are profitable and which are not
- ✔ To give bankers and other sources of finance confidence that your business is being well managed and that their money is in good hands
- ✔ To allow you to accurately calculate your tax bill
- ✔ To help you prepare timely financial forecasts and projections
- ✔ To make sure you both collect and pay money due correctly
- ✔ To keep accountancy and audit costs to a minimum

Starting simple with single entry

If you are doing books by hand and don't have a lot of transactions, the single-entry method is the easiest acceptable way to go. *Single entry* means you write down each transaction in your records once, preferably on a ledger sheet. You record the flow of income and expenses through your business by making a running total of money taken in (gross receipts) and money paid out (payments or, as they are sometimes called, *disbursements*). Receipts and payments should be kept and summarised daily, weekly, or monthly, as the business needs require. At the end of the year, the 12 monthly summaries are totalled up. You are ready for tax time.

It is useful to separate different types of income and expense into categories, for example stock, vehicles, telephone, as in Figure 13-1. This will let you see how much is being spent or received from each.

Payments				Analysis			
Date	Name	Details	Amount £	Stocks	Vehicles	Telephone	Other
4 June	Gibbs	Stock purchase	310	310			
8 June	Gibbs	Stock purchase	130	130			
12 June	ABC Telecoms	Telephone charges	55.23			55.23	
18 June	Colt Rentals	Vehicle hire	87.26		87.26		
22 June	VV Mobiles	Mobile phone	53.24			53.24	
27 June	Gibbs	Stock purchase	36.28	36.28			
Totals			672.01	476.28	87.26	108.47	

Figure 13-1: An example of an analysed cash book.

You need to keep copies of paid and unpaid sales invoices and the same for purchases, as well as your bank statements. The bank statements should then be 'reconciled' to your cash book to tie everything together.

If you are taking or giving credit then you need to keep some more information as well as the cash book, whether analysed or not.

Dealing with double entry

If you operate a partnership, trade as a company, then you may need a double-entry bookkeeping system from the start.

A double-entry bookkeeping system requires two entries for each transaction, hence the name, and every transaction has two effects on the accounts. For example when you buy an item of stock for sale and pay for it in cash, your cash balance goes down and your amount of stock goes up by the same amount, keeping everything in balance.

Choosing the right accounting program

With the cost of a basic computerised accounting system starting at barely £50, and a reasonable package costing between £200 and £500, it makes good sense to plan to use such a system from the outset.

With a computer you have no more arithmetic errors. As long as you enter the information correctly, the computer adds it up correctly. With a computer, the £53.24 mobile phone expenditure in Figure 13-1 is input as an expense (a debit), and then the computer automatically posts it to the mobile phone account as a credit. In effect, the computer eliminates the extra step or the need to master the difference between debit and credit.

A computerised accounting program is only as good as the data entered into it. Introduce strict end of month controls to make sure that all stock has been counted and valued, that all the month's invoices have been dealt with, and so on. Without this, your computer program will be reflecting inaccurate data.

Routine tasks, such as filling in the tax and VAT returns, take minutes rather than days with a computer. The system can ensure your returns are accurate and fully reconciled. With a computerised system, invoices are always accurate. You can see at a glance which customers regularly take too long to pay.

You have two main options in your choice of a first accounting system. If you think a manual system is best for your purposes, you can get sheets of analysis paper with accounting entry printed columns, and put in your own headings as appropriate. Or you can buy off-the-shelf manual sets of books from any office stationer's outlet. These will cost anything from £10 to £20 for a full set of ledgers. Hingston Publishing Co (www.hingston-publishing.co.uk) produce small business accounts systems for both VAT and non-VAT registered business for about £15.

If you decide to take the plunge and go straight for accounting software then there are a myriad of software providers to choose from who serve the small business market with software for bookkeeping. These are some of the more popular packages.

The personal and business edition of Microsoft's Money (www.microsoft.co.uk) includes tools for managing your personal finances and keeping track of business accounts within the same product. It's not a suitable product for any business that expects to expand quickly or might require extra add-ons such as payroll facilities in the future, but it has some good features to offer sole traders.

It is an inexpensive product, between £25 and £35 depending on the version you buy, and there's no yearly support cost.

MYOB 10's (www.myob.co.uk) is an all-round small-business tool, which includes payroll and stock control capabilities as standard and costs £235. One year's support is £111.63 (including VAT).

TAS Books Small Business Edition (SBE) (www.tassoftware.co.uk) is aimed specifically at the needs of new, smaller companies, and, in general, online support within the product is comprehensive and there's a manual that helps to explain more advanced features. There is a £117 (excluding VAT) a year support cost and a purchase price of £199 (excluding VAT).

QuickBooks (www.intuit.co.uk/quickbooks) can integrate with Microsoft Office and can grow with your business by adding an integrated payroll. The basic version is £139.85 (including VAT) and the professional version is £259.90 (including VAT).

Sage's entry product Instant Accounting (www.uk.sage.com) at £149 including VAT bears reasonable comparison with some of the other products on the market. It's one of the more basic packages available, offering none of the fancy features, such as multiple currency support, available elsewhere.

Outsourcing bookkeeping

Accountants and freelance bookkeepers can do all your bookkeeping work at a price. The rate will be anything from £20 per hour upwards.

Bookkeeping services range from a basic write up of the entries and leave the rest to you approach, through to providing weekly or monthly accounts, perhaps with pointers as to what might be going wrong. There are even services that act as a virtual finance director, giving you access to a senior accountant who may even sit on your board.

Most bookkeeping services will have a computer system, which you will have to plug into.

The most routine but vital task may be doing the payroll. If you don't get this done on time and correctly both staff and the Inland Revenue, for whom you have to collect PAYE (Pay As You Earn), will become restless. A weekly payroll service for up to ten employees will cost upwards of £85 per month. If you pay everyone monthly, this will drop to about a third of that figure.

It's probably best to get someone local if you go this route, so ask around to find someone who uses someone and is satisfied. Alternatively use the phone book.

Understanding the Accounts

It is one thing keeping the books, but it is quite another thing to be able to make good use of the information contained in the accounts. The raw accounting data has to be turned from columns of figures into statements of account. Those accounts in turn tell how much cash your business has, its profit or loss numbers, and how much money is being tied up in the business to produce those results.

Forecasting Cash Flow

In the language of accounting, income is recognised when a product or service has been sold, delivered, or executed, and the invoice raised. Whilst that rule holds good for calculating profit it does not apply in forecasting cash flow.

You can think of cash flow as the cold shower of reality, bringing you sharply back to your senses. Profit, on the other hand, is what may be generated if all goes well and customers pay up. (Preparing a cash flow forecast is covered in Chapter 8.)

Overtrading describes a business that is expanding beyond its financial resources. As sales expand, the amount of cash tied up in stocks and customers' credit grows rapidly. Pressure also comes from suppliers of goods and services and from additional employees who all expect to be paid. The natural escape valve for pressures on working capital is an overdraft (or a substantial increase in the existing one).

Reporting Your Profits

A key use of the bookkeeping information is to prepare the profit and loss account.

In carrying out any business activity, two very different actions go on. One is selling your goods and services and getting paid for them. Money comes in, perhaps not immediately, but it eventually shows up. This money goes by a variety of names including, *revenues, income,* and *sales income.* The second transaction is the outlay you make in order to provide the goods and services you sell to your customers. Some of the costs you incur are for raw materials, salaries, rents, and so forth. These costs are also known as *expenses.* By deducting your expenses from your income, you end up with the profit (or loss) for the particular period under review.

At its simplest, the profit and loss account has at its head the period covered, followed by the income, from which all the expenses of the business are deducted to arrive at the profit (or loss) made in the period. Figure 13-2 shows a sample account.

Figure 13-2:
A basic
profit and
loss
account.

Profit and Loss Account for year to 31 March 200X	£
Income	1,416,071
Less expenses	1,389,698
Profit	26,373

Whilst the information shown in the profit and loss account is certainly better than nothing, you can use the basic bookkeeping information to give you a much richer picture of events within the business. Provided, that is, that you have set up the right analysis headings in the first place.

The following sections show, step-by-step, how to build up the profit and loss account to give you a more complete picture of the trading events of the past year at Safari Europe, the example I use in the following sections.

Calculating gross profit

One of the most important figures in the profit and loss account is the gross profit. Whatever your activity, you have to buy certain 'raw materials'. Those include anything you have to buy to produce the goods and services you are selling. So if you sell cars, the cost of buying in the cars is a raw materials cost. In Safari's case, as they are in the travel business, the cost of airline tickets and hotel rooms are the raw material of a package holiday.

What's left from our sales revenues after deducting the cost of sales, as these costs of 'making' are known, is the gross profit. This is really the only discretionary money coming into the business, which we have some say over how it is spent. So the higher the gross profit the more valuable the product or service we are providing is in the eye of our customer. Figure 13-3 shows a sample profit calculation.

In the account shown in Figure 13-3 you can see that Safari have two sources of income, one from tours and one from insurance and other related services. They also, of course, have the costs associated with buying in holidays and insurance policies from suppliers.

The difference between the income of £1,416,071 and the cost of these 'goods' they have sold is just £160,948. That is the sum that the management have to run the business and not the much larger headline-making figure of nearly £1.5 million.

Safari Europe

Profit and Loss Account for year to   31 March 200X

Income

Tours sold	1,402,500
Insurance & other services	13,571
Non-operating revenue	0
Total income	1,416,071

Figure 13-3:
An example
of gross
profit
calculation.

Less Cost of goods sold

Tours bought	1,251,052
Insurance & other services	4,071
Total cost of goods sold	1,255,123
Gross profit	160,948

Figure 13-4 shows how gross profit is calculated in a business that makes things.

Figure 13-4:
A man-
ufacturer's
gross profit.

	£
Sales	100,000
Cost of goods sold	65,000
Gross profit	35,000

In the example in Figure 13-4, the basic sum is the same as for a service business, as shown in Figure 13-3. Take the cost of goods from the sales income and what's left is gross profit. However in a business that makes things you hold raw materials and we only want to count into cost of goods sold the materials actually used. We do this by noting the stock at the start of the period, adding in any purchases made and deducting the closing stock.

You also need to build in the labour cost in production and any overheads, such as workshop usage, and deduct those in order to arrive at the gross profit, as shown in Figure 13-5.

Reckoning expenses

After you calculate the gross profit, you have to allow for all the expenses that are likely to arise in running the business. Using the Safari case as a working example, Figure 13-6 shows all the costs usually associated with running the business, such as rent, rates, telephone, marketing and promotion, and so forth. Whilst all these expenses are correctly included, they are not all allowable for tax purposes in all countries. I look at taxation in Chapter 14.

The Total expenditure heading in Figure 13-6 is not quite accurate. There are other expenses associated with running a business that aren't included here, but these expenses are treated in a slightly different way for reasons that will become apparent when we look at profit.

	£	£	£
Sales			**100,000**
Manufacturing costs			
Raw materials opening stock	30,000		
Purchases in period	25,000		
	55,000		
Less Raw materials closing stock	15,500		
Cost of materials used		39,500	
Direct labour cost		18,000	
Manufacturing overhead cost			
Indirect labour	4,000		
Workshop heat, light, and power	3,500		
Total manufacturing costs		7,500	
Cost of goods sold			65,000
Gross profit			35,000

Figure 13-5: Expanded gross profit calculation.

Appreciating the different types of profit

Profit can be measured in several ways:

- **Gross profit** is the profit left after all costs related to making what you sell are deducted from income.

- **Operating profit** is what's left after you take away the expenses (or expenditure) away from the gross profit.

- **Profit before tax** is what you get after deducting any financing costs.

  The reasoning here is that the operating management can have little influence over the way in which the business is financed (no borrowings means no interest expenses, for example), or the level of interest charges.

Safari Europe

Profit and Loss Account for the year to 31 March 200X	Year 1
Income	
Tours sold	1,402,500
Insurance & other services	13,571
Non-operating revenue	0
Total income	1,416,071
Less Cost of goods sold	
Tours bought	1,251,052
Insurance & other services	4,071
Total cost of goods sold	1,255,123
Gross profit	160,948
Expenditure	
Rent & rates	18,000
Heat, light, & power	3,500
Telephone system lease	2,000
Computer leasing	5,000
Marketing & promotion	12,500
Postage & stationery	3,250
Telephone	3,575
Insurance & legal	3,500
Wages (not Karen's)	36,000
Consultancy services	25,000
Membership & subscription	1,500
Travel & subsistence	4,250
Training & staff development	6,000
Depreciation of fixtures	5,500
Total expenditure	129,575

Figure 13-6:
Business
expenses.

Interestingly enough, when it comes to valuing the business, it's the operating profit that is generally used as the multiplying factor (so many times earnings is a typical valuation mechanism and it is operating profit that is used).

Taking away the financing costs, in our example of £5,000 interest charges, we are left with a profit before tax of £26,373, as shown in Figure 13-7. Finally tax is deducted to leave the net profit after tax, the bottom line. This is the sum that belongs to the owners of the business and, if we are dealing with a limited company, is what dividends could be paid from.

Safari Europe

Profit and Loss Account for the year to 31 March 200X	
Income	
Tours sold	1,402,500
Insurance & other services	13,571
Non-operating revenue	0
Total income	1,416,071
Less **Cost of goods sold**	
Tours bought	1,251,052
Insurance & other services	4,071
Total cost of goods sold	1,255,123
Gross profit	160,948
Expenditure	
Rent & rates	18,000
Heat, light, & power	3,500
Telephone system lease	2,000
Computer leasing	5,000
Marketing & promotion	12,500
Postage & stationery	3,250
Telephone	3,575
Insurance & legal	3,500
Wages (not Karen's)	36,000
Consultancy services	25,000
Membership & subscription	1,500
Travel & subsistence	4,250
Training & staff development	6,000
Depreciation of fixtures	5,500
Total expenditure	129,575
Operating profit	31,373
Less interest charges	5,000
Net profit before tax	26,373
Tax	5,538
Net profit after tax	20,835

Figure 13-7:
Levels of
profit.

Balancing the Books

You have to know where you are now before making any plans to go anywhere else. Without a starting point any journey is bound to be a confusing experience. For a business, summing up your current position is done in the balance sheet, the primary reporting document of the business. The balance sheet contains evidence of all the financial events over the entire life of the business, showing where money has come from and what has been done with that money. Logically, the two sums must balance.

In practical terms, balancing your sums takes quite a bit of work, not the least of which isn't necessarily the balancing part, but figuring out the numbers. Your cash-in-hand figure is probably dead right, but can you say the same of the value of the assets? Accountants have their own rules on how to arrive at these figures, but they do not pretend to be anything more than an approximation. Every measuring device has inherent inaccuracies, and financial controls are no exception.

A balance sheet

In formal accounts the figures are set out vertically rather than in horizontal fashion, reflected in Figure 13-8. In effect the long-term borrowings, in this case the mortgage and hire purchase charges, are named *Creditors, amounts falling due in over 1 year* and deducted from the total assets to show the *net total assets* being employed.

The bottom of the balance sheet in Figure 13-8 shows how the owners of the business have supported these assets, in this case by their own funds. As you will see later, they could also have invested profit made in earlier years back into the business (see reserves). I have also assumed her house is now a business premises owned by her company. (This assumption has wider implications, but none that are relevant to the arithmetic or the balance sheet.)

Categorising assets

Accountants describe *assets* as valuable resources, owned by a business, which were acquired at a measurable money cost. The three key points in the definition are:

 ✔ **Valuable resources:** To be valuable, the resource must be cash, or of some use in generating current or future profits. For example, a *debtor* (someone who owes a business money for goods or services provided) usually pays up. When that happens, the debt becomes cash and so meets this test. If there is no hope of getting payment, then you can hardly view the sum as an asset.

	£	£
NET ASSETS EMPLOYED		
Fixed assets		
Premises	150,000	
Car	7,000	
Furniture	1500	
Jewellery and paintings	350	
Book value		158,850
Current assets		
Money owed by sister	135	
Cash	50	
Total current assets	185	
Less Current liabilities		
Overdraft	100	
Credit cards	50	
Total current liabilities	150	
Net current assets		35
Total assets		158,885
Less: Creditors, amounts falling due in over 1 year		45,500
Net total assets		**113,385**
FINANCED BY		
My capital	113,385	
Total owners' funds		113,385

Figure 13-8: Jane Smith Limited Balance Sheet at 5 April, 200X.

- ✔ **Owned:** Ownership, in its legal sense, is different from possession or control. In a business, possession and control are not enough to make a resource an asset. For example, a leased machine may be possessed and controlled by a business but be owned by the leasing company. So not only is it not an asset, it is a regular expense. To be an asset the business must either own or be in the process of buying the item concerned.

- ✔ **Measurable money cost:** Often, this test is all too painfully obvious. If you pay cash for an asset, or promise to pay at a later date, it clearly has a measurable cost. If you manufacture an asset during the course of doing business, you pay money in wages, materials, and so on during that process. You may have problems in deciding exactly how to measure the cost, but there is no problem in seeing that money has been spent.

In simpler terms, an asset is a valuable possession the business paid for.

The exception to the *paid for* part is the grey area of goodwill. *Goodwill* is the value placed upon the reputation and other intangible assets – a brand name, for example – of a business. Assessing the value of this asset is of particular interest to those buying or selling a business.

One useful convention recommends listing assets in the balance sheet in their order of permanence, that is, starting out with the most difficult to turn into cash and working down to cash itself. This structure is very practical when you are looking at someone else's balance sheet, or comparing balance sheets. It can also help you to recognise obvious information gaps quickly.

Accounting for liabilities

Liabilities are claims against the business. These claims may include such items as: tax, accruals (which are expenses for items used but not yet billed for such as telephone and other utilities), deferred income, overdrafts, loans, hire purchase, and money owed to suppliers. Liabilities can also be less easy to identify and even harder to put a figure to, bad debts being a prime example.

Understanding reserves

Reserves are the accumulated profits made by a business over its working life, which have been ploughed back into the business rather than taken out by the owner(s).

In the final version of Jane Smith's balance sheet we showed her capital as being the sole support for the liabilities of the business. The implication was that she had put this whole sum in at once. In practice, this is much more likely to have happened over time, and in a variety of ways.

Perhaps she started out in business, as that is how we must now look at her affairs, with a sum say of £25,000. In the period since she has been in business she has made a net profit after tax of £50,000 and put this back into her business to finance growth. In addition the premises that she bought a few years ago for £111,615 have just been revalued at £150,000, a paper gain of £38,385.

We could now recast the bottom portion of her company balance sheet as shown in Figure 13-9.

	£	£
FINANCED BY		
Capital introduced		25,000
Reserves		
Capital reserve	38,385	
Revenue reserve	50,000	88,385
		113,385

Figure 13-9:
Jane's
reserves.

The profit of £50,000 ploughed back into the business is called a *revenue reserve*, which means the money actually exists and could be used to buy stock or more assets. The increase in value of the business premises is, on the other hand, a *paper* increase. The £38,385 increase in *capital reserves* could not be used to buy anything, as it will not be in money form until the premises are sold. However that paper reserve could be used to underpin a loan from the bank, so turning a paper profit into a cash resource. Both reserves and the capital introduced represent all the money invested by the shareholder in this venture.

Analysing Performance

Gathering and recording financial information is a lead-up to analysing a business to see how well (or badly) it is doing. This analytical process requires tools, in this case ratios, and their usefulness and limitations need to be understood, before they can be used to good effect.

Using ratios

All analysis of financial information involves comparisons. As a business is constantly changing, the most useful way to measure activity is through ratios. A ratio is simply one number expressed as a proportion of another. Travelling 100 miles may not sound too impressive, until you realise it was done in one hour. The ratio here is 100 miles per hour. If you knew that the vehicle in question had a top speed of 120 miles per hour, you would have some means of comparing it to other vehicles, at least in respect of their speed. In finance, too, ratios can turn sterile data into valuable information in a wide range of different ways and help you make choices.

The key financial ratios that you will need from the outset are described below. These should all be monitored at least on a monthly basis.

Sophisticated accounting software have 'report generator' programs that produce standard ratio reports with analysis commentary suggesting areas worthy of more detailed analysis. The process is a bit like plugging your car engine into a programme designed to test its present condition. By monitoring rpm, gas emissions, fuel usage, and the like, and comparing performance against the specification for the vehicle, it is possible to say how well, or badly, the vehicle is running and what should be done to raise its performance.

Gross profit percentage

To figure gross profit percentage, you deduct the cost of sales from the sales and express the result as a percentage of sales. The higher the percentage, the greater the value you're adding to the goods and services you're producing. Figure 13-10 shows the calculation.

Figure 13-10:
Formula for figuring gross profit percentage.

$$\text{Gross profit percentage} = \frac{\text{Profit}}{\text{Sales} - \text{Cost of sales}} \times 100$$

Operating profit percentage

Figuring the operating profit percentage gives you a measure of how well the management is running the business, because operating expenses that the management is responsible for are a component. Financing decisions are presumed to be the owner's responsibility; interest and taxation are set by the government, so those numbers are out of management control and accountability.

To calculate this number, you deduct not only the cost of sales but also expenses from profit, as shown in Figure 13-11.

Figure 13-11:
Calculating operating profit.

$$\text{Operating profit percentage} = \frac{\text{Profit}}{\text{Sales} - (\text{Cost of sales} + \text{Cost of operations})} \times 100$$

Net profit percentage

Figuring your net profit essentially gives you your business's *bottom line,* telling you how much money is left for you to take out, or re-invest in your business. A higher percentage means you are making more money from each pound of sales generated.

You can calculate net profit either after you pay tax or before – earnings before interest and tax, known as EBIT.

In its after-tax form, which Figure 13-12 shows, net profit percentage represents the sum available either to be distributed as dividends or retained by the business to invest in its future.

Figure 13-12:
Figuring net profit percentage.

$$\text{Net profit percentage} = \frac{\text{Profit}}{\text{Sales} - (\text{Cost of sales} + \text{Cost of operations} + \text{Taxes paid})} \times 100$$

Return on capital employed

This number, frequently abbreviated as ROCE, is the primary measure of performance for most businesses. If, for example, you invested £10,000 in a bank and at the end of the year they gave you £500 interest, then the return on your capital is 5 per cent (£500/10,000 × 100 = 5%).

In a business this ratio is calculated by expressing the operating profit (profit before interest and tax) as a percentage of the total capital employed – both in fixed assets and in working capital, called *net current assets* in the balance sheet. Figure 13-13 shows the formula for figuring ROCE. Refer to Figure 13-11 to figure the operating profit number.

Figure 13-13:
Figuring return on capital employed.

$$\text{ROCE} = \frac{\text{Operating profit}}{\text{Fixed assets} + \text{Working capital}} \times 100$$

If you think about it, return on capital employed is the same as saying the return on the shareholders' funds plus the long-term loans, or the 'financed by' bit of the balance sheet.

Current ratio

This is calculated by dividing your current assets by your current liabilities. There is really only one rule about how high (or low) the current ratio should be. It should be as close to 1:1 as the safe conduct of the business will allow. This will not be the same for every type of business.

A shop buying in finished goods on credit and selling them for cash could run safely at 1.3:1. A manufacturer, with raw material to store and customers to finance, may need over 2:1. This is because the period between paying cash out for raw materials and receiving cash in from customers is longer in a manufacturing business than in a retail business.

Average days collection period

Any small business selling on credit knows just how quickly cash flow can become a problem. The average collection period ratio is calculated by dividing your debtors by the amount of credit sales, and then multiplying that by the days in the period in question. The result is expressed in days, so you can see in effect how many days it takes for your customers to pay up, on average.

Sixty days is a fairly normal period for customers to take before paying up. Forty-five days would be a good target to aim for and ninety days is too long to let go without chasing.

This is a good control ratio, which has the great merit of being quickly translatable into a figure any businessperson can understand, showing how much it is costing to give credit.

If you are selling into overseas markets the practice on punctual payments can vary widely.

Stock control ratio

A simple way to tackle stock control is to see how many times your stock is turned over each year. Dividing the cost of sales by the stock arrives at this ratio. The more times you can turn your stock over the better.

Gearing down

The more borrowed money a business uses, as opposed to that put in by the shareholders (either through initial capital or by leaving profits in the business), the more highly *geared* the business is. Highly geared businesses can be vulnerable when either sales dip sharply, as in a recession, or when interest rates rocket as in a boom. Figure 13-14 shows how to calculate gearing percentage.

Figure 13-14:
Figuring
gearing
percentage.

$$\text{Gearing percentage} = \frac{\text{Debt (long-term borrowings)}}{\text{Debt + Shareholders' funds}} \times 100$$

Gearing levels in small firms average from 60 per cent down to 30 per cent. Many small firms are probably seriously over-geared, especially so as they go into the first stages of growth.

Keeping on the right side of the law

Whether the money in the business is yours alone, provided by family and friends, or supplied by outside financial institutions, you have a legal responsibility to make sure your accounts are kept in good order at all times. If you are successful and need more money to expand, you will need the financial information to prove your case. If things are not going so well and you need to strengthen your position to weather a financial storm, then you will have even greater need of good accounting information.

Whatever the circumstances in the background there are always the tax and VAT authorities who will need to be certain that your figures are correct and timely.

Carrying out an audit

Most companies will be required to appoint an auditor and have their accounts audited. It is the job of the auditor to report to the members (shareholders) of the company as to whether the accounts have been properly prepared taking notice of the appropriate accounting rules. The auditor must also report as to whether the accounts give a *true and fair* view of the state of the company's affairs. In order to arrive at their conclusion, the auditor will carry out an examination of the records on a test basis to ensure that the accounts are not materially incorrect. This does not mean that the auditor will check every detail, but they will look at a representative sample of transactions to get a feel for whether or not the books are being properly kept.

If your bookkeeping records are poorly kept, inaccurate, or missing, then expect a hefty bill and a lot of your time being spent in answering questions about long gone, and often fairly trivial, financial events.

If you have a computerised system, the year-end audit is made much simpler for you and your accountant. In fact, with some accounting software, you can do much of the work for the accountant before she or he sets foot on your premises. You can, for example, produce reports which all auditors will require, such as the trial balance. Some packages have utilities which enable the auditor to run random checks on the transactions and postings and some have facilities for the pre-production of debtors' confirmation letters. Auditors will normally send those out to debtors to check that the transaction did take place. In this way, the auditor's life is made much simpler and, hopefully, it will take less time to conduct the audit, your personnel will be free to carry on with their work sooner, there will be a smaller fee for you to pay, and, if you require it, your accountant can get on with some work that will be of rather more benefit to the business. For example they could recommend on how you could tighten up on credit control, stock taking, or get better and more timely management accounts, all infinitely more valuable to the owner-manager than a set of audited accounts.

Filing your accounts

If you are trading as a company then your accounts have to be filed with Companies House (www.companieshouse.co.uk) each year.

Late filing penalties were introduced in 1992 to encourage directors of limited companies to file their accounts on time because they must provide this statutory information for the public record. The amount of the penalty depends on how late the accounts reach the Registrar.

Penalties for filing your accounts late are shown in Table 13-1.

Table 13-1	Late Filing Penalties
Length of delay, measured from the date the accounts are due	**Private company**
3 months or less	£100
3 months and one day to 6 months	£250
6 months and one day to 12 months	£500
More than 12 months	£1,000

Unless you are filing your company's first accounts, the time normally allowed for delivering accounts to Companies House is ten months from the end of the relevant accounting period for private companies. If you are filing your company's first accounts and they cover a period of more than 12 months, they must be delivered to the Registrar within 22 months of the date of incorporation for private companies.

Whilst all companies must prepare full accounts for presentation to the company's shareholders, small and medium-sized companies can send abbreviated accounts to the Registrar of Companies. Abbreviated accounts contain very little information that could be of use to a competitor. Nothing is given away on turnover or margins, for example, a luxury denied to larger companies. Small companies' accounts (ones with less than £350,000 turnover, balance sheet totals less than £1.4 million, and fewer than 50 employees on average, to be precise) delivered to the Registrar must contain:

✔ An abbreviated balance sheet.

✔ Selected notes to the accounts including accounting policies, share capital, particulars of creditors payable in more than five years, and the basis of any foreign currency transactions.

✔ A special auditor's report (unless exempt).

The rules of disclosure are complex and this is only a brief outline of the requirements. If you are unsure about the information that you have to provide then you should take professional advice. Where a company files abbreviated accounts it must have a special auditor's report confirming that the exemptions have been satisfied and the directors must make a statement at the foot of the balance sheet saying that they have relied upon the exemptions.

Part III
Staying in Business

"This is not only a tax investigation, Mr Grimble,
this is a <u>thorough</u> tax investigation."

In this part . . .

Once your business is up and running the problems don't stop or slow down. They just change. Selling successfully may have looked like your biggest problem before you started out, but once you get going managing the money takes on at least as much importance.

Even if you make piles of profit, you have to keep alert to ways to make sure that the taxman gets no more than his fair share of the proceeds. You will find you have to manage not only your own money, but VAT (Value Added Tax), PAYE (Pay as You Earn), and NI (National Insurance).

Chapter 14

Managing Your Tax Position

. . . .

. . . .

*I*f you think that all, or even most, of the profit you make in your business comes your way, think again. The government takes a sizeable slice of everything you make, in one way or another, and gets very nasty if you try to evade their clutches. Whilst you may be starting your first business, government agencies have had centuries to hone their skills in extracting their pound of flesh. Since 1842, when income tax was reintroduced into Britain, everyone in business has been required to account for their income and profits.

Before you reach for your passport and head offshore, taxing entrepreneurs is a fact of life in almost every country in the world, though both the amounts and methods of assessment vary widely. Surprisingly enough the tax climate in the UK is relatively benign and we pay less than most.

Still, whilst you may have to pay tax, you don't have to pay too much. As one law lord eloquently expresses it, 'No-one has to so arrange their affairs as to allow the Inland Revenue to dig the biggest shovel into their affairs.'

Tackling Taxes for Different Types of Businesses

Sole traders, partnerships, and limited companies are treated differently for tax purposes, so I look at each in turn.

Managing your tax position is one area in which timely professional advice is essential. This is made even more important because tax rules can change every year. Good advice can both help to reduce the overall tax bill and so increase the value of profits to the business.

Figuring out sole traders and partnerships

A partnership is treated as a collection of sole traders for tax purposes, and each partner's share of that collective liability has to be worked out. If you're a *sole trader* (in other words, self-employed) your income from every source is brought together and the profit is taxed altogether. Income from business is one of a number of headings on your general tax return form.

In the UK the taxes that need to be calculated are:

- ✔ Income tax on profits

- ✔ Class 4 national insurance on profits

- ✔ Capital gains tax, on the disposal of *fixed assets* such as property at a profit, or when the whole business is sold

- ✔ Inheritance tax, paid on death or when certain gifts are made

Neither of the last two taxes is likely to occur on a regular basis, nor will they occur in the first few years in business, so I don't cover them here. When those taxes do come into play the sums involved are likely to be significant and professional advice should be taken from the outset. The following sections go into income tax and national insurance.

Adding up income tax

Under the self-assessment tax system in the UK, you pay taxes for your accounting year in the year in which your accounting year ends. So if you made up your accounts to 31 December, the basis period for income tax year 2003/2004 is 6 April 2004 to 5 April 2005. There are special rules that apply for the first year and the last year of trading that should ensure tax is charged fairly.

If your turnover is low, currently in the UK less than £15,000 per year, you can summarise your income on three lines: Sales, expenses, and profit. If your turnover is above the minimum, you have to summarise your accounts to show turnover, gross profit, and expenses by account categories, such as vehicle running costs, advertising, telephone and rents.

No matter how you account for your business income, you get to deduct a personal allowance amount from your profit figure. You pay income tax on the difference between your profit minus your personal allowance. The personal allowance is the current threshold below which you don't pay tax.

Figuring class 4

You figure class 4 national insurance based on taxable profits. The percentage you pay depends on what range your profits fall in. You pay 7 per cent if the number falls in a range that currently goes from £8,000 to £30,000. Above the £30,000 mark, you pay 9 per cent. This is paid in addition to the flat rate Class 2 contributions of about £7 per week.

All these rates and amounts change in March of every year, but the broad principles remain the same.

Looking at levies on companies

Companies have a legal identity separate from those who work in them, whether or not those workers also own the company. Everyone working in the business is taxed as an employee. The company is responsible in the UK, through the PAYE (Pay As You Earn) system for collecting tax and passing it to the tax authorities.

Directors' salaries are a business expense, just as with any other wages, and are deducted from the company's revenues in arriving at its taxable profits.

Companies in the UK pay tax in three main ways:

- **Corporation tax** is paid on the company's profits for the year, as calculated in the tax adjusted profits. The rate of corporation tax in the UK, and in many other countries, depends on the amount of profits made. In the UK, if the profits are less than £300,000 the small companies rate of 20 per cent applies. Above £1.5 million the full rate of 30 per cent is charged. For figures in between a taper applies (all these figures are subject to annual review in the budget). Corporation tax is payable nine months after the end of the accounting period.

  As a concession to persuade sole traders to convert to limited company status the Inland Revenue allows a company to earn the first £10,000 tax free in any year. For profits between £10,001 and £50,000 a special marginal rate of tax is paid. This is covered in more detail elsewhere in this chapter.

- **Dividend payment taxes** are levied on the distribution of profit to the shareholders. This gives the appearance of taxing the same profit twice, but through a process of tax credits this double taxation doesn't generally occur. When a shareholder gets a dividend from a company it comes with a tax credit attached. This means that any shareholder on the basic rate of tax won't have to pay any further tax. Higher rate taxpayers, however, have a further amount of tax to pay.

✔ **Capital gains tax** is owed if an asset, say a business property, is sold at a profit. This capital gain is taxed along the general lines of corporation tax, with lower rates applying to smaller companies.

Assessing the Best Legal Structure

The most important rule is 'never let the tax tail wag the business dog.' Tax is just one aspect of business life. If you want to keep your business finances private then the public filing of accounts required of companies isn't for you. On the other hand if you want to protect your private assets from creditors if things go wrong, then being a sole trader or partner is probably not the best route to take.

Company profits and losses are locked into the company, so if you have several lines of business using different trading entities you cannot easily settle losses in one area against profits in another. But as sole traders are treated as one entity for all their sources of income, there is more scope for netting off gains and losses. Some points to bear in mind here are:

✔ If your profits are likely to be small, say below £50,000, for some time, then from a purely tax point of view you may pay less tax as a sole trader. This is because as an individual you get a tax-free allowance. Your first few thousand pound of income are not taxable. This amount varies with personal circumstances, married or single, for example, and can be changed in the budget each year.

✔ If you expect to be making higher rates of profit (above £50,000) and want to reinvest a large portion of those profits back into your business, then you could be better off forming a company. Companies don't start paying higher rates of tax until their profits are £300,000. Even then, they don't pay tax at 40 per cent. A sole trader would be taxed at the 40 per cent rate by the time their profits had reached about £30,000, taking allowances into account. So a company making £300,000 taxable profits could have £54,000 more to reinvest in financing future growth than would a sole trader in the same line of work.

✔ Non-salary benefits are more favourably treated for the sole trader. You can generally get tax relief on the business element of costs that are only partly business related, such a running a vehicle. A director of a company is taxed on the value of the vehicle's list price and is not allowed travel to and from work as a business expense.

But the whole area is complicated and depends heavily on what you want to achieve. For example if you want to maximise your entitlement to make pension contributions, then a strategy that is tax efficient, for example incorporating, as turning yourself into a limited company is known, may be a bad idea. Get professional financial advice before you make the decision.

Paying Taxes/Calculating Tax Rates

The Inland Revenue Web site (www.inlandrevenue.gov.uk) contains all the latest tax rates and details of almost everything you are likely to need to complete your tax return correctly.

The main corporation tax rate is 30 per cent. The rate is 19 per cent for companies with taxable profits between £50,000 and £300,000 and companies with taxable profits of £10,000 or below pay nothing.

The good news, a rare enough event when it comes to paying taxes, is that small businesses are generally treated more favourably than their bigger brothers. In summary, you aren't hit for the full potential tax bill until you are making over £300,000 a year in profits. Most businesses avoid that position until their turnover exceeds £2 million.

Valuing value-added tax

As if paying tax on profits wasn't enough pain, every business over a certain size has to, in effect, collect taxes too. VAT (value-added tax) is a tax on consumer spending. It is a European tax system, although most countries have significant variations in VAT rates, starting thresholds, and in the schemes themselves.

Essentially, you must register to collect VAT if your taxable turnover, that is, your sales (not profit), exceeds £52,000 in any 12-month period, or looks as though it might reasonably be expected to do so. This rate is reviewed each year in the budget and is frequently changed. (The UK is significantly out of line with many other countries in Europe, where VAT entry rates are much lower.)

You get no reward for collecting VAT, but you are penalised for making mistakes or for making late returns.

The Customs and Excise website (www.hmce.gov.uk) has bags of useful information on every aspect of the subject including details of all VAT rates and procedures.

Registering and sending in VAT

VAT is complicated tax. The general rule is that all supplies of goods and services are taxable at the standard rate (17.5 per cent) unless the law specifically states they are to be zero-rated or exempt.

In deciding whether your turnover exceeds the limit, you have to include your zero-rated sales (things like most foods, books, and children's clothing), as they are technically taxable; it's just that the rate of tax is 0 per cent. You leave out exempt items such as the provision of health and welfare, finance, and land.

Customs and Excise issues three free booklets on registering for VAT: a simple introductory booklet called *Should you be registered for VAT?* and two more detailed booklets called *General Guide* and *Scope and Coverage*. If in doubt (and the language is not easy to understand) ask your accountant or the local branch of the Customs and Excise; after all, they would rather help you to get it right in the first place than have to sort it out later when you have made a mess of it.

Each quarter, or each year if you take that option, you have to complete a return that shows your purchases and the VAT you paid on them, and your sales and the VAT you collected on them. The VAT paid and collected are offset against each other and the balance sent to the Customs and Excise. If you paid more VAT in any quarter than you collected, you get a refund.

To help smaller businesses that might struggle with the more traditional VAT return (explained above) the Customs and Excise have introduced The Flat Rate Scheme (FRS). It enables eligible businesses to calculate their VAT payment as a percentage of their total turnover. You still have to put VAT on your sales invoices but you don't have to do the input and output tax return to settle up your VAT. Your VAT liability is agreed as a percentage of all your sales. This percentage will be given to you by Customs and Excise based on the type of trade your business carries out.

It sometimes pays to register even if you don't have to – if you are selling mostly zero-rated items for example, as you can reclaim VAT that you have paid out on purchases. Also, being registered for VAT may make your business look more professional and less amateurish to your potential customers.

Calculating VAT

The simple bookkeeping system I describe in Chapter 13 may need to be extended to accommodate VAT records. So the analysed cashbook you use in a simple system needs additional columns to accommodate the pre-VAT sales, the amount of VAT, and the total of those two figures.

Calculating the VAT element of any transaction can be a confusing sum. Following these simple steps will help you always get it right.

1. Take the gross amount of any sum (items you sell or buy), that is the total including any VAT and divide it by 117.5 – if the VAT rate is 17.5 per cent. (If the rate is different, add 100 to the VAT percentage rate and divide by that number.)

   All this means is that we are saying that the sum we have paid out on a purchase or have sent out on an item we are selling is 100 per cent of the net bill with another 17.5 per cent on top.

2. Multiply the result from Step 1 by 100 to get the pre-VAT total.

3. Multiply the result from Step 1 by 17.5 to arrive at the VAT element of the bill.

Completing the VAT return

This has to be where a computer-based bookkeeping system wins hands down. VAT returns are automatically generated by the accounting package. All you have to do is enter the current VAT rate. If you take web-enabled software updates you may not even have to do this.

Basically, the VAT inspectors are interested in three figures:

- ✔ The amount of VAT you collected on the goods and services you sold.

- ✔ The amount of VAT collected from you by those who have sold you goods and services.

- ✔ The difference between those two sums. If the difference is positive, that's the amount of VAT due to be paid. If the number is negative, you are entitled to reclaim that amount.

For a business VAT is a zero-sum game – you don't make money and you don't pay money – it's the end consumer who picks up the tab.

The final two numbers are a check on the reasonableness of the whole sum. You have to show the value of your sales and purchases, minus of VAT, for the period in question.

The VAT return has to be signed by the person registered for VAT. It's important to remember that a named person is responsible for VAT, a limited company being treated as a person in this instance. Not only are you acting as an unpaid tax collector but also there are penalties for filing your return late or incorrectly. Your VAT records have to be kept for six years and periodically you can expect a visit from a VAT inspector.

Choosing cash or income

Generally VAT is levied on invoiced sales, so in theory and often in practice there can be occasions when you have to pay VAT on sums you have not collected yourself. (See Chapter 13 for accounting rules.) This unhappy state of affairs can happen if you send out an invoice at the end of the quarter and have not been paid by your customer by the time you have to make the VAT return. If this proves a major problem you can usually elect to pay VAT on a cash basis, rather than the strictly more correct income recognition basis that is triggered when you send out your invoices.

One important source of problems is the gap that exists between what the VAT rules allow as business expenses and the (usually more liberal) rules applied by the Inland Revenue. In general, any expenditure 'wholly and exclusively for business purposes' is tax deductible for Inland Revenue purposes. If you are going to reclaim VAT, expenditure must also be directly attributable to the taxable supplies you are making. These must be goods or services that are taxable at either the standard rate or the zero rate (that is, not exempt). If you cannot attribute your expenditure to the taxable supplies you are making, you will be treated as the end-consumer, so will not be able to reclaim the VAT.

Minimising taxes

There is no reason to arrange your financial affairs in such a way as to pay the most tax. Whilst staying within the law by a safe margin you should explore ways to *avoid* as opposed to *evade* tax liability. This is a complex area and one subject to frequent change. The tax authorities try most years to close loopholes in the tax system, whilst highly paid tax accountants and lawyers try even harder to find new ways around the rules.

Some of the areas to keep in mind when assessing your tax liability are:

- ✔ Make sure to include all allowable business expenses. Especially when you have recently set up in business, you may not be fully aware of all the expenses that can be claimed. For example whilst entertaining clients is not an allowable business expense, the cost of your meals may well be allowable if you are away from home and staying overnight.

- ✔ If you have made losses in any tax period, these may under certain circumstances be carried forward to offset future taxable profits or backwards against past profits.

- ✔ You can defer paying capital gains tax if you plan to buy another asset with the proceeds. This is known as 'rollover relief' and it can be used normally up to three years after the taxable event.

- ✔ Pension contributions reduce your taxable profits. You may even be able to set up a pension scheme that allows you some say over how those funds are used. For example your pension fund could be used to finance your business premises. The pension fund would in effect become your landlord. The company then pays rent, an allowable business expense, into your pension fund, which grows tax-free.

- ✔ If you do intend to buy capital assets for your business, bring forward your spending plans so as to maximise the use of the *writing down allowance*, which is the portion of the cost of the asset you can set against tax in any year. For example, if you propose to buy a computer you are allowed to charge 100 per cent of the cost in the year you make the purchase. For a car, the proportion would be just 25 per cent (up to a maximum vehicle cost of £12,000). If, for example, you know in March that you intend to buy a new computer later that year, by making purchase before 5 April, you can take the writing down allowance in that tax year. If you wait until after that date you will have to wait until the following tax year to get the benefit of a lower tax bill.

✔ Identify non-cash benefits that you and others working for you could take instead of taxable salary. For example, a share option scheme may achieve the same, or better, level of reward for employees, with less tax payable.

✔ Examine the pros and cons of taking your money out of a limited company by way of dividends or salary. These routes are taxed differently and may provide scope for tax reduction.

✔ If your spouse has no other income from employment, they could earn a sum equivalent to their annual tax-free allowance (currently about £4,000) by working for your business.

✔ If you incurred any pre-trading expenses at any stage over the seven years before you started up in business, you can probably treat them as if you incurred them after trading started. Such expenses could include market research, designing and testing your product or service, capital items such as a computer bought before you started trading and then brought into the assets of your business.

✔ You may be able to treat the full purchase price of business assets you bought through hire-purchase in your capital allowances calculation.

This list is indicative rather than comprehensive. It is a field in which timely professional advice can produce substantial benefits in the form of lower tax bills.

Handling Employment Taxes

Not only must you pay tax on your businesses profits and collect value-added tax from suppliers for onward transmission to an ever-hungry exchequer, you have to look after your employees' tax affairs too. Don't think for one moment that this is considered an act of generosity or simply a convenience because you have an accounting system in place and a bookkeeper with time on their hands. You as an employer have a legal responsibility to ensure an employee's taxes are paid and in the last resort could end up picking up the tab yourself, if they fail to.

Paying PAYE

Income tax is collected from employees through the PAYE system, or Pay As You Earn. The employee's liability to income tax is collected as it is earned instead of by tax assessment at some later date. If the business is run as a limited company then the directors of the company are employees. PAYE must be operated on all salaries and bonuses paid to them, yourself included.

The Inland Revenue now issues booklets in reasonably plain English, explaining how PAYE works. The main documents you need to operate PAYE are:

 ✔ A deduction working sheet (Form P11) for each employee

 ✔ The PAYE Tables. There are two books of tax tables in general use, which are updated in line with the prevailing tax rates

 • Table A Pay Adjustment Tables – Shows the amount an employee can earn in any particular week or month before the payment of tax

 • Tables B to D and LR – Taxable Pay Tables that show the tax due on an employee's taxable pay

 ✔ Form P45, which is given to an employee when transferring from one employer to another

 ✔ Form P46, which is used when a new employee does not have a P45 from a previous employer (such as a student starting work for the first time)

 ✔ Form P60, which is used so that the employer can certify an employee's pay at the end of the income tax year in April

 ✔ Form P35, the year-end declaration and certificate for each employee. This is used to summarise all the tax and National Insurance deductions from employees for the tax year

 ✔ Form P6, the tax codes advice notice issued by the Inspector of Taxes telling you which tax code number to use for each employee

You work out the tax deduction for each employee using the following steps. (For *week* read *month*, if that is the payment interval.)

1. Add the current week's gross pay to the previous total of gross pay to date, so as to show the total gross pay to and including this week of the tax year.

2. Check the tax code number of the employee on Table A, to arrive at the figure of tax-free pay for that particular week.

3. Deduct the amount of tax-free pay from the total pay to date, to get the amount of taxable pay.

4. Work out the tax due on the total taxable pay for the year to date using Table B. Then make the appropriate deduction to allow for the tax due.

5. Deduct the amount of tax already accounted for in previous weeks from the total tax due, to work out the tax due for the week.

Allocating National Insurance

As well as deducting income tax, as an employer you must also deduct National Insurance (NI) contributions. There are three rates of contributions for NI purposes:

- ✔ Table A – the most common rate, used in all cases except for those who qualify for Table B or C
- ✔ Table B – used for certain married women who have a certificate for payment at reduced rate
- ✔ Table C – used for employees who are over pension age

For Tables A and B there are two amounts to calculate: the employee's contribution and the employer's contribution. For Table C there is no employee's contribution. The amounts of contributions are recorded on the same deduction working sheets as used for income tax purposes.

The amounts of NI due are found by referring to the appropriate table. The tables show both the employee's liability and also the total liability for the week or month. Both these figures must be recorded on the deduction working sheet.

Accounting for employment taxes

When you pay out wages and salaries to your staff you need to record the net pay in your cashbook as well as the PAYE and NI paid to the Collector of Taxes.

If you have only one or two employees then the record of the payments in the cashbook, together with the other PAYE documentation, will probably do. But if you have any more you should keep a wages book.

The deductions working sheet gives you a record of the payments made to each employee throughout the year. You also need a summary of the payments made to all employees on one particular date.

The law requires that employees *must* provide their staff with itemised pay statements, known as payslips. These must show:

- ✔ Gross pay
- ✔ Net pay
- ✔ Any deductions (stating the amounts of each item and the reason why the deductions are made)

The Inland Revenue website has details on these employment taxes.

Surviving a Tax Investigation

Hopefully with good bookkeeping and accounting systems you will avoid any disputes over tax and other matters. Complete records are vital if you are to successfully defend yourself from mistaken allegations of wrongdoing.

Keeping the factors in the following sections in mind will help you understand better how tax enquiries get started and what might happen if one does.

Rationalising the reasons

The Inland Revenue gets their information from three sources. Their own investigations and tips from the public account for the vast majority of their information received. However an increasingly effective third measure is to ask people to inform on themselves. Crazy as that may sound, it seems to work. Whilst not quite amounting to an amnesty, those self-employed who have strayed across the boundary between tax avoidance and tax evasion can contact tax authorities anonymously and get confidential advice on how to sort themselves out.

Sometimes the tax authorities look closely at whole industries. In recent years, for instance, they have looked long and hard at the amusement arcade business, construction, betting and gaming, commodities dealing, and some doctors and dentists.

Tax inspectors also may do any of the following:

- ✔ Drive around exclusive residential areas and look carefully at any expensive-looking renovation work

- ✔ Use the services of pubs, restaurants, hotels, copy shops, and other cash businesses, looking carefully at the businesses' cost structures

- ✔ Read local newspapers and use press-cutting agencies to cross-check people's claimed lifestyle with their actual one

- ✔ Access company databases and on-line records from Companies House

- ✔ Check up on local authority parking permits in certain areas

- ✔ Examine the land registry to monitor house purchases and property prices and sales and keep an eye on the yachting register

The tax authorities put all the information that it gathers into its computers and all these sources of data are cross-correlated with each other. They have a skilled project team looking specifically at the uses of information technology for tax investigations and they can usually uncover anything that does not look quite right. For example if someone is claiming to make no profit from their business, but own a yacht, have a residence parking permit for inner city parking in an area they don't appear to live in, and are having a new swimming pool installed, alarm bells ring.

But what is much more likely is that someone tips the tax inspectors off. Informers are often aggrieved spouses or employees, competitors, jealous neighbours, or jilted lovers. Some of this information is second-hand and dangerously wrong, but that is how gossip works. Some people like to brag about how they load their expenses, or take cash payments that are not entered in the books, so it's not exactly surprising that gossip starts up. If that gossip reaches the wrong ears then an investigation may begin.

The duration of an investigation varies according to the complexity of the case and availability of information. It would be surprising if a case – from beginning to end – has not been cleared within 18 months. With a technically-based case, however, it can take much longer – if, for example, both sides need to seek tax counsel's advice. When parts have to be taken to the Commissioners, a case can stretch for years.

Recognising the signs that you're under scrutiny

It's not too difficult to know a tax investigation is underway. You will as likely as not get a standard letter from the Special Compliance Office, or your accountant will. It will state that enquiries have begun under Code of Practice 8 for less serious matters and Code of Practice 9 for series matters. Booklets will accompany the letter, to explain the procedure. By this stage you can be sure that a lot of information has already been gathered.

Anticipating the worst that can happen

The Inland Revenue has sweeping powers to demand documents from the taxpayer and from third parties under section 20 or section 745 of the Taxes Management Act. They are always entitled to obtain papers and documents under a notice if the notice is valid. And they can go back 20 years into a person's affairs in cases of suspected fraud. That is way beyond the six years that you are required to keep your own accounting records. So if you have stuck strictly to the six-year rule you may be at something of a disadvantage in a tax enquiry.

What they are not entitled to do is to insist upon an interview with the taxpayer or third parties. They cannot force people to speak.

The Revenue is allowed to search premises and remove documents if they have a warrant. If they raid your premises, don't obstruct them. But do follow a few simple rules:

- ✔ Make sure your professional adviser gets round to the premises as fast as possible.

- ✔ Read the warrant and make sure that you understand it.

- ✔ Remember you are under no legal obligation to talk.

- ✔ Make sure also that your staff are aware they are under no legal obligation to talk.

- ✔ Ask for the purpose of the search.

- ✔ Obtain a receipt for any materials that they take away.

- ✔ Get the name and office of the investigator-in-charge.

The Revenue understands the real world and that people in it have complex financial, commercial, and personal lives. They go to great lengths to protect confidences and save embarrassments.

This means in practice that disclosures can be made on a managed basis. Two spouses, say, can go through one joint disclosure as appropriate, and then have separate meetings with the Revenue in which they can make disclosures of which the other will be unaware. Likewise, directors of a business can make disclosures of which fellow directors will remain ignorant.

Negotiating around penalties

The penalties can theoretically be as high as 100 per cent of the unpaid tax; in practice they are nearly always dwarfed by the amount of tax to be paid and in the worst case you would go to jail. But in practice, the Revenue prosecutes very rarely. So the number of investigations that end up with someone in prison is relatively small.

If the Revenue says they are going to prosecute, the consequences can be very serious. You must seek professional advice immediately.

Bargaining is inevitable in most cases. The Revenue's main aim is to ensure that taxpayers pay the right amount of tax. But what is the right amount of tax is open to discussion. They are also concerned with hitting their own sales targets in an efficient manner. They have goals as to how much unpaid tax they have to collect each year and deadlines to meet along the way. Anyone with a goal and a deadline can be negotiated with.

Insuring against loss

Tax investigations can be costly. Apart from any fine, you will have to bear the cost of your own advisers answering the tax inspector's questions. This can run into a substantial four-figure sum, even for a relatively trivial case. Even if you win you won't get those costs back.

You can protect yourself from some problems by getting insurance against a tax, VAT, or NHI investigation, which will at least ensure you get good timely advice at no additional cost. The Association of British Insurers (www.abi.org.uk) can put you in contact with a source of such insurance as well as advice.

Chapter 15

Improving Performance

. . . .

In This Chapter

▶ Seeing why retaining customers matters

▶ Measuring customer satisfaction

▶ Discovering ways to cut costs and work smarter

▶ Evaluating market growth strategies

▶ Looking at new product opportunities

. . . .

*A*n unpleasant truism in business, and in much else, is that once resources are allocated they become misallocated over time. Another way of looking at this problem is to say that just because something 'ain't broke' it doesn't mean it can't be made to perform better still. To get your business to grow and keep growing needs a continuous effort to improve every aspect of your business.

In this chapter, I tell you how to keep your business going strong by keeping your customers happy, improving your efficiency and effectiveness, and increasing and expanding your business.

Checking Your Internal Systems

In order to improve performance you have to have systems in operation that help you measure performance in the first place. The two sub-sections following give you tips for evaluating how you spend your time and how to keep on top of your markets.

Keeping track of your routine

A good test of whether you are allocating enough time to the task of improving performance is to keep a track of how you spend your time, say, over a month. As well as recording the work you do and the time you spend on each major task, put the letter R, for routine, S for strategic, or I for improving performance next to the task.

A routine task is something like meeting a customer or the bank manager, delivering a product or service, or taking on a new employee. Strategic tasks would include considering a major shift of activities, say from making a product to just marketing it, forming a joint venture, or buying out a competitor. Improvement activities include all the elements I talk about in this chapter – activities focused on getting more mileage, lower costs, or higher yields out of the existing business.

Most owner managers spend 95 per cent of their day on routine tasks and only tackle improvement and strategic issues when they hit the buffers. For example most entrepreneurs don't worry too much about cash until it runs out. Then they pick up the phone and press customers into paying up. What they should have done, however, is introduce new procedures for collecting cash *before* the crunch.

If you are not spending at least 30 per cent of your time on improving your business and strategic issues, then you're probably heading for the buffers.

Analysing market position

A *SWOT analysis* is a way of consolidating everything you know about your competitive market position. SWOT stands for Strengths, Weaknesses, Opportunities, and Threats. Many businesses use SWOT analysis regularly, and very few people try it once and never again. For my money, SWOT is the way to go.

A SWOT analysis can't be carried out on the business as a whole. You have to analyse each important market segment separately. Because customer needs in each segment are different, it follows that you have to do different things in each segment to satisfy those needs. You may be up against different competitors in each segment so your strengths and weaknesses will be particular to that competitive environment. For example, look at travel methods: for families, car, coach, and to a lesser extent, train compete with each other; for business people, car, plane, and first-class rail travel are the biggest competitors.

Discovering strengths and weaknesses

A strength or weakness is an element that matters to the customers concerned. In fact it has to be such an important factor in the customer's mind that they would not buy without it. These are known as Critical Success Factors and it is your performance against these that confirm your strengths and weaknesses.

Find out the five or so things you have to get right to succeed in your market. For retail booksellers, location, range of books, hours of operation, knowledgeable staff, and ambiance may be the top five elements. Rank how well you think your competitors perform in these critical areas, or better still ask their existing, soon to be your, customers. If they score badly, you may have a strength.

Keeping an eye on opportunities and threats

It is important to recognise that an idea, invention or innovation is not necessarily an opportunity to grow your business. An opportunity has to be attractive, durable and timely. It is centred on a product or service that creates or adds value for its buyer or end user.

Working out what is attractive to you is fairly straightforward. Estimating the likely life of an opportunity or whether the time is right for its launch is not so easy. In a way that is the essence of an entrepreneur's skill. With opportunities you are looking for those that will bring the maximum benefit to the business whilst at the same time having a high probability of success. The benefits you are looking for may vary over time. In the early years cash flow may feature high on the list. Later fast growth and high margins may be more important.

Threats can come from all directions. Changes in the political or economic climate, new legislation or hackers and computer viruses can all have an impact on your business. For example, one business founder found to his dismay that his new Web site linked into dozens of pornography sites – the work of professional hackers. This set his operation back two months.

Changes in the demographic profile of populations (more older people and fewer of working age) or changing fashions, hit all businesses, old and new economy alike.

There are always too many potential threats for you to consider so you need to focus on those with the greatest possible impact that seem most likely to occur.

Doing the actual analysis

The actual SWOT process is asking various groups to share their thoughts on your company's greatest strength, its most glaring weakness, the area of greatest opportunity, and the direction of greatest threat.

To carry out a SWOT analysis, you need to consider each element separately for each major market segment.

Use the following steps to find out your SWOT quotient in each SWOT area:

1. **Determine your own view.**

    Decide what you think your business's best feature is, what the greatest weakness is, where your opportunities to gain more customers lie, and what the biggest threat facing your business is.

2. Find out what other entrepreneurs and your management team think about these issues.

3. Ask your newest front-line staff the same questions.

4. Form a customer focus group to consider the same questions.

5. Analyse how far apart the views of each group are.

   If you are close to your customers and to your market, there should be little difference among the various groups. If there is a large difference, figure out what you can do to make sure the gap is narrowed and stays that way.

The question 'so what?' is a good one to apply to all aspects of your SWOT analysis. That will help you concentrate only on the important issues. Once completed the SWOT will provide the ingredients and framework for developing your marketing strategy, which I look at in Chapter 10.

Retaining Customers

Businesses spend an awful lot of time and money winning customers and nothing like enough time and money on keeping them. This behaviour is as pointless as pouring water, or perhaps molten gold might be a better material to keep in mind, into a bucket with a big hole in the bottom. Most if not all of the flow is required to keep the bucket partially full. However fast the flow in, the flow out is just as fast.

Virtually all managers agree that customer care is important. A recent survey of major UK companies showed that 75 per cent had recently instituted customer care quality schemes. Sadly another survey, conducted by Bain and Company, the American consultants, also revealed that less than a third of those companies saw any payback for their efforts in terms of improved market share or profitability.

Bain suggests that the reason companies are disappointed with their attempts to improve customer care is that they don't have anything tangible to measure. To help overcome that problem Bain suggests that managers focus on the Customer Retention Ratio, a Bain invention. For example, if you have 100 customers in January and 110 in December, but only 85 of the original customers are still with you, then your retention rate is 85 per cent. Bain's study demonstrated that a 5 per cent improvement in retention had a fairly dramatic effect on clients. For a credit card client it boosted profits by 125 per cent; for an insurance broker there was a 5 per cent increase in profits; and for a software house a 35 per cent improvement in profits. Bain claims that the longer customers stay with you the more profitable they become. The next section explains why.

Realising why retaining customers matters

Studies and common sense indicate several principal reasons why retaining customers is so vitally important:

- ✔ It costs more to acquire new customers than to retain the ones you have. What with market research, prospecting, selling time, and so on, it costs between three and seven times as much to acquire a new customer as to retain an old one.

  This is nothing more than the old military maxim applied by Montgomery, that attacking forces need several times the strength of the defenders to guarantee success.

- ✔ The longer you retain a customer, the more years you have to allocate the costs of acquiring that customer. By spreading the costs of acquiring new customers over ten years, instead of one or two, the annual profit per customer will be higher. Suppose it costs you £500 to get a new customer, and that customer makes you £1,000 profit each year you keep them. If you keep the customer one year, your annual profit is £500 (£1,000 minus £500). However, if you keep the customer ten years, your annual profit is £950 (£1,000 minus £500/10). Customers who stay tend, over time, to spend more.

- ✔ Regular customers cost less to serve than new customers. Insurance and underwriting costs as a percentage of sales fall by 40 per cent for renewal policies. You don't incur up-front costs again.

- ✔ Long-term customers are often willing to pay a premium for service. Long-term customers also are less prone to check your competitors because they know and like you.

Avoiding the consequences of losing customers is a powerful motivator for keeping in your customers' good graces. Some of those consequences are:

- ✔ Dissatisfied customers tell between eight and 15 others about their experience. Just avoiding this negative publicity has a value.

- ✔ Your former customers are fertile ground for your competitors. If you keep your customers, your competitors have to offer inducements to dislodge your customers and this is expensive and time-consuming for them.

Working to retain customers

Use these five rules to make sure you retain customers and so improve your profit growth:

- ✔ Make customer care and retention a specific goal, and reward people for keeping customers not just for getting them.

✔ Find out why you lose customers. Don't just let them go – have either a follow-up questionnaire or get someone other than the salesperson concerned to visit former customers to find out why they changed supplier. You'd be surprised how pleased people are to tell you why they didn't stay with you, if you explain that it may help you serve them better the next time.

✔ Research your competitors' service levels as well as their products. If it's practical, buy from them on a regular basis. If you can't buy from competitors, keep close to people that do.

✔ If one part of your organisation is good at caring for customers, get them to teach everyone else what they do.

✔ Recognise that the best people to provide customer care are those staff who work directly with customers. But this means you have to train them and give them the authority to make decisions on the spot. Ciphers don't convince customers that you really want to keep their business.

Retaining customers is not the passive activity it sounds. The next sections offer concrete ways to keep your customers happy.

Monitoring complaints

One terrifying statistic is that 98 per cent of complaints never happen. People just don't get round to making the complaint, or worse still, they can find no one to complain to. You would have to be a hermit never to have experienced something to complain about, but just try finding someone to complain to at 8 p.m. on a Sunday at Paddington Station and you will get a fair impression of how the Gobi Desert feels.

You can never be confident that just because you're not hearing complaints your customers and clients aren't dissatisfied and about to defect. It also doesn't mean that they won't run around bad mouthing you and your business. It's as well to remember that on average people share their complaint with a score of others, who in turn are equally eager to share the tidings with others. The viral effect of e-mail has the potential to make any particularly juicy story run around the world in days if not hours.

Set up a system that will ensure your customers have ample opportunity to let you know what they think about your product or service. This could involve a short questionnaire, a follow up phone call or an area on your Web site devoted to customer feedback. As a bonus you will probably get some great ideas on how to improve your business.

One entrepreneur who is more than aware of the problems (and incidentally opportunities) presented by complaints is Julian Richer, founder of the retail hi-fi chain, Richer Sounds. His maxim is that his staff should maximise customers' opportunities to complain. The operative word in that sentence is *opportunities*, which should not be confused with *reasons*. In order to put this policy into effect Richer has a range of techniques in place. The whole customer satisfaction monitoring process starts from the moment customers enter one of his retail outlets. A bell near the door invites those in the shop to ring it if they have had particularly good service or help whilst in the shop. That help could be simply getting some great advice, or may be finding a product they want to buy at a very competitive price. Customers find that when they get their hi-fi equipment home there is a short questionnaire on a postcard asking them for their immediate post-purchase feelings. Does the product work as specified, is it damaged in any way, were they delighted with the service they have had? The postcard is addressed to 'Julian Richer, Founder' and not, as is the case with so many other big businesses, to 'Customer Services, Department 126754, PO Box, blah blah blah'. Richer does surveys on customer satisfaction and encourages his staff to come up with their own ideas for monitoring customer reactions. In fact he insists that they hit minimum targets for getting customer feedback. Silence on the customer satisfaction front is not an option for management in his business. Richer is clearly aware of the other great statistic when it comes to complaining customers.

Ninety-eight per cent of customers who have a complaint will buy from you again if you handle their complaint effectively and promptly. Not only will they buy from you again, but also they will spread the gospel about how clever they were in getting you to respond to their complaint. Nothing makes people happier than having something to complain about that ends up costing them next to nothing.

Setting customer service standards

Customer service is all those activities that support a customer's purchase, from the time they become aware that you could supply them with a particular product or service, to the point at which they own that product or service and are able to enjoy all the benefits they were led to believe were on offer.

The largest part of the value of many products and services lies in how customer service is delivered. It is also the area most likely to influence whether customers come back again or recommend you to others. Customer service works best when:

- ✔ Customers are encouraged to tell you about any problems.
- ✔ Customers know their rights and responsibilities from the beginning.
- ✔ Customers know the circumstances under which they are entitled to get their money back and how to take advantage of other rights.
- ✔ Customers feel in control. It's far better to provide a full refund if the customer is dissatisfied than to demand that the customer come up with a good reason for the refund. A refund, or any other recourse you offer, should be prompt.

Repeat business is another key profit-maker. Repeat business comes from ensuring customers are genuinely completely satisfied with – and preferably pleasantly surprised by – the quality of your product. Repeat sales save unnecessary expenditure on advertising and promotion to attract new customers.

It is certain that as standards of living rise, the more that quality, convenience, and service will become important relative to price. An investment in a strategy of quality customer service now is an investment in greater future profitability.

You need to have a model to follow for effective customer service and you should consider using mystery shopping as a way to keep tabs on your customer service standards – both issues are covered in the next sections.

Customer service is often the difference between keeping customers for life and losing customers in droves. You and your staff have to deliver outstanding customer service at all times.

In order to do this everyone has to know what the important elements of good customer service are and everyone needs to incorporate those elements into their everyday customer interactions.

The key elements of your customer service plan should include:

- ✔ **Initial contact:** The customer's first contact with staff creates a lasting impression and can win and sustain customers. All your staff need to be aware of how to handle enquiries quickly and competently. They should know how to leave potential customers feeling confident that their requirements will be met.

- ✔ **Information flow:** Keeping customers informed of where their orders are in the process influences their feelings about the way you do business. Your action plan needs to specify each step of your process: quotation; order confirmation; delivery notification; installation instructions. A regular flow of information throughout this period makes your customers feel that they matter to you.

- ✔ **Delivery:** Delivering the goods or service is a key part of customer service. Your product needs to be available in a timely manner, delivery lead times must be reasonable, and the delivery itself must be in a way that meets the customer's requirements.

- ✔ **After-sales support:** Good coverage in areas such as maintenance, repairs, help-lines, upgrade notification, instruction manuals, returns policy, and fault tracing help customers feel that you care about their total experience with your products and business.

- ✔ **Problem solving:** Often the acid test of customer service; your staff need to be able to recognise when a customer has a real crisis and what your procedure is for helping them.

High customer service standards enable many firms to charge a premium for their products. Yet in many ways, good customer service can be a nil-cost item. After all it takes as much effort to answer the phone politely as it does with a surly and off-putting tone. So improved customer service is one route to increased profitability.

Carrying out mystery shopping

No, mystery shopping is not the feeling of surprise that comes over you when you unpack the result of your weekly family shop at the supermarket. Mystery shopping is the process that investigates your staff's service, friendliness, speed, and product knowledge to ensure that your customers are being well cared for.

Mystery shopping is the evaluation, measurement, and reporting of customer service standards by use of agents acting as if they were customers. It is arguably the fastest and most effective method of obtaining hard objective management data about customer service levels. Your employees have to be on their toes for every customer, since any of them could be a mystery shopper.

Companies such as the aptly named Mystery Shoppers (www.mystery-shoppers.co.uk) or National Opinion Polls (www.nop.co.uk/mystery) employ thousands of people around the country who routinely visit thousands of locations, make tens of thousands of phone calls, and ask for millions of quotations or pieces of advice, none of which will result in an order for the business concerned.

Key aspects that mystery shopping can measure:

- Are the staff knowledgeable, helpful and polite?
- Are the staff competent at selling your products and services?
- Do the staff try to sell products or services that are related to the one(s) they are enquiring about?
- How are customers treated when they are complaining or returning products?
- Do the staff comply with all the regulations governing your industry?
- How competitive are your prices and other terms?
- Is your product being properly displayed with the right literature and any other point-of-sale materials?
- Are the premises in a clean workmanlike condition?
- How do your staff perform on the telephone?
- How effective is your Web site?

Rewarding loyalty

The reasons that loyalty improves profitability are: retaining customers costs less than finding and capturing new ones; loyal customers tend to place larger orders; and loyal customers don't always place price first, whilst new ones do. So what works and what doesn't when it comes to keeping customers loyal?

One of the things that hasn't lived up to its promise is customer loyalty cards. When they were launched, retailers made big claims of how they would be gathering tons of invaluable data about customers. But mostly they have been left with huge virtual warehouses of information that hasn't been used.

Analysing the buying habits of millions of shoppers as their cards are swiped at the till can be prohibitively expensive and few companies have used much of the data gathered to make their customers feel special and hence want to stay loyal.

Asked to give reasons for their loyalty, the top five elements consumers list are:

- ✔ Convenience
- ✔ Price
- ✔ Range
- ✔ Customer service
- ✔ Quality

What this means is that you have to get your basic marketing strategy right and understand what your customer wants and how much they are prepared to pay. If that is wrong no loyalty scheme will keep them on board. Customer service and quality are about getting it right first time, every time. This can usually be helped if you always under promise and over deliver.

The way you handle a customer's complaint can make all the difference between whether a customer comes back or not. Most people who complain will buy from you again if their complaint is handled well.

Care and help-lines, where customers are encouraged to call for advice, information or help with problems, will keep customers loyal and make them more likely to buy from you in the future. If the line is a free phone service it will be even more effective.

Keeping in touch with customers can also bind them more securely. Questionnaires, newsletters, magazines, letters about incentive, customer service calls, invitations to sales events, and 'member get member' schemes are all ways of achieving this result.

Improving Productivity

Improving productivity is a constant requirement for a growth-minded business, not simply an activity during periods of economic recession (when it is still, nonetheless, important – much better than adopting the 'turtle position', pulling in your head and your hands and getting off the road!). Productivity needs to be improved by acting on both your costs and your margins.

Increasing margins can be achieved by changing the mix of products and services you sell to focus on those yielding the best return, or by raising your selling price. Cutting cost has the merit of showing quick and certain returns.

Cutting costs

Costs need to be constantly controlled and balanced against the need for good quality and good service. In particular you need to separate and act on your variable and your fixed costs (see Chapter 5 for more on fixed and variable costs).

Variable cost cutting is always in evidence in recession; witness the automotive and banking staff cuts in the early 1990s and in 2002–3. Cutting variable costs include such things as wages and materials that are directly related to the volume of sales.

Cutting fixed cost such as cars, computers and equipment that do not change directly with the volume of sales should not include scrapping investments in technology that could bring economies and extra nimbleness in the future (like flexible-manufacturing facilities, where, for example, Peugeot has invested in product lines that can turn out two models at once). Many firms, following Japanese practice, increase their use of subcontractors to help offset increased risk.

Equally, alliances between firms, aiming to reduce fixed cost investments, can be advantageous. In the soft drinks industry, Perrier provide distribution for Pepsi in France, while Bulmers reciprocated for Perrier in England, avoiding the need for extra investment in warehousing and transport.

Focusing attention on the 20 per cent of items that make up 80 per cent of your costs will probably yield your biggest savings. The 80/20 rule is helpful in getting costs back into line, but what if the line was completely wrong in the first place?

Budgeting from zero

When you sit down with your team and discuss budgets, the arguments always revolve around how much more each section will need next year. The starting point is usually this year's costs, which are taken as the only facts upon which to build. So, for example, if you spent £25,000 on advertising last year and achieved sales of £1 million, your advertising expense was 2.5 per cent of sales. If the sales budget for next year is £1.5 million, then it seems logical to spend £37,500 next year on advertising. That, however, presupposes last year's sum was wisely and effectively spent in the first place, which it almost certainly was not.

Zero-based budgeting turns the cost argument on its head. It assumes that each year every cost centre starts from zero spending and, based on the goals of the business and the resources available, arguments are presented for every pound spent, *not just for the increase*.

Increasing margins

To achieve increased *profit margins*, which is the difference between the costs associated with the product or service you sell and the price you get in the market, you need first to review your sales. This requires accurate costs and gross margins for each of your products or services (see Chapter 12). Armed with that information you can select particular product groups or market segments that are less price sensitive and potentially more profitable.

No-one rushes out to buy expensive overpriced products when cheaper ones that are just as good are readily available. The chances are that your most profitable products are also the ones that your customers value the most. You should start your efforts to increase margins by concentrating on trying to sell the products and services that make you the most money

Pricing is the biggest decision your business has to make, one it needs to keep constantly under review. Your decision on pricing is the one that has the biggest impact on company profitability. Try the consultants' favourite exercise of computing and comparing the impact on profits of a 5 per cent:

- ✔ Cut in your overheads
- ✔ Increase in volume sales
- ✔ Cut in materials purchased
- ✔ Price increase

All these actions are usually considered to be within an owner-manager's normal reach. Almost invariably, the 5 per cent price increase scores the highest, as it passes straight to the net profit, bottom line. Even if volume falls, because of the effect price has on growth margin, it is usually more profitable to sell fewer items at a higher price. For example, at a constant gross margin of 30 per cent with a 5 per cent price increase, profits would be unchanged even if sales declined 14 per cent. Yet if prices were cut 5 per cent, an extra 21 per cent increase in sales would be needed to make the same amount of profit.

Frequently, resistance to increasing prices, even in the face of inflationary cost rises, can come from your own team members, eager to apportion blame for performance lapses. In these instances it is important to make detailed price comparisons with competitors.

Working smarter

Making more money doesn't always have to mean working longer hours. You could just work smarter and who knows you may even end up working fewer hours than you do now and still make more money.

One way to get everyone's grey matter working overtime is to create smart circles, comprising of people working in different areas of your business who are challenged to come up with ideas to make the business better (and smart rewards, which include extra resources, holidays and recognition for their achievements, rather than cash). You could formalise the process of encouraging employees to rethink the way they work and reward them in such a way as to make their working environment better still.

Rewarding results

If you can get the people who work for you to increase their output, you can improve productivity. The maxim 'What gets measured gets done and what gets rewarded gets done again' is the guiding principle behind rewards, and setting objectives is the starting point in the process.

The objectives you want people to achieve in order to be rewarded beyond their basic pay need to be challenging but achievable too, which is something of a contradiction in terms. Problems start to arise as soon as professional managers and supervisors come on board with experience of working in big companies. They, and probably you yourself, tend to take objectives and the ensuing budgets very seriously. They have to be hit, so it makes sense to pitch on the conservative side.

Rewarding excellent results

Nick White's Ecotravel company sends people to off-the-beaten-track exotic locations and to conservation areas where money goes into research projects. Ecotourists who book with Ecotravel pay to see animals in conservation areas and a proportion of the money they spend on the holiday goes directly to conservation projects.

White expanded slowly until two years ago when he introduced a 'rewarding excellence'

initiative and sales shot up by 40 per cent in just six months. The basis of the reward is an accelerating bonus. If the company hits its sales targets staff share in a 5 per cent bonus. If it exceeds targets the bonus rates rise too. For every 20 per cent of achievement above target the bonus rate goes up 1 per cent. Targets are reset each year using a similar formula but starting from a new and higher base level.

But in a small business growth and improvement percentages have the potential to be much greater than in larger firms. A big business with a third of its market can only grow very quickly by acquisition or if the market itself is growing very fast. A small firm, on the other hand, can grow by very large amounts very quickly. Moving from 0.01 per cent of a market to 0.02 per cent is hardly likely to upset many other players, but it represents a doubling in size for the small firm. However exceptional performance, even in a small firm, will only be attainable with breakthrough thinking and performance. The question may not be how can we grow the business by 20 per cent a year, but how can we grow it by 20 per cent a month.

But if goals are set too aggressively people may leave. Even, perhaps especially, great performers will balk if the hurdle is put too high. You can read about some of the types of reward schemes common in small business in Chapter 11.

A way to get the best of both worlds is to have a performance band rather than just one number. The reward for achieving a really great result should be massive, but if this high goal is missed slightly, the employee is rewarded as if the goal had been set at the level reached. The reward is proportionately smaller, so your rewards budget still balances. This technique can get an 'inspiration dividend'. Teams can be persuaded to set higher goals than they might otherwise have set, and even when they miss them, the year-on-year improvements can be stunning.

Increasing Sales

The most obvious way to grow a business is to get more sales. This is often easier said than done, but there are some tried and proven techniques that usually deliver the goods. A helpful framework to keep in mind is the one developed by the business guru, Igor Ansoff, and named after him as Ansoff's Growth Matrix.

Ansoff's model has four major elements:

- ✔ Business development, which is about getting more customers like the ones you already have and getting them to buy more from you.

- ✔ Market development, which involves entering new markets in your home country or overseas.

- ✔ Product or service development, which involves launching new products or extensions to existing products or services. A courier service adding an overnight delivery service to its existing 48-hour service is an example of this activity.

- ✔ Diversification, which means, in a nutshell, launching off into the unknown.

Getting customers to buy more

This is a no-brainer starting point for achieving profitable growth. Winning a new customer can be an expensive and time-consuming activity, so once you have them the more you can get them to spend with you rather than a competitor, the better your bottom line will be.

You can avoid this experience if you use this framework to categorise your customers:

- ✔ **Courtship:** This is the stage before a customer has bought anything from you. At this stage the customer is suspicious and your objective is to get your first order. Any order will do just to get the relationship underway.

- ✔ **Engagement:** Having got your first order in the bag, your customer may still be moderately suspicious of you and is still not sure if your intentions are wholly honourable. Your goal is to get your first repeat order and cement the relationship. Getting to this stage means that your first order must go well and your customer must be at least satisfied, or delighted if you want to get to the honeymoon stage in your relationship. To make that happen you need to stand out from the crowd and go the extra mile to make that customer feel special by meeting their particular needs.

- ✔ **Honeymoon:** With several repeat orders successfully fulfilled, your customer now trusts you and is susceptible to new ideas. Here you should be looking to increase sales volume. It is almost certain that as a new supplier your customer has not put all their eggs in your basket. Now your task is to get as many eggs as you can and build up to being the preferred and perhaps only supplier.

✔ **Wedlock:** When you first started talking to your customer you were the new kid on the block, to them at least. Your ideas and products or services were refreshingly new and their existing suppliers had had ample opportunity to disappoint them and let them down. Now you have become, or are fast becoming, that old boring supplier. You need to think of ways to keep your relationship exciting and fresh.

✔ **Deadlock:** Your customer has become disenchanted and is considering divorce. The time has come to bring on new products and services to whet their appetite and make them see you as the exciting vigorous supplier you appeared when your relationship started.

Encouraging referrals

Referrals are the most valuable marketing asset any business can have. Whether you are selling direct to an end consumer or user, or operate in the business-to-business arena your goal is the same – to get those using your product or service to talk in glowing terms about their experience with your business.

Passive word of mouth is rarely as effective as encouraging satisfied customers to pass on the glad tidings. Happy customers tell an average of 0.7 other people if they have had a positive experience with you. Unhappy customers tell 11 to 20 other people.

You can make word-of-mouth advertising work, however. It just requires discipline and a programmed effort to ask your customers for referrals. Make it easy for them – give them brochures, flyers, samples, or whatever it takes to make your case. Then follow up.

Discounts for introductions come out of your advertising budget. So you need to work out how much an introduction to a prospect is worth before you can decide on the discount. The rules to follow are:

✔ Be specific in the type of introductions you want. In particular make the sales volume and product specifications clear. There is no point in giving a discount for products on which your margins are already tight.

✔ Have a sliding scale of discount. The more introductions you get the more you give.

✔ Make it easy for people to give you introductions. Send them fax back forms or have a place on your Web site for them to tap in minimum details. A name and company should be enough for you to find the other details you need.

✔ Follow up and let people know that their introduction paid off. People are usually interested in more than just the discount when they give introductions.

✔ Have a specific programme such as member-gets-member and run it as a campaign for a set period of time. Then change the programme and the discounts. That keeps people interested.

✔ Give the discount promptly, but not until the new introduction has bought and paid their bill.

✔ Give extra discount for introductions to loyal customers. Perhaps when the new customer has placed their third or fourth order you can give the extra discount.

✔ Research the market and find out what introductory schemes are on offer in your sector.

✔ Set up a database to monitor the effectiveness of your introductory discount scheme.

Entering new markets at home

Generally the most rewarding market growth for small businesses comes in the first few months and years when the whole of what is known as the home market is up for grabs. New markets can take a number of shapes. The two most common of these are:

✔ Geographic. Once you are confident that you have extracted as much business as you can get from your immediate business area, be that a town, city, or region, move onto another one. You need to make sure that the new geographic area is broadly similar to the one you have been successful in already. For example, Bristol and Bath are broadly similar to Bradford and Sheffield as cities, but if your business has tourists as customers, the last two cities will be less appealing as a new market than the first two.

✔ Demographic. This covers factors particular to customer groups. If you make clothes for women in Bristol, you could consider making clothes for children, men or teenagers also sticking to the Bristol area.

You can get help and advice from Business Link (www.businesslink.org) who can provide practical support in this area and in most other areas of marketing your business.

Selling overseas

Motley Fool's entry into the German market involved a modest change in a well-proven product, as for its entry to the British, French, and Italian markets between 1998 and 2001. But expanding overseas is not quite as easy as it looks.

Painting the landscape with art shops

Megan started her first reproduction modern art shop in St Ives, Cornwall in 2000. That went well, so using the same basic criteria for layout and location, she opened her second shop in Padstow a year later and a third in Falmouth in the following year.

Megan reckoned that tourists, who make up 80 per cent of her market, spend most of their time within a dozen miles of their holiday cottage, caravan, or hotel. So by opening more outlets at least 12 miles apart she is not in danger of cannibalising her sales from an existing shop.

Marks and Spencer made a mess of its foray into America and retired in some ignominy from the French market, closing 38 stores virtually overnight and exciting the wrath of the French trade unions on the way. The Body Shop, a world business if ever there was one, found it hard going in the French market, where people take beauty, as they do wine, rather more seriously than most.

Don't let these stories of failure discourage you. After all, millions of businesses export successfully and you can always get some help in getting started.

You can get a package of help put together by Trade Partners UK (www.tradepartners.gov.uk/exportusa/overview/introduction/introduction.shtml), the government's export advisory organisation. Trade Partners UK tackles the issues identified as the most important ones facing companies exporting to the US market for the first time.

To be eligible to apply for Export USA, a service to help small firms find customers in that market, you should have an established record of trading in the UK; be new to the US market although not necessarily new to exporting; and be nominated by your local Business Link or Trade Association as being likely to succeed. The final choice of those to be supported through Export USA is made by Trade Partners UK and the British Trade Office in New York.

Companies selected for Export USA are expected to pay a one-off fee of £1,000 (including VAT) before they can access the package of help. Successful applicants have access to all five elements of the package as set out below:

- ✔ Ongoing contact with a named trade officer at one of the British Consulates in the US

- ✔ An initial market assessment, and advice on how to proceed, from the trade officer

- ✔ Participation in a two- or three-day course at a university business school, on marketing to the US, arranged by Trade Partners UK

✔ A visit to a US trade fair or event relevant to the individual company's particular industry and needs

✔ Advice on commercial publicity, including a *New Product from Britain* press release

Once accepted onto the Export USA programme you receive one year's free membership with the British-American Chamber of Commerce.

Adding new products or services

At one end of a spectrum are truly new and innovative products; at the other are relatively modest product or service line extensions. For example, Amazon's Music and Video/DVD business could be seen as product line extensions of their book trade. Their Tools and Hardware operation looks more like a new product. New to them, of course, not to the thousands of other businesses in that sector.

Most new products are unsuccessful. A new product has to be two or three times better in some respect – price, performance, convenience, availability – to dislodge a well-entrenched rival.

They don't necessarily have to be your new products and services, of course. Alliances, affiliations, joint ventures, and the like abound.

The sources of successful new products include:

✔ Listening to customers, who can tell you their needs and dissatisfactions with current products and services.

✔ Your sales team, who are also close to the market and so can form a view as to what might sell well.

✔ Competitors who are first to market usually make lots of mistakes on the way. Following in their wake you can avoid the worst of their errors and succeed where they have not.

✔ Exhibitions and trade fairs are where other firms, not necessarily competitors, but those on the margins of your sector meet and exchange ideas. Products and services that work well in one environment may be adapted for use in your market with little cost.

✔ Markets that are known to be in advance of your own. Many new ideas start their lives in the US and only arrive in Europe 18 months to five years later. Following trends there will give you useful pointers for successful new products in your own market.

✔ Research and development departments often throw up innovative ideas for which there are no obvious market need. You may know of profitable ways to exploit those technologies.

Sitting pretty together

Online women's network, iVillage, and personal care products merchant Unilever have created an independently managed dot.com to market beauty products online. For Unilever this represents a new channel to market. The company will focus on beauty needs, beauty-related services, content, and commerce solutions. iVillage's contribution was its beauty channel along with several other properties and advertising support.

This venture increased iVillage's reach from its home market in the USA to the 88 countries in which Unilever has a physical presence. The new company, based in New York, will look to generate revenues through advertising, sponsorships, and e-commerce sales of beauty and personal care products. iVillage.com's rich, independent editorial content coupled with Unilever's marketing prowess hopes to create an unparalleled force in the beauty and personal care marketplace, both parties hope.

Diversifying as a last resort

Diversification involves moving away from the products, service and markets that you currently operate in, to completely new areas of business. This is the riskiest strategy of all – selling things you know little about to people you know even less about. Sure you can do market research and buy in industry expertise but there is still a risk.

Companies that succeed in diversifying do so by hastening slowly, sometimes by acquisition, and above all by listening to customers and front-line staff.

Unless you can quantify the value added in an acquisition or diversification, for example in better buying with quantity discounts or by being able to spread your costs over a bigger sales volume, don't bother.

However, if you can get acquisitions right, the growth through diversification can be phenomenal.

Part IV
Making the Business Grow

"Are you hiding something from us, Mr Dingwall?"

In this part . . .

Growing your business will be the biggest and most rewarding challenge of all – if you can get it right. Running a bigger business takes no more hours a day than running a small one, but it can be a whole lot more profitable.

A growing business usually means taking on more people, and more people means a change in your role. The best way to move forward is to get others to do what you want them to do, because they want to do it. The trick in accomplishing that small miracle involves building teams and delegating tasks for them to carry out, with your key task to become an effective leader and motivator.

Chapter 16

Franchising for Growth

· ·

In This Chapter

▶ Seeing if adding a franchise could help your business grow

▶ Reviewing the range of franchise options

▶ Establishing the procedures for getting a franchise pilot off the ground

▶ Understanding the risks

· ·

*F*ranchising is a great way into business; it's a great way to grow a business too. Over 652 different types of franchise are on offer somewhere in the world so it's hard to see how you can't find one that suits your needs and aspirations.

Franchising is a marketing technique used to improve and expand the distribution of a product or service. The franchiser supplies the product or teaches the service to the franchisee, who in his turn sells it to the public. In return for this, the franchisee pays a fee and a continuing royalty based usually on turnover. They may also be required to buy materials or ingredients from the franchiser, giving them an additional income stream.

You have two possible strategies for harnessing the power of franchising to your business. You could consider taking on a franchise that is complementary to your existing business or you could franchise your own business concept, taking on self-employed franchisees instead of hired-in managers to run your new branches or outlets.

Finding the Right Franchise

Over 400 different types of franchise are currently on offer in the UK. This pool of franchise opportunities is being added to each year with the steady influx of new franchise chains, particularly from the US and Canada, who have between them over 4,000 franchisers, operating 310,000 franchised outlets.

Adding a franchise

In August 2003, Harrods, London's up-market department store, opened the first UK outlet of Krispy Kreme Doughnuts. For Harrods the sales of doughnuts are complementary to their other food and beverage sales, so it represents pure extra revenue. For Krispy Kreme, it's a chance to enter the UK market that they believe is ripe for development as there is no dominant doughnut brand in the market.

The aim in adding a franchise to your existing business is to *leverage,* as the business gurus would say, your customer or resource base, in order to get more sales per customer or square metre of space.

So if your customers are buying chocolate, sweets, and stationery from you, adding a freezer with ice cream is no big deal. Chances are the ice cream supplier will be so keen to extend their distribution that they will throw in the freezer cabinet for free. You are taking someone else's business model, product, and support systems and bolting them on to your business to add turnover and profits.

Knowing what to look for

So how should you go about looking for a franchise? Well, for a start it should meet all the criteria you can identify in Chapter 3 that lead you to start up your main business.

The franchise you are considering may be new or it may be already established. There is nothing wrong with a product or service being new, provided it has been tested and found to work, preferably for at least a couple of years in a location or community similar to that for which it is now being offered (as is a condition for membership of the British Franchise Association) and provided also that the franchisee is satisfied that it enjoys a good reputation among users and customers. Equally, there is no automatic guarantee of success in dealing with an established product or service. You must check whether the market is growing, static, or declining. Where the franchise relates to a new or established product or service, you need to be satisfied that it has staying power, to what extent the demand is seasonal (people in the UK are less addicted to ice cream in winter than in some other countries) and whether its appeal is to any extent confined to a specific age group or sector of the community.

Check whether the franchise product has some unique feature protected by a patent or trademark. If its success is tied to a celebrity name, you will have to find out how active the celebrity is in promoting it and judge how durable his or her fame is likely to be.

Judge how competitive the product or service is in price and quality with similar ones on the market and, in particular, available in your vicinity.

These points are all brought painfully home each year by the well-publicised failures of one or two franchisers that were thought, even by the banks, to be soundly based. In each case, though, questions addressed to the actual franchisees would have shown that all was far from well. In other words, there is no substitute for first-hand investigation and research – not even expert hearsay.

Searching for a business

There are literally dozens of ways of finding out more about franchise opportunities. The best starting point is a discussion with your bank manager. This may seem a bit far-fetched – after all you may not necessarily be looking for money. But the chances are that the franchiser who runs the chain will have run their plans past one of the major clearing banks to ensure that they will view with favour any business plans put forward by their potential franchisees. The big five banks have lent over £150 million to franchisees and even have special departments to oversee their franchise business. They track the performance of major franchise chains and can offer advice and assistance in evaluating them. The Royal Bank of Scotland (www.rbs.co.uk/franchise) and Barclays (www.barclays.co.uk/business.html) are particularly strong in the franchise area, but the others are well represented too.

If you are taking up a franchise you may find that some banks offer a special franchise funding facility, which has been put together with the help of the franchiser. This will make getting that loan much easier than going to the bank with your own business idea and plan.

After the banks come a number of consultancy businesses specialising in the sector. Big accountancy practices such as BDO Stoy Hayward (www.bdo.co.uk) and legal firms such as Brodies (www.brodies.co.uk) and Mundays (www.mundays.co.uk) all offer high quality advice and contacts in the field.

The sector has a sprinkling of magazines describing franchises in detail, giving case histories and listing current franchise opportunities. *Franchise World* (www.franchiseworld.co.uk) and *The Franchise Magazine* (www.franchise-magazine.co.uk) are amongst the leaders in the sector. Newspapers such as *The Daily Telegraph*, *Daily Mail*, and *The Sunday Times* all have franchise sections each week and sponsor exhibitions in London and Birmingham where you can meet both franchisers and franchisees. Don't forget that great book, *Franchising For Dummies*, by Dave Thomas, that covers pretty well everything you could possibly need to know.

There are dozens of Web sites that offer franchises for sale. These include: *Daltons Weekly* (www.daltons.co.uk), *Grant Thornton* (www.companiesfor-sale.uk.com) and *Which Franchise?* (www.whichfranchise.com).

Investigating and appraising

Most franchisers have discovered that the hard sell is neither in their own interest nor that of the franchisee. Successful franchising is a question of mutual dependence and a franchisee who finds or feels that they has been sold a pup is not likely to be a co-operative member of the franchise family.

The 1973 Fair Trading Act offers very little specific legal protection to the franchisee. Basically, what protection there is, is embodied in the franchise agreement but that document is subject to omissions and commissions of wording which can make a great deal of difference to the deal that is being offered to the franchisee. The franchise agreement can also throw much light on the good intent or experience of the franchiser. You should ask a great many questions about the agreement in order to put the provisions of the contract into context. Three areas, aside from the product or service, which may not be fully covered in the contract but which require close investigation and scrutiny are covered in the following sections.

Checking out the territory

Though the franchiser should provide a map showing the exact extent of the territory, this is not in itself a guarantee of absolute protection. Under EC competition laws the franchiser cannot prevent one franchisee trading in another's exclusive territory, though he may decline to license a competitor within it. You can do very little about this except to check for the location or planned location of the next nearest operator of the same franchise.

You should also check whether the agreement specifies any circumstances under which your territory could be reduced.

Examine the rationale behind the territory assignment. Has the franchiser picked it out arbitrarily or has he conducted – as he should have done – market surveys to indicate that the franchise is likely to be viable in that territory? Market research should cover aspects like traffic flows, access, population mix by age and class, and so forth, and the information should be made available to the franchisee.

Checking out the franchiser

The most important questions to put to the franchiser are:

- ✔ How long have you been in the UK?
- ✔ How many outlets have you established?
- ✔ How successful are your franchises?
- ✔ How many franchises have been shut down and why?

Failing a track record in the UK, you need to find out how well they have performed elsewhere and to what extent they have been successful in those markets. You need to make sure those markets are similar to the one you will be operating in, as success in one market is no guarantee of success in other markets.

Investigating the franchise package

Franchisers make their money in a variety of ways. Every franchiser charges an initial fee, a royalty on turnover, and/or a mark-up on goods supplied for resale. However, there can be considerable – and significant – differences in the amounts and the way they are collected.

My advice is to be very careful about franchises with a high initial fee and a low royalty (unless, of course, the franchiser receives part of his income in the form of a mark-up on goods supplied): the franchiser may be of the take-your-money-and-run variety. Equally, low royalties may reflect a high mark-up on the goods and services you're required to buy from the home company. The question then is whether the product being offered is competitive in price.

A low initial fee is not necessarily favourable either – it may mask high royalties or hidden charges. Another point to watch out for is whether the franchiser sets a minimum figure the franchisee must pay, irrespective of income from the franchise. If so, is the amount reasonable? The advice of an accountant would be invaluable.

Related to the question of fees is that of advertising. Increasingly, advertising is a separate and additional charge, currently an average of 2.6 per cent of turnover. As the franchisee, you need to be satisfied that the advertising is good and relevant, both as regards content and medium. Local press, radio, TV, and cinema advertising can be helpful to the franchisee. National campaigns are costly and the purpose behind them may be to sell franchises rather than to further the franchisee's particular business. Nevertheless, some national advertising may be essential if a nationwide franchise chain is to be developed, with its knock-on benefits to individual franchisees.

Franchising Your Business Idea

If your business concept looks as though it could be replicated in several other places, you have a number of choices. The most obvious is to open up more branches. But you could consider a faster, and in some ways safer route, by franchising your business for others to roll out and share the risk.

Weighing the advantages and disadvantages

From the franchiser's point of view, one huge financial advantage is that you don't have any direct investment in any of your franchises. The inventory and equipment are owned by the franchisee.

Because of the shortage of prime sites, there is a growing trend for franchisers to acquire leases on behalf of franchisees or at any rate to stand as guarantors. Nevertheless, the effect on the liquidity of the franchiser, in contrast to expansion by opening branches, is enormous.

However, you do face heavy start-up costs in piloting the franchise and in setting up and maintaining training if you do the job properly. Thereafter there are further costs in providing a continuing service to franchisees in such matters as research and development, promotion, administrative back up, and feedback and communication within the network. The expectation is that these costs are offset because:

✔ The franchisee, as the owner of the business, is more likely to be highly motivated than an employee and more responsive to local market needs and conditions.

✔ As the franchiser, you receive an income from the franchises.

✔ As the franchiser, you can save on personnel and administrative costs by running your operation from a central location. You can negotiate quantity discounts from your suppliers by ordering for all your franchises at the same time.

✔ As the franchiser, you realise some of the benefits of expanding your business without direct financial involvement.

On the other hand, the failure of an individual franchise may reflect badly on your entire business, even though you have no direct control. In extreme cases, you may terminate or not renew a franchisee's agreement, but you cannot fire the franchisee as you could an employee.

As a franchiser, you are dependent on the willingness of the franchisee to observe the rules and play the game, and any failure of the franchisee to do so is equally and perhaps more damaging to you and to other franchisees than it is to the wayward franchisee.

Sometimes the mixture of dependence and independence of franchising produces a curious problem. The franchisee is encouraged to think of him or herself as an independent business entity and to a large extent this is indeed the situation. Nevertheless, he or she is operating your business concept under a license and pays a fee to do so. The franchisee may identify so closely with the business that he or she resents having to pay a fee, feeling that the franchise's success is due to his or her own efforts, not to the franchise concept or to you, the franchiser. This is apt to be particularly so if the franchiser adopts a low profile, either in terms of direct help or in matters such as national advertising. Clearly, of course, the franchisee is obliged to pay under the terms of the agreement, but a sour relationship is not good for either party, so it is up to you to maintain your part of the bargain both in letter and in spirit. Franchises are a matter of mutual interest and obligation.

Doing the pilot

After a franchise concept has been developed, a pilot operation should be run for a period of at least a year. The pilot should be run by someone as similar to the intended typical franchisee for the chain as is practicable. The aim is to test not just the business concept, but to see if the operating systems have been described well enough for people outside the founding business organisation to run.

Let's use as an example a fast food outlet offering slimmers' lunches. You already own a couple of outlets for which you have found a catchy name, Calorie Counter. You have established a standard image in terms of décor, layout, tableware, menus, and graphics and your staff have a stylish uniform. Your gimmick is that every dish has a calorie rating and a breakdown of the fibre and salt content on the menu, and along with their bill customers get a calorie and fibre count for what they have bought. You also have some recipes that you have pioneered.

In the year since you opened you have ironed out most of the start-up bugs and learned a lot about the catering, accounting, and staffing problems in running a business of this kind.

The indication is that there is demand for more restaurants like yours, but you have neither the capital nor the inclination to take on restaurant managers. Being a thorough sort of person you have documented every aspect of running your restaurant, covering everything from recipes, ingredients, and cooking times, to opening hours, wages, incentives, and dress code. You have also standardised your accounting system and linked the electronic till to your raw material and stock systems, so that key ingredients can be re-ordered automatically. From your experience in opening two of your own restaurants you know how and where to advertise, how much to spend, and how sales demand is likely to grow in the early weeks and months. You have captured all this knowledge in a sort of manual, which you propose to use as a guide for whosoever you select to open your next outlet.

You are now ready to run your first pilot franchise. This involves using your manual and procedures with a real live franchisee. True, you may have to give them some incentive to join you in the risk. But whatever you end up negotiating, as long as it gives you the benefits of franchising listed above, you are ahead of the game.

Once your pilot franchisee gets under way you will have the opportunity to test your manual in action. You, after all, invented the business, so you should know what to do in every situation, but seeing if a green franchisee straight off the street can follow your map and get a result is the acid test.

Put what you learn from the pilot into a revised franchise manual, sort out your charging and support systems, and you are ready to start to roll the franchise out.

Finding franchisees

Sorry, but that last sentence in the previous section was a bit misleading. Despite having a great business, a robust and proven business manual, and a couple of pilot runs under your belt, you are not quite ready to roll the franchise out around the world, or even around your neighbourhood. The most recent NatWest/British Franchise Association survey (they do one every year and have done for the last 20) asked franchisers what they consider to be the biggest barrier to the growth of the number of franchises they operate. By far the greatest number of respondents – 41 per cent – said it was the lack of suitable franchisees.

Visit any franchise exhibition, and you visit many if you are serious about growing in this way, and the thousands of people milling around the stands and in the seminar rooms will convince you that there is no lack of interest amongst the general public to taking up a franchise.

 Finding potential franchisees is not a problem. Use the contact details earlier in the chapter to advertise for applicants and attend as many exhibitions as you can and you will have applicants coming out of your ears. Yet turning that latent demand into done deals is not so easy. One international franchise chain only offer franchises to 30 per cent of the people they interview, and they only interview a small fraction of the number of people they see at exhibitions.

This begs the obvious question. What sort of person makes the ideal franchisee? Well, looking at past career patterns may not be much help. Les Gray, chairperson of Chemical Express, the 104-outlet cleaning products franchise chain, lists a postman, a sales manager, a buyer, a farmer, and a shipping agent as the occupations of their most successful franchisees.

Franchisers say they have the most success with franchisees that are motivated, able to work hard, have some management aptitude, good communication and people skills and are *not* too entrepreneurial. They are not looking for people with relevant industry skills and experience, as they want to inculcate candidates into their formula.

Look at Chapter 11 for some other tips on how to recruit and select great people.

Rolling out the franchise

So now you have a proven formula and a steady stream of candidates you are ready for the big roll out. But you still have some choices to make about the best way to expand.

Starting with strategy-led expansion

Taking the strategy-led approach means you carefully select locations and areas that most closely fit your business model. For example, the Hard Rock Café model is what is known as a capital city business. In other words there is room for one only in each major international city. ProntaPrint, on the other hand, can accommodate an outlet in each major business area within a city, or a single outlet in any major town with a population over around 30,000 people.

Your equation depends on your customer profile. A fast print outlet might find the going tough in a seaside town with 20,000 pensioners and 10,000 holidaymakers.

Opting for opportunity-led expansion

Using the opportunity model you build the business around the key resources you find. So if great premises comes on the market 100 miles from your headquarters, it may make good business sense to go for it. Premises only come on the market every seven to ten years, so waiting around can be an impractical option if you are impatient for growth.

The same goes with franchisees. You may want to launch in Brighton, but if you find a great franchisee in Scarborough then maybe that's the place to go for.

Investing in international expansion

Only about 400 of the US's 3,500 franchisers are doing business abroad, but that 11 per cent are doing good business. Chico's Tacos, based in Temulco, Southern California, launched their first overseas franchise in Cairo, the Egyptian capital, only three years after starting up in the US.

The factors that drive franchisers to look at overseas markets are:

- ✔ Saturation of the existing domestic market
- ✔ Relaxation of trade barriers
- ✔ Heightened awareness of global markets and brands
- ✔ Improved transportation and communication systems, which make doing business internationally easier

In addition franchisers are benefiting from the growing awareness of franchising as a concept in countries where it was virtually unknown only a few years ago.

Perhaps the best way into international markets is to sell a master franchise for a particular country or region – the master franchise owner in that region can then develop and sell units there, following your model. You can advertise your master franchise via any of the magazines or networks listed earlier in the chapter. But don't expect a rush until you can prove the concept in your home market.

Chapter 17

Becoming a Great Manager

. . . .

In This Chapter

▶ Seeing why you need a team and how to build one

▶ Planning for your own succession

▶ Learning how to delegate effectively

▶ Developing the right leadership style

▶ Preparing for change

. . . .

*I*n business, one of the simplest profit calculations is profit per employee. Until you become a massive company with more than 500 employees, each employee you add increases your profit. Still we need not worry too much about what happens when you have 500 employees on your hands. Well, not in this book, anyway.

But employees are not a trouble-free resource. To maximise the employee-profit ratio, you have to manage your employees so that they produce quality work for you. You have to build them into teams, and lead and manage them to prepare them for the roller-coaster life of change that is the inevitable lot of a small growing business.

In this chapter, I give you the tools you need to become a successful and effective manager.

Building a Team

Teams are a powerful way to get superb results out of even the most average individual employees. With effective team-work , a small firm can raise its efficiency levels to world-class standards. Some small firms have built their entire success around teams.

A group of people working together is not necessarily a team. A successful sports team will have the right number of players for the game, each with a clearly defined role. There will be a coach, to train and improve players' performances, and there will be measurable goals to achieve in the shape of obvious competitors to beat. Contrast that with the situation that usually prevails in a typical small firm. The number of players is the number who turn up on a particular day, and few have specific roles to play. Some are trained and properly equipped and some are not. For the most part the business's objectives are not clearly explained to employees, nor are any performance measuring tools disclosed. It is highly likely that most of the players in the home team do not even know the name or characteristics of the enemy against whom they are competing.

Clearly a successful sports team and an unorganised group of co-workers have little in common, but what needs to be done to weld people at work into a team is also clearly visible.

Successful teams have certain features in common. They all have strong and effective leadership; have clear objectives; appropriate resources; the ability to communicate freely throughout the organisation; the authority to act quickly on decisions; a good balance of team members, with complementary skills and talents; the ability to work collectively; and a size appropriate to the task.

However talented the soloists are in a small business, in the end it's orchestras that make enough noise to wake up a slumbering customer and make them aware of your virtues as a supplier. But teams don't just happen. However neat the CVs and convincing the organisational chart, you can't just turn out a team-in-a-box. The presumption that people are naturally going to work together is usually a mistake. Chaos is more likely than teamwork.

Looking at types of teams

Just like employees themselves, teams come in all shapes and sizes – or at least a few different types, explained in the following list:

- ✔ **Management teams:** These are groups of people tasked with managing functions and achieving specific results over the long term. You may have, for example, three teams to cover sales, support, and warehousing. The sales team is expected to meet sales targets and the warehouse team to get goods to customers on time. In practice every firm will have its own definition of business functions.

- ✔ **Project teams:** Often cross-functional, made up of people from different areas, project teams can be assembled for any period of time to look at a particular project. That project may be improving customer service, or increasing overall efficiency, or cutting costs. The value of having someone from other functions in these teams is to ensure that too parochial a view is not taken.

- ✔ **Taskforces:** A taskforce is a team put together for a short period of time to look at one narrow issue or specific problem of immediate concern. For example if you propose changing your working hours, you may put together a taskforce to report on the implications for everyone inside and outside the firm. Then a decision based on the best information provided by people most affected by the change can be made.

Small company teams can be made up of anything from two to six people. Anything above six is frankly too unwieldy and will take up more resources than a small firm can afford to devote to one aspect of the business. Even quite small businesses can find they have several teams running at the same time.

Founding principles

Successful teams share common principles, outlined in the following list:

- **Balanced team roles:** Every team member must have a valuable team role. Experts in team behaviour such as R Meredith Belbin have identified the key team profiles that are essential if a team is to function well (full details on Belbin can be found at www.belbin.com or by calling 01223 264975). Any one person may perform more than one of these roles. But if too many people are competing to perform one of the roles, or one or more of these roles are neglected, the team will be unbalanced. They will perform in much the same way as a car does when a cylinder misfires. The key roles as described by Belbin, who developed the team role evaluation system used my many organisations, are:

  - **Chairperson/team leader:** Stable, dominant, extrovert. Concentrates on objectives. Does not originate ideas. Focuses people on what they do best.

  - **Plant:** Dominant, high IQ, introvert. A 'scatterer of seeds' who originates ideas. Misses out on detail. Thrusting but easily offended.

  - **Resource investigator:** Stable, dominant, extrovert, and sociable. Lots of contacts with the outside world. Strong on networks. Salesperson/diplomat/liaison officer. Not an original thinker.

  - **Shaper:** Anxious, dominant, extrovert. Emotional and impulsive. Quick to challenge and to respond to a challenge. Unites ideas, objectives, and possibilities. Competitive. Intolerant of woollyness and vagueness.

  - **Company worker:** Stable, controlled. A practical organiser. Can be inflexible but likely to adapt to established systems. Not an innovator.

  - **Monitor evaluator:** High IQ, stable, introvert. Goes in for measured analysis not innovation. Unambiguous and often lacking enthusiasm, but solid and dependable.

  - **Team worker:** Stable, extrovert, but not really dominant. Much concerned with individuals' needs. Builds on others' ideas. Cools things down when tempers fray.

- **Finisher:** Anxious introvert. Worries over what could go wrong. Permanent sense of urgency. Preoccupied with order. Concerned with 'following through'.

✔ **Shared vision and goal:** It is essential that the team has ownership of its own measurable and clearly defined goals. This means involving the team in business planning. It also means keeping the communication channels open as the business grows. The founding team knew clearly what they were trying to achieve and as they probably shared an office they shared information as they worked. But as the group gets larger and new people join, it becomes necessary to help the informal communication systems work better. Briefing meetings, social events, and bulletin boards are all ways to get teams together and keep them facing the right way.

✔ **A shared language:** To be a member of a business team people have to have a reasonable grasp of the language of business. It's not much use extolling people to improve return on capital employed or reduce debtor days if they have only the haziest notion of what those terms mean, why they matter, or how they can influence the results. So you need to develop rounded business skills across all the core team members through continuous training, development, and coaching.

✔ **Compatible personalities:** Whilst having different team profiles are important, it is equally vital to have a team who can get on with one another. They have to be able to listen to and respect each other's ideas and views. They need to support and trust one another. They need to be able to accept conflict as a healthy reality and work through it to a successful outcome.

✔ **Good leadership:** First-class leadership is perhaps the most important characteristic that distinguishes winning teams from the also-rans. However good the constituent parts, without leadership a team rapidly disintegrates into a rabble bound by little but a pay cheque.

People cannot just be picked and put into teams because of their particular professional or job skills. If the team is to function effectively the balance of behavioural styles has to mesh too.

Coaching and Training

Coaching and *Training* are two ways to help individuals and teams improve their performance. Coaching is carried out by a skilled and experienced person watching an individual or small group performing a task. The coach shows them individually how they can improve their performance. The emphasis is on personalised instruction. Training is usually a more formal process where the trainer has a set agenda for the event based on the knowledge required by the trainees. Everyone being trained goes through much the same process, at the same time.

Small firms are notoriously bad at recognising the need for training of any type. Over 40 per cent of small firms devote only one day or less to staff training each year. Only 13 per cent invest five days or more in training. Amateur football teams spend more time in training than the average small firm, so it is hardly surprising that few teams in that firm ever realise their true potential, or come anywhere near becoming professionals.

And yet all the evidence is that training pays a handsome and quick return.

The choices a small firm has for training are:

✔ **On-the-job coaching:** This is where people learn from someone more experienced about how a job should be done. The advantages are that it is free and involves no time away from work. It should also be directly related to an individual's training needs. However it is only as good as the coach and if they are untrained you could end up simply replicating poor working standards.

✔ **In-house classroom training:** This is the most traditional and familiar form of training. Some, or all, of your employees gather in a 'classroom' either on your premises or in a local hotel. You hire in a trainer or use one of your own experienced staff. This method provides plenty of opportunity for group interaction and the instructor can motivate the class and pay some attention to individual needs. The disadvantages, particularly if it is help away from your premises, are that you incur large costs that are more to do with hospitality than training and it is time-consuming and difficult for a small firm to release a number of its employees at the same time.

✔ **Public courses:** These are less expensive than running a training pro-gramme in a hotel. You can also select different courses for different employees and so tailor the training more precisely to their needs. Most public courses are generic and the other attendees are more likely to come from big business or even the public sector so much of what is covered may be of little direct relevance to your business. Quality can be patchy.

✔ **Interactive distance learning:** This kind of training can be delivered by a combination of traditional training materials, teleconferencing, and the Internet and e-mail discussions. You miss out on the personal contact, but the costs are much lower than traditional training. Most of the learn-ing programmes are aimed at larger firms, so some material may not be so relevant. Check Chapter 19 for information on e-training.

✔ **Off-the-shelf training programmes:** These come in packaged kits, which may consist of a training manual, video, and/or a CD-ROM. Once again the cost is lower than for face-to-face training, but you miss out on a pro-fessional trainer's input.

✔ **College courses:** Many universities and business schools now offer pro-grammes tailored for the needs of small firms. Professional instructors who understand the needs of small firms deliver these. They are rela-tively expensive but can often be very effective.

✓ **Government initiatives:** Governments have an interest in encouraging training in small firms. As well as providing information on where their training schemes are being run, governments often provide training grants to help with the costs.

To make sure you get the best out of your training, follow these guidelines:

✓ Introduce a routine that ensures all employees attending training are briefed at least a week beforehand on what to expect and what is expected of them.

✓ Ensure that all employees discuss with you or their manager or supervisor what they got out of the training programme – in particular did it meet both their expectations? This should take place no later than a week after the programme.

✓ You or their manager need to check within a month, and then again at regular intervals, to see whether skills have been improved, and that those skills are being put into practice.

Evaluate the costs and financial benefits of your training and development plans, and use this information to help set next year's training budget.

Appraising Performance

Appraising performance of both teams and individuals is not primarily concerned with blame, reward, or praise. Its purpose is to develop people and help them perform better and be able to achieve career goals. The end result of an appraisal is a personal development plan.

Appraisal lies at the heart of assessing, improving, and developing people's performance for the future of the business. However, to be an effective tool, appraisal needs to be approached seriously and professionally by all involved. The appraisal has to be a discussion between people who work together rather than simply a boss dictating to a subordinate. It should be an open two-way discussion for which both the appraiser and appraisee prepare in advance.

The ground rules for successful appraisals are:

✓ It should be results orientated. The appraisal interview starts with a review against objectives and finishes by setting objectives for the year to come.

Set intermediate goals and objectives for new staff even if final goals can't be realistically set. For example, challenge new salespeople to acquire product knowledge and visit all the key customers, leaving actual sales achievement objectives until later in the year.

✔ The appraisal discussion should be separate from salary review. A discussion about salary is unlikely to encourage people to be open and frank, but an appraisal must be both those things. The salary review and the appraisal must be seen as different events and if possible carried out at different times of the year.

✔ The appraisal format is a narrative rather than tick boxes and ratings schedules. It covers a discussion of achievements, areas for improvement, overall performance, training and development, and career expectations.

Allow plenty of time for each appraisal interview (one and a half hours on average). The setting should be free from interruptions and unthreatening.

Carry out appraisals at least once a year, with more regular quarterly reviews – new staff should be reviewed after three months. Some owner-managers question the necessity of a formal annual appraisal when they feel that they are already appraising their team informally on a day-to-day basis. This approach would be rather like trying to assess a business by its daily trading figures rather than its annual profit and loss account. The changes in behaviour and performance you're trying to assess happen over a longer time-span and may not be easy to see on a day-to-day basis. Also your assessments on a day-to-day basis are likely to be influenced by pressures and feelings on the day and may not reflect the true longer-term picture.

Use appraisals to identify training needs and incorporate any deficiencies into a personal or company-wide training plan.

Developing a Leadership Style

Most large organisations today have grown up according to basic management principles. If you started your business career working for a bigger firm, or your present managers worked in such enterprises, you know the scenario. Managers in these organisations plan, organise, and control in a way that produces consistent, if unexciting results. It's a formula that worked remarkably well for much of the 20th century when all a successful company had to do to prosper was more of the same. But management which is all about maintaining order and predictability is ill-equipped to deal with change, which is the order of the day for the 21st century. To cope with it effectively you need to be a leader as well as a competent manager and young businesses are in greater need of leaders than they are of managers, at the outset at least.

Understanding leadership

Leadership and management are not the same thing, although many business people fail to make the distinction. Peter Drucker, a professor at the University of Southern California, sums up the difference between leaders and managers thus: 'A leader challenges the status quo; a manager accepts it.'

In a world where product life cycles are shrinking, new technologies have an ever-shorter shelf life, and customers demand faster delivery and higher quality, the leader's job increasingly means defining and inspiring change within a company. By setting a company's direction, communicating this to its workforce, motivating employees and taking a long-range perspective, a leader adapts the firm to whatever volatile environment it does business in. In short, the leader becomes the change master in their own firm.

Delegating

Overwork is a common complaint of those running their own business. There is never enough time to think or plan. But if you don't make time to plan you will never move forward.

Delegating some tasks would ease the stress. *Delegation* is the art of getting things done your way by other people. Or as one entrepreneur succinctly put it, 'making other people happy to make you rich'.

Many owner-managers are unable to delegate either because they draw comfort from sticking to routine tasks such as sending out invoices, rather than tackling new and unfamiliar ones such as keeping up on developments in the industry, or because they just don't know how to delegate. Either way, neither the business nor those in it can grow until delegation becomes the normal way to operate.

Delegating brings benefits to everyone involved in the process.

Benefits for the boss include:

- ✔ **More time** to both achieve more today and to plan for the future. In this way time can be freed up to tackle high value-added tasks such as recruitment and selection, or motivation.

- ✔ **Back up** for emergencies and day-to-day tasks. By delegating, you have a reserve of skilled people who can keep the business running profitably if you're not there. This can also give customers and financial backers the comfort of knowing that they are not dealing with a one-man-band whose operation would fall apart without him or her.

Benefits for employees include:

- ✔ **The opportunity to develop new skills:** Failing to delegate deprives employees of the opportunity to learn new skills and to grow themselves, and drives good employees, just the ones a growing organisation desperately needs, away for greater challenges. Employees who have assumed the responsibility for new tasks train their staff in the same way. Then the organisation can grow and have management in depth.

✔ **Greater involvement:** Research consistently shows that employees rank job satisfaction to be of equal or greater value than pay in their working life. Delegation encourages people to take ownership of their decisions and will increase their enthusiasm and initiative for their work, and so get more satisfaction from their work.

Benefits for the business are:

✔ **Efficiency improves** by allowing those closest to the problems and issues being faced to take the decisions in a timely manner.

✔ **Flexibility of operations increases** because several people are able to perform key tasks. In this way teams and tasks can be rotated and expanded or contracted to meet changing circumstances. Delegation also results in more people being prepared for promotion.

Delegating successfully

Delegation is a management process not to be confused with 'dumping', in which unpopular, difficult, or tedious tasks are unceremoniously shoved onto the shoulders of the first person who comes to hand. To make it work successfully you should adopt the following five-point plan for delegating.

1. **Decide what and what not to delegate.**

   The general questions for deciding what should be delegated are:

   - Can anyone else do or be trained to do the work to a satisfactory standard?

   - Is all the information necessary to carry out the task available to the person(s) to whom the task could be delegated?

   - Is the task largely operational rather than strategic?

   - Would delegating the task save you a reasonable amount of time?

   - Would some initial teething problems whilst the new person settles into the task cause undue problems? Delegation itself is a form of risk-taking, so if you can't deal with a few mistakes delegation will prove difficult.

   - Can someone other than you properly exercise direct control over the task?

   Any routine jobs, or information gathering, or assignments involving extensive detail or calculations, can usually be readily delegated. Tasks that are less easy to delegate include all confidential work, discipline, staff evaluation, and complex or sensitive issues.

2. **Decide whom to delegate to.**

The factors to consider here are:

- Who has the necessary skills?

- Who could or should be groomed for future promotion?

- Who is most likely to respond well to the challenge?

- Who is most likely to be or continue to be a loyal employee?

- Whose workload will allow them to take on the task(s)?

3. **Communicate your decision.**

Factors to consider here are:

- Discuss the task you propose to delegate one to one with the individual concerned.

- Confirm that they feel up to the task or agree any necessary training, back-up, or extra resources.

- Set out clearly in writing the task broken down into its main components, the measurable outcomes, the timescales, and any other important factors.

- Allow time for the implications to sink in and then discuss with the person concerned how they propose going about the task.

- Let others in the business know of your decision.

4. **Manage and evaluate.**

From the beginning clearly establish set times to meet with the person delegated to and review their performance. Make the time intervals between these reviews short at first, lengthening the period when their performance is satisfactory. The secret of successful delegation is to follow up.

5. **Reward results.**

Things that get measured get done and those that are rewarded get done over again. The reward need not be financial. Recognition or praise for a job well done are often more valuable to an ambitious person than money.

Barriers to delegation

Delegation is difficult and most people experience a loss of control or a fear that the people they are delegating to are not really capable of doing the task well. You have to understand and manage these natural fears and concerns if you're to succeed at delegating.

These problems are further compounded by the fact that the manager of a small firm is usually the owner or at least part-owner too. As the business owner that means that the ultimate penalty if the person delegated to fails falls back onto you with potentially serious consequences. After all the responsibility for all borrowings rests with the owner and if poor delegation leads to poor business results then the owner will be the one to suffer the most. Also if the business is a limited company, you will be a director. Directors have particular legal obligations that they are not absolved from simply because they delegated responsibility.

The main reasons owner-managers give for being unable to delegate are:

- ✔ **I can do it better and quicker myself.** This may well be true when you start up, but will inevitably lead to being overworked and overburdened. Some key tasks will just not get done or will wait until they become a crisis. Employees will never develop the skills to help you if you don't delegate to them, so working long and often unproductive hours will become the norm for you.

- ✔ **I don't want to lose control.** This is natural and also a major problem for small firms with unsophisticated information systems. It's something of a chicken-and-egg type problem. Without good control systems you will never be able to delegate and still feel in control. But if you do everything yourself, why would you need systems to show others what is going on. For example until you have an accounting system that shows how much money you are owed, by whom, and for how long, it's impossible to effectively delegate the task of collecting money owed to the firm. Without such a system there is no way to define or investigate the task, nor are there the tools to allow the person who has been delegated, to do a good job.

- ✔ **I'm too busy to delegate.** This is a variation of the first barrier. Overworked owner-managers are often disorganised, and have no personal plan. They deal with things as they occur. Without a way to categorise tasks they misallocate their time and so leave insufficient time for key tasks. This creates more problems, taking up more time, and so a vicious spiral begins. Every day starts behind schedule. Until the boss organises their own schedule, building in enough time to plan and delegate properly, the process can't start.

- ✔ **I've tried delegating, but it doesn't save me any time.** Delegation probably won't save the boss any time. All it will do is let them spend the time they want to dedicate to work more productively, profitably, and enjoyably.

- ✔ **I've tried delegating, but they made a mess of it and I had to do it myself anyway.** Like anything else in management things will fail. Learning to how to delegate effectively takes time and practice. It won't happen overnight, but if it doesn't happen the business will never realise its potential.

Evolving leadership styles for growth

Whilst all businesses require leadership, they don't require the same type or amount of leadership all the time. As with children, businesses do not grow seamlessly from being babies to adulthood. They pass through phases: infancy, adolescence, teenage, and so on. Businesses also move through phases if they are to grow successfully. Each of these phases is punctuated by a crisis, a word which derives from Greek and translates loosely as dangerous opportunity.

Researchers have identified several distinctive phases in a firm's growth pattern, and provided an insight into the changes in organisational structure, strategy, and behaviour that are needed to move successfully on to the next phase of growth. This inability to recognise the phases of growth and to manage the transition through them is probably the single most important reason why most owner-managed firms fail to achieve their true potential, let alone their founder's dreams.

Typically a business starts out taking on any customers it can get, operating informally, with little management and few controls. The founder, who usually provides all the ideas, all the drive, makes all the decisions, and signs the cheques, becomes overloaded with administrative detail and operational problems. Unless the founder can change the organisational structure, any further growth will leave the business more vulnerable. The crises of leadership, autonomy, and control loom large.

Over time, the successful owner-manager tackles these crises and finds a clear focus, builds a first-class team, delegates key tasks, appraises performance, institutes control and reporting systems, and ensures that progress towards objectives is monitored and rewarded. The firm itself consistently delivers good results. There is no set time that each of these phases should last. An old economy firm may take anything from three to ten years to reach the third phase of growth.

Each phase of growth calls for a different approach to leading the business. Sometimes strong leadership is required; at others a more consultative approach is appropriate. Some phases call for more systems and procedures, some for more co-operation between staff. Unfortunately, as the business gets bigger most founders try to run their business in much the same way as they did when it was small. They end up with a big small company, rather than the small big company that is required if successful growth is to be achieved. They believe taking on another salesperson, a few hundred square metres' of space, or another bank loan can solve the problems of growth. This approach is rather like suggesting that the transition from infancy to adulthood could be accomplished by nothing more significant than providing larger clothes.

Managing change

Peter Drucker, the management guru, claims that the first task of a leader is to define the company's mission. In a world in which product and service life-cycles are shrinking, new technologies have an ever-shorter shelf life and customers demand ever higher levels of both quality and innovation. Entrepreneurial leadership means inspiring change.

Being flexible enough to change

In adapting the business to an increasingly volatile and competitive environment, the boss must become the change master in the firm. Small firms are usually better at handling change than big firms. A speedboat can always alter course faster than a supertanker. However small firms often have to adapt to much more change than big established firms. Big firms usually define the standards in an industry and it's the small firms who have to scramble to keep up.

Also the turbulence created by changes in the economy can create a wash that can sink small firms unless they can adapt and change quickly. Those small firms most able to adapt and change, and of course those who are most prepared are most likely to survive and prosper during turbulent times.

But recognising the need for change falls a long way short of being able to implement it successfully. Few people like change and even fewer can adapt to new circumstances quickly and without missing a heartbeat.

By definition a small business seeking growth must be able to manage a fast rate of change. Entrepreneurs must see change as the norm and not as a temporary and unexpected disruption, which will go away when things improve.

Planning for change

Change management is a business process, like any other business process. Following a tried and proven procedure can improve your chances of getting it right more often.

These four steps show how you can break down change management into its elements.

1. **Tell staff why change is necessary (or better still help them to find out for themselves).**

   The benefits of change are not always obvious. So spell them out in much the same way as you would explain the benefits of your product or service to a prospective customer.

   Explaining the background to the changes you want to make will help people see the changes as an opportunity to be competitive rather than a threat to existing work practices.

   Better than just explaining is to encourage staff to look outside the business for themselves and identify potential problems and suggest their own solutions. Not only might they have great ideas for change – perhaps better than yours – they will be more willing to accept them and take responsibility for making the changes succeed.

2. **Make the change manageable.**

Even when people are dissatisfied with the present position and know exactly what needs to be done to improve things, the change may still not happen. The change may be just too big for anyone to handle. But if you break it down into manageable bits it can be made to happen.

3. **Take a shared approach.**

Involve people early on. Asking them to join you in managing change only at the implementation stage is too late to get their full co-operation. Give your key participants some say in shaping the change right from the start. This will mean that nobody feels the change is being imposed and more brains will be brought to bear on the problem.

Individual resistance to change is a normal reaction. By understanding why people are resisting you can help them overcome their doubts and embrace the change. Try to anticipate the impact of the change on the people involved:

- Get an overview of the forces at work both in favour of and against the change.

- Make a list of those most affected by the change. Put each person into one of four categories: no commitment; will let it happen if others want it; will help it happen; will make it happen.

    Examine how each person will be affected by the change. Look at career prospects, working hours and conditions, team membership, and so forth.

- Anticipate retraining. Often a fear of failing is the principal reason people won't try something new.

Open, face-to-face communication is the backbone of successful change. It gets across the 'why' of change and allows people to face up to problems openly. It also builds confidence and clears up misunderstandings.

Whilst open communication is vital, it is risky to announce intended changes until you have some committed participants alongside you.

4. **Reinforce individual and team identity.**

People are more willing to accept change and to move from the known to the unknown if they have confidence in themselves and their boss. Confidence is most likely to exist where people have a high degree of self-esteem. Building up self-esteem involves laying stress on the positive rather than the negative aspects of each person's contribution. Exhortations such as 'you guys have had it too easy for too long' are unlikely to do much for people when you are faced with major competitive pressure.

The importance to the change project of each person, both as an individual and where appropriate as a team member, needs to be emphasised. To survive a positive, confident climate for change needs lots of reinforcement, such as:

- Reward achievement of new goals and achieving them quickly

- Highlight success stories and create as many winners as possible

- Have social events to celebrate milestones

- Pay personal attention to those most affected by the change

Change takes longer than you think. Most major changes make things worse before they make them better. More often than not the immediate impact of change is a decrease in productivity as people struggle to cope with new ways of working, whilst they move up their own learning curve.

The doubters will gloat and even the change champions may waver. But the greatest danger now is pulling the plug on the plan and either adopting a new plan or reverting to the status quo.

To prevent this 'disappointment' it is vital to both set realistic goals for the change period and to anticipate the time lag between change and results.

Measuring Morale

How your employees feel about their jobs, their co-workers, the company, and you and other bosses has a direct effect on how well or poorly they do their jobs. You need to stay on top of morale issues to keep your business running smoothly.

The most reliable way to measure morale at work is to carry out an attitude survey. In a big company, such surveys may be accompanied by one-to-one interviews and focus groups. But in a small firm that is not really an option.

In much the same way as you might survey customers to find out how happy they are with your products and services, survey your employees to find out what they feel about their employment conditions. Attitude surveys provide an objective measure to counterbalance the more descriptive view obtained from discussions and gossip. They also provide a useful way to see if morale is getting better or worse over time.

You may decide to introduce attitude surveys because of a particular event, such as a number of key staff leaving at the same time, or some other obvious problem. Change can upset morale and that can have a knock-on effect on business performance. But once started it makes sense to keep the practice up. At the very least, surveying your employees demonstrates your concern, and at the best it gives you valuable pointers to raising morale, output, and profits.

A word of warning: your attitude survey will reveal two basic facts that every attitude survey reveals. The first is that everyone believes himself or herself to be underpaid. The second is that everyone believes that communication is awful. Both these feelings are fairly normal and you can at least draw comfort from that.

Most people believe they are underpaid both by market standards and in relation to the effort they put in. They also believe that the gap between levels is too great. This belief that they are poorly rewarded exists irrespective of how much people are actually paid, or indeed how hard they work. If you ask them why they don't leave, they will tell you about loyalty to a small firm or perhaps, more flatteringly, loyalty to you.

Nearly all employees also believe their boss knows a secret that directly affects them that he or she is not willing to divulge. It may be about restructuring, moving, merging, or outsourcing. This phenomenon happens at all levels. The shop floor believes supervisors have secrets; supervisors believe managers withhold crucial information on plans that involve them; while those remaining managers know the directors are planning their future in secret. So they become convinced there is a communication problem in the organisation because no one will tell them what is *really* going on.

You have to take all the information from your employees into consideration when sizing up the situation, and not just the results of one attitude survey.

Introducing attitude surveys

John Huggett, a young and abrasive entrepreneur, moved south from Yorkshire and bought up a small but seriously troubled engineering factory. The company employed twenty-two people and had shrunk over the years from more than fifty. The business had suffered losses for over a year. Huggett succeeded brilliantly in solving the problems that had built up over the years.

In the process, by his own admission, he came close to committing murder – telephone directories and occasionally the telephone itself flew through the air. John was perceived, not unnaturally given his style and the rescue job he was attempting, as a fire-eating monster. No one saw the human behind the gruff exterior.

At that time it didn't matter. However, as the factory moved into a period of growth and expansion, John recognised that he and the management

team needed to make a conscious effort to change towards a more consensual style of management. People didn't feel empowered and they weren't about to stick their necks out when the blood still ran from the walls. John stood up in front of the workforce of and said, 'We are going to have a different management style, and we are going to change.' He introduced an attitude survey to take the temperature of the water and committed himself, in advance of the survey, to live by its results.

This he and the management team have done, introducing exceptionally effective team briefings, management walkabout and other consultative mechanisms. It took time for the work force to be convinced, but they came to greatly respect John's integrity and open style.

Part V
The Part of Tens

"As we're a new company with a new product, we have to carry out stringent crash tests."

In this part . . .

You probably have a file somewhere marked 'Miscellaneous', which contains all the information that you know you will find really useful *one day*. You can think of this part as being a collection of tips, cautions and suggestions that will help you start-up and grow your business. Read on!

Chapter 18

Ten Pitfalls to Avoid

. . . .

. . . .

Some 400,000 small businesses close down each year in the UK and over half of those closures occur in the first year of trading. Whilst not all of those closures come under the heading of home-busting events, no-one likes to have a personal failure on their hands even if it doesn't wipe them out financially.

This chapter lists the main problems that cripple most small businesses that have to shut their doors in the first year or so.

Knowing Too Little

Running your own business calls for a well-rounded range of expertise. In the early morning you may have to be coach and trainer to a new employee, by mid-morning, coffee-break time in big business parlance, you will be negotiating with the bank for an extra line of credit, mid-day will be spent drafting a marketing strategy, the early afternoon could be spent looking for suppliers for a new product you are thinking of launching. The late afternoon could find you delivering a rush order to a key customer followed by a quick shufty around a competitor's premises and a couple of possible premises for you to move into if you grow as planned. The evening is devoted to drafting a job advertisement and a leaflet, leaving the weekend to get the books up-to-date and the VAT return done.

 Take the time out before you start up to brush up on the range of skills that you are going to need. There are now more opportunities for education and training, at every level, in the small business and management field than ever before. No formal academic qualifications are required for most of the courses and costs are generally modest. In certain cases, participants may be eligible for grants or subsidised training. The bulk of the activities are concentrated in universities and colleges throughout the whole of the UK (see Chapter 7). However, there are a growing number of opportunities for the less mobile to take up some form of home study in the business field in general, and small-business opportunities in particular. With the growth of the Internet it is now practical and worthwhile for UK-based entrepreneurs to get their learning experience from virtually any part of the world (see Chapter 17).

Being Overly Optimistic about the Market

Business starters are by nature optimistic. You have to be to overcome the hurdles both natural and man-made that will appear in your path. But the one area you can't afford to be over-optimistic about is the market itself. That is the one thing you can't change. People can be replaced, products can be improved, and money can be found, as can new premises. But the raw ingredient of any business, the potential market, is a given that cannot be easily changed. True, big businesses talk grandly about educating the market to appreciate their wonderful product or service, but educating markets calls for deep wallets and long time horizons, both in short supply in the small-business world.

Take care not to develop the 'iceberg syndrome'. Don't believe the small number of customers you can see is a sure indication of the great mass of other customers lying hidden below the water-line just waiting to be sold to. It is a fundamental mistake to believe that customers are simply waiting to be sold to and that competitors are either blind or lazy.

Underestimating Start-up Time

Everything in business seems to take longer than you think. Premises take ages to find and even longer to kit out and be ready for use. If you start up before you are ready there is a good chance customers will be disappointed and rush around sharing their displeasure.

Make a chart showing the key tasks that have to be carried out before you can start up your business in the left-hand column, with the timescale in days, weeks or months, as appropriate to your business, across the top of the chart. In the right-hand column show who is responsible for each task.

Draw a bar between the start and finish date for each key task, showing how long the task will take. Some of the tasks will overlap others and some will be dependant on the successful completion of earlier tasks. For example you can't install the oven in a restaurant until you have found the premises and signed the lease. You can, however, research oven suppliers and negotiate the price and delivery. Use the chart to monitor progress and take corrective action as you go.

Spending Too Much to Start

New businesses should be lean and mean. Don't spend too much on fixtures, fittings, and equipment too soon. People with a background in big business often start with extravagantly high standards. They expect the latest computer equipment, broadband ISP, colour photocopier, and cappuccino maker close to hand, and to sit in an executive-style office from the outset. These overheads have to be spread across the products/service sold and you can lose your competitive edge by being too expensive. See Chapter 8 for information on start-up costs

Mistaking Cash for Profit

The cash that flows into the business hasn't had any of the automatic deductions knocked off it, as has a pay cheque from an employer. So the money that comes in is 'gross' cash flow. It may be real cash, but it is not really yours, or at least not all of it. There may be a temptation to use this cash to maintain your living standards, but don't yield to it. When the bills come in – from the suppliers, for National Insurance, for VAT – as they inevitably will, you may be stuck for the cash to pay them. The Inland Revenue and Customs and Excise put more businesses into liquidation than anyone else.

Maintain a cash flow forecast on a rolling quarterly basis. In that way you will always have a one-year view as to what is likely to happen to the cash in the business. Use the cash flow projection to anticipate peaks and troughs in cash flow.

Use a spreadsheet and either write the program yourself or use the template that comes with your accounting software. Manual cash flow systems are inefficient and discourage regular updates. On the other hand spreadsheet updates are simple, efficient, and free of arithmetic errors, at least.

Choosing the Wrong Partner

A partnership is to business life what a marriage is to the rest of your life – a long-term, all pervading relationship that spills over into and impacts on everything you do. Partnerships are complicated affairs, relying as much on chemistry as on personal attributes, skills, or knowledge. Just as you should never embark on a marriage without a few months of dating, at the very least, you should find a way to test out a partnership before you formalise the relationship. (See Chapter 4 for the legal aspects of partnerships.)

Take on a project together that involves using the skills and expertise you hope your prospective partner will be bringing to the business. If you want them to do the buying, for example, go to a trade show together, preferably one that involves a couple of days travelling to and from the venue. Watch them at work talking to exhibitors and opening up negotiations. Get them to meet others involved with your business, your spouse, bank manager, key clients, in fact anyone who knows you well, and get their reaction.

The big thing to keep in mind is that a business partnership is likely to last longer than the average marriage. So if you can't face that, don't start it.

Ignoring Accounting

Many owner managers see accounting as a bureaucratic waste of time that is only carried out to keep the tax authorities off their backs and make it easier for those authorities to carve a deeper trough in their hard won profits. Now whilst it is possible to have some sympathy with that point of view it can't be condoned. For too many new businesses their first year's accounts are also their last. By the time they really know what is going on it may be too late to put things right.

Part of the problem is that accounting is seen as a historic process tracking events that have already happened. So if it has already happened it's too late to worry about it – right? Wrong. If you have the financial information quickly you can take corrective action quickly and perhaps save a bundle. Suppose your raw material costs are rising sharply. Unless you reflect this promptly in your prices, or reduce costs in some other way, your gross margin will come down and profits will dip. Now if you don't get to hear about this margin dip until the auditors tell you when they put your accounts together from the bundles of bills you keep in those shoe boxes, you will be in deep trouble. Instead of a small problem you may well have a disaster on your hands. 'Frequent accounting makes for long friendships', at least that is what Paccioli claimed in 1494 in his book on double-entry bookkeeping.

Forgetting Working Capital

Most business starters can work out how much the big-ticket items will cost – computers, vehicles, and office furniture for example. But they often forget to allow for the recurring items such as money owed by customers, stock-in-trade, and 'invisible' items such as insurances. To make matters more complicated these items often have time lags associated with them. A customer who owes you money has to be financed until they pay up, as does your raw materials until they can be turned into saleable product that has been delivered and paid for. These items constitute a business's working capital (Chapter 12 talks about working capital), and the more successful you are the more of a problem working capital will become.

Think about it. The first thing that happens when you get a new big order is you need the ingredients or raw materials to put it together. Your suppliers expect payment within 30 days, or perhaps even on a pro forma basis (cash with delivery) in your early months of trading. But the snag is that you have to work up your product using bought-in raw materials, which may take weeks or months, and then wait for months for payment. In the meantime you are hung out with a growing need for working capital. The paradox is that nearly as many businesses go bust with the sales curve going up, as with it going down. The technical term for this is overtrading and the cure is to allow for it in your business plans and make sure you have sufficient working capital in place to survive.

Having No Clear Competitive Advantage

There has to be something unique about either you or your product or service that makes you stand out from your competitors. It could be something as obvious as being open later or longer. Or it may be a policy such as the John Lewis Partnership's 'never knowingly undersold' message. Whatever your unique selling proposition is, communicate it effectively. (See Chapter 6 for more on competitive advantage.)

Choosing the Wrong Location

Where you conduct your business and how much rent you pay is vital. Don't be tempted to take premises just because the rent is cheap – there is usually a reason, such as few customers pass that route or transport links are poor making it difficult for employees and suppliers to get to.

Equally don't take on an expensive town centre site if your turnover is unlikely to cover your outgoings. Your market research (see Chapter 5 for more on this) should help you identify a suitable location.

Chapter 19

Ten People to Talk to Before You Start

In This Chapter

▶ Identifying all the key people who can help you get started

▶ Leveraging your network of contacts to maximum advantage

▶ Getting the lowdown on what people really think are your strengths and weakness

Starting up a business can be a lonely business, but you don't have to do it all on your own. There are hundreds of people, some just a few feet away, who can give you useful insights into your skills and attributes and they may even have a useful perspective on the viability of your business idea.

Speaking with Your Spouse

Your spouse may not know a great deal about your great business idea, but you can be sure they know a lot about you. Your spouse can remind you of your weaknesses and help you play to your strengths. They also need to be prepared for the long hours and lack of holidays that are sure to feature in the early months and years as you get your business established. This may mean that the existing share out of household and family tasks such as taking children to school, family visits and painting and decorating, have to be re-divided to reflect the new balance of work. That may prove contentious, so talking the issues through at the outset will save conflict and arguments when time constraints really start to bite.

The money put into the business will have an impact on the money available for other areas of family expenditure so your spouse will also have to be comfortable with the financial commitments you are taking on. Unlike most other investments you may have made, on houses and cars for example, the money put into a business could all be lost irrevocably.

One would-be entrepreneur who set out to open a bookshop was reminded by their partner how they disliked dealing with the general public. They loved books and delighted in visiting book fares and auctions. But once reminded that essentially the job entailed opening and closing a shop six days a week, the enthusiasm level took a dive. Better take a dive before you start up than have your cash take a dive a few weeks afterwards.

Making Use of Your Professional Network

The people in your network of associates have large chunks of the knowledge you need to get your business successfully launched. The ability to create and maintain strong professional relationships is an important key to business success. Networking is the vital business skill that lets you cultivate lasting business relationships and create a large sphere of influence from which you can find new clients, contacts, referrals, and opportunities.

You can use a network for just about anything from finding a new supplier to getting introductions to overseas sales agents. You can find a reliable bank manager, a new accounting software package, or a great venue for your next business meeting. Your network contacts, unlike almost everyone else in the business world, are usually unbiased and authoritative. You should make few major decisions without recourse to network contacts.

Benefiting from Entrepreneurs Who Started a Similar Business

Now it may come as a complete surprise but there is nothing people like more than to talk about themselves and their successes. Obviously if someone thinks you are going to steal their customers they will shut up like a clam. But if the business you plan to start is unlikely to infringe on their sphere of activities then most established entrepreneurs will be only too happy to pass on some of their hard-earned tips.

First establish that you are not going to tread on their toes. For example if you plan to start up in the same line of business 30 miles away, there is little chance you will cause each other much trouble. You might be able to open a shop at the far end of the same town as a competitor without doing them any serious damage.

Use your common sense as to who to approach and, to be on the safe side, double the distance that you feel is a safe gap between you.

You might also find someone who has had a business failure in the field you plan to start up in and would be prepared to talk. You can find such people by scouring the press or talking to trade associations and other operators in your sector.

Spending Time with a Friendly Banker

Bankers see a lot of different people about a lot of different businesses. You can draw on their wide range of knowledge and experience. Your banker may be familiar with your type of business, the location you're interested in, or have advice on different financing options.

Start by talking with a bank manager you don't want to borrow money from. Begin the conversation by asking for advice, rather than their money. Only when you have convinced yourself that your proposition is an appropriate one for a bank should you make the pitch. (See Chapter 8 for more about banks and bank managers.)

Tapping into Your Local Enterprise Agency Director

There are over 1,000 business experts sitting in a local office somewhere near you just waiting to offer advice, help, encouragement, and support to anyone thinking about starting a business. The even better news is that the services they provide are either free or low cost. Enterprise Agencies (see Chapter 7) have been around for 25 years and are an initiative started by big business to help small business.

Bank managers, business executives on loan as part of their career development, and the occasional civil servant, accountant, and lawyer, staff these agencies. Make sure you grab your fair share of this expertise.

Communicating with Your Current Boss

Talking to your boss about anything other than the job in hand is always a tricky decision. Talk about your entrepreneurial vision too soon and you will find yourself sidetracked for promotion and pay rises and perhaps even first in line for the next downsizing event. Leave it too late and they will see your action as disloyalty at best and betrayal at worst. If you plan to start up in the same line of work and maybe even try to take some key accounts with you, then better talk to a lawyer rather than your boss. But if the climate is right and you can talk to your boss then a number of valuable things could happen. She or he could be a source of investment capital, a business partner, or a useful source of business advice and contacts.

Your boss could even become your first customer, if the businesses are compatible.

Calling Your Colleagues

Those you have worked alongside over the years have formed a view about your talents. Whilst your spouse has seen you after work, they have seen you at work. If they don't know your strengths, weaknesses, foibles, and desires, then no one does. At the worst they will tell you that you are barmy and explain why, at best they will join you in the venture or invest their hard earned savings in your business.

If you were thinking about taking a partner then casting your eye around your colleagues would be a good place to start looking. Remember, it cuts both ways. Whilst they may know a lot about how you perform at work, you know as much about them.

Find someone compatible and trustworthy and give him or her some idea of your plans. If they are enthusiastic and offer to help with the legwork, per-haps investigating the market or looking out for premises, then you could have a result. They may even have been harbouring similar dreams them-selves and just needed the spur of your approaching them to trigger them into action.

Bringing in Your Best Friend

On the assumption that your best friend is not your spouse, then here is someone else who should be able to tell you if you are the right sort of person to start up the particular business you have in mind. You could start out by asking them to review your skills and knowledge inventory (see Chapter 3) and so provide a valuable crosscheck on your self-assessment. In fact you should always find someone who knows you really well to go through this and the business idea evaluation process (also in Chapter 3). Unfortunately everyone's capacity for self-deception is unlimited, and no opportunity for a reality check should be missed.

Reporting to an Accountant

You need an accountant in any event (I explain the process of finding one in Chapter 11). However you should not miss out on making the maximum use of as many accountants as possible when researching to establish your business. Take all the free advice you can get, as most accountants will give you a free first meeting in the hope of signing you up as a client.

Pump them for as much as you can for any tips, pointers, or advice on the business you have in mind.

✔ Accountants are the first port of call for any entrepreneur seeking help and advice, ahead of bank managers, small firms advisers, and business associates. As a consequence they are the repositories of an enormous amount of information on every aspect of business, not just finance.

✔ Accountants draw an increasing amount of their revenue from non-accounting tasks and some even make more money from providing general business advice than they do from auditing.

✔ Most accountants are sole traders or in small partnerships operating in much the same way as you plan to do when you set up your business. So unlike bank managers, who all work in large organisations, accountants can identify with your problems and concerns.

Plugging into a Business Angel Network

Business angels (see Chapter 8) have some attractive attributes. They are not so risk averse as venture capital firms, they act more quickly, putting up money in weeks rather than months, and they are not so fussy about your pedigree. But when it comes to giving a helping hand they are absolute stars. Using the business angel networks you can find an angel with expertise in the sector you have an interest in.

Chapter 20

Ten Ways to Make E-Training Work For You

● ●

In This Chapter

▶ Getting the smartest brains on the planet to train and develop you for absolutely nothing

▶ Imbedding e-learning into every aspect of your business

● ●

*T*here is absolutely no way a small business can routinely afford high quality classroom-based training. It costs too much and in any case small firms simply can't afford to have their staff off the premises for days at a time. In a business with 1,000 employees, having ten people away being trained is fine. In a business with ten employees, having three away is a disaster in the making.

So whilst it is both possible and desirable to do some of your training in the classroom you will have to consider a more innovative and cost-effective way to ensure you and your team can outsmart your competitors. Luckily help is at hand. At a press conference on 4 April 2001, the Massachusetts Institute of Technology (MIT) announced its commitment to making virtually all of its courses freely available on the World Wide Web for non-commercial use as part of its long-standing objective to focus the contributions of both its faculty and its new technologies on broad, societal benefits. MIT is just one of hundreds of universities and institutions around the world that are making knowledge widely available either for free or at a fraction of the cost of classroom-based training. To get the best out of e-learning follow these ten guidelines.

Linking Training Goals to Business Strategy

Training and development are core elements of your business strategy. The starting point in the process is to decide on your business goals and objectives (see Chapter 5) and decide how training will support them. For example if your primary goal is to capture new customers then everyone who works in the business, not just the sales team, needs to be induced with the basic selling skills.

Determining What Training Your Staff Needs

Once you know the skills, attributes, attitudes, and abilities required by your employees to meet your goals, then the next logical task is to find out their current state of knowledge. If this has not been done during routine performance appraisals (see Chapter 15), then it will have to be done as a one-off exercise before training and development can commence.

One great strength of e-training is that you can pick training packages to meet both the content needs and time constraints of each individual employee. Conventional classroom-based training is rarely cost effective unless there are eight or ten people to be trained, numbers that few small firms are likely to have. So all you need to do is look down your list of training needs and match those up to the resources listed in the e-training catalogue of a particular provider.

Don't forget that employees don't stay put for very long. On average people stay with one firm less than ten years and in some industries five might be closer to the norm. So you have to allow for that in your thinking and may consider building any new skills required into your recruitment job specification.

Choosing the Best Means

The worrying number to remember here is that fewer than 30 per cent of trainees complete a typical e-training program and achieve the desired output. To overcome the fickleness of e-learners you will have to ensure the content is as interesting as possible. Based on your budget, media format, and bandwidth, choose among video, audio, digital photos, animations, drawings, and clip-art to capture the learner's attention.

When it comes to visual material, do try not to confine your training programme usage to that which can be found on a standard PowerPoint program. Good though these are, they are unlikely to provoke surprise, and surprise is a useful way to maintain interest over the life of a program. Try to select an e-learning program that involves people by including thought-provoking questions, case studies, surveys, analogies, quizzes, and tests.

Include real world examples from your business environment; photos, sample documents, charts, and interviews and so forth will all help to make the content more relevant to the job and hence be more likely to be used and useful.

Build in practise time as each new concept is presented. Make sure the program includes assessment questions after each major concept to test for understanding throughout, not just at the end. Create case studies or scenarios in which learners are asked to apply the knowledge and skills learned rather than just demonstrate recall.

Use a blended approach. Just because you are using e-training doesn't mean you have to chuck over tried and proven classroom methods. Put the learning methods to the tasks they are best suited to. Decide which parts of the curriculum need to be offered asynchronously, synchronously, and face-to-face. Consider whether topics need in-person interaction and support (face-to-face), require guided instruction and facilitation (synchronous e-learning), or can be done independently with minimal support (asynchronous e-learning).

Asynchronous training is e-learning in the more traditional sense of the word. It involves self-paced learning, CD-ROM-based, network-based, intranet-based, or Internet-based. It may include access to instructors through online bulletin boards, online discussion groups, and e-mail. Or, it may be totally self-contained with links to reference materials in place of a live instructor.

Synchronous training is done in real time with a live instructor facilitating the training. Everyone logs in at a set time and can communicate directly with the instructor and with each other. Trainees can ask questions and even view a whiteboard, in much the same way as they would in a conventional classroom. Training lasts for a set amount of time – from a single session of ten minutes upwards to several weeks, months, or even years. This type of training usually takes place via Internet Web sites, audio- or video-conferencing, Internet telephony, or even two-way live broadcasts to students in a classroom.

You can get online support for both synchronous and asynchronous training methods. Online support comes in the form of forums, chat rooms, online bulletin boards, e-mail, live instant-messaging support and knowledge databases offering indexed explanations and guidance. Online support offers the opportunity for more specific questions and answers, as well as more immediate answers.

Create a curriculum of courses rather than one long master course designed to teach all people all things. Divide material into modules that can be completed in less than 30 minutes and include some shorter and longer modules, too, for those occasions when learners have more or less time to devote to their studies. Be sure to specify how each piece of learning fits in with the others and what essentials are needed before completing each section.

Preparing Training and Development Plans

Break down the curriculum into concise skills based on job needs. Be sure to relate each training skill to a job skill. List objectives in terms of skills, not prior courses taken. For example, rather than stating that the *Introduction to Access* course is a pre-requisite to the training, list the skills the learners must have mastered, such as creating a database, carried out a query, prepared a report, and so forth.

A comprehensive e-learning system will have one or more of these components:

- ✔ A learning management system to contain and facilitate e-learning
- ✔ Content tools for creating and managing content
- ✔ Curricula directive tools for assessment, testing, skill-gap analysis, certification
- ✔ Tracking matchmaking tools that can connect learning resources with employees' needs
- ✔ Tools that can push customised content to people depending on their performance needs, available connectivity, and preferred learning modes

Some people think e-learning is almost solitary, but it doesn't have to be. It is beneficial to students to give them plenty of group work and to encourage their participation in online discussions.

Making the Business Case

An e-training and development strategy will require budget allocation. Whilst you may already have a training and development budget, that should not prevent you making the business case for using the e-route. The following points help to justify such expenditure:

- ✔ e-learning is more efficient. It has been shown that learning time can be reduced by as much as 75 per cent when using e-learning compared to traditional classroom methods. Cutting out dead time, such as delegate introductions and lunch breaks, saves time. Learners can also skip through or omit material they already know, are not held up when others need more time to grasp the content, and can move at a quicker pace through instructional material rather than having to follow a trainer's formal scripted presentation.

- e-learning is quicker to deliver. A trainer may typically be only able to train one or two groups per week and if the group is large it may well take months to complete, or hold the organisation back if a quicker delivery is required. Also over long periods of time, the content may change and without a formula for providing quick updates, by the end of the training period, out-of-date content could be being delivered. e-learning can be delivered to tens or even hundreds of people at one time. The sometimes higher development costs for e-learning are more than surpassed by the delivery cost savings. The savings from delivering e-learning compared to offering a more traditional approach are so significant that initial outlays are often incidental when the project is viewed as a whole, over its entire lifespan.

- Perhaps the greatest cost savings are in the form of opportunity costs from keeping the employee longer on the job. Taking an average salary of £20,000, with the employee working 225 days per year, their average daily cost (excluding other benefits) is £89. Therefore, a typical five-day course costs the organisation £444 in terms of lost productivity, at the very least, even before their outputs are taken into account. If this training can be reduced to as little as three days of e-learning, then the immediate productivity gain is at least equivalent to the additional two days the person will be back on the job, or £178 on average. Also consider that by training more people, more quickly, the implementation of whatever they are being trained on will be much more rapid, filtering through to increased productivity for the whole initiative. If there was a high turnover of staff, then if the same training could be used year after year the savings would be even higher.

 If you design or buy in e-learning the basic training framework could last many years. Amortising the costs over such a relatively long time period would certainly make an e-solution an attractive investment for most training and development activities.

Identifying Training Providers

Many companies outsource portions of their e-learning to one or more suppliers, opting to buy or lease content, infrastructure, or services rather than create them. The supplier market is consolidating and changing rapidly so it pays to research the market rigorously. At a minimum, compare the cost, effectiveness, scale, and pricing of various e-learning solutions.

Check out these Web sites to fide out more about e-learning suppliers.

- Cisco Systems. This site has commercialised resources for e-learning including case studies: `www.cisco.com/warp/public/10/wwtraining/elearning`

✔ Cybrary. The e-Learning Cybrary is an ontology-based collection of annotated links to e-learning sites, news, documents, portals, and other e-learning resources available on the Web: `www.co-i-l.com/elearning`

✔ eclipse. A comprehensive one-stop resource for e-learning that provides structured access to thousands of links of *selected* and *reviewed* e-learning: `www.e-learningcentre.co.uk/eclipse/Default.htm`

E-Learning Portals, where you can find out more about e-learning include:

✔ Click2Learn.com (`www.click2learn.com`). Founded by Microsoft co-founder Paul Allen, their customers include more than half of the Fortune 100 as well as thousands of small businesses.

✔ CyberU (`www.my.cyberu.com`). This site gives you access to over 3,000 online classes. You can try one of their demo classes and start your online learning immediately.

✔ Learndirect (`www.learndirect.co.uk`). They have hundreds of specially created online courses in computers, office skills and self-development designed to fit in with your own timetable.

Briefing Trainees

One aspect missing from many training and development programmes is the pre-training briefing. Whilst the management team may be fully aware of the organisation's future needs in terms of skills, attitudes and abilities, those being trained may be less clear.

So the business case for e-training has to be transformed into a personal case. The relationship between the employees' current and future prospects need to be explained in terms of their current skill level and the level they will achieve once they have successfully completed the e-training programme.

Delivering the Training

Successful e-training delivery is an operational matter. You need to make sure the facilities in terms of access to the Internet or intranet are made available at appropriate times. People travelling off site, both locally and internationally, have to be brought into the equation. After all, that is one of the key features of e-learning. It is 24/7 anytime, anywhere, anyhow. But it will only be so if you plan it to be so. In the early days of CBT and CD-ROM training, access to hardware was almost always a bottleneck.

Today, with widespread access to computers and the Internet either using laptops, Internet cafés or hotel facilities, there is really no reason why someone should miss out on a training assignment. With e-learning there will be even fewer reasons for falling behind with the learning schedule.

Evaluating Training

You and your managers care about results of the business: money, time, and impact. You care less about the happy sheets and course evaluations that are the staple diet of most training organisations. You want to do things better, faster, cheaper, easier. Which of e-learning's potential strengths could help achieve this? Is it global consistency of content? Is it learners being able to learn at the most convenient time and place? Is it learners being able to learn just the blocks they need? Is it easier identification of who has what competency? Is it the opportunity to test and require mastery? Is it the use of simulation? Is it having access to a wide range of outside content? Is it some other capability or feature of e-learning?

This doesn't mean you shouldn't also track trainees and check in with them regularly. Online trainees can easily lie low, so monitoring their progress is crucial. Check whether trainees turn in assignments on time and call them if they haven't and use a course management system to track how long trainees stay online.

Making E-Training Lifetime Training

The more different ways that you use e-learning tools and technologies, the more accepted e-learning will become as a standard corporate practice, and the more efficient it will be. The goal should be to get e-training ingrained into the culture so it becomes part of lifetime learning.

Index

• C •

• D •

Darling, David (entrepreneur), 119
debt
  bad, 38, 126
  defined, 15
  subordinated, 138–139
debt capital
  bank loans, 133–136
  equity capital versus, 127–129
  loans from family and friends, 137–138
delegation of tasks, 308–311
delivery of products, 125, 276
Department of Trade and Industry (DTI),
    23, 144
design registration, 178–179
Design Registry, 178–179
Diffusion of Innovations (Rogers,
    Everett), 76
Direct Access Government (DAG), 112
Direct Selling Association (trade
    association), 57
directors, 222–224, 311
Directors Insurance, 223
disabled employees, 205
disbursements, 231
disclosure, 249, 266
discrimination, 205–206
distance learning, 305
Distance Selling Regulations, 180
distribution channels
  push and pull, 172
  researching, 14
  retailers, 172
  selecting, 172–174
diversification, 288
dividends, 255, 261
domain name registration, 176
door-to-door selling, 173
Drucker, Peter (management teacher),
    307–308, 312
DTI (Department of Trade and Industry),
    23, 144
due diligence process, 100, 102, 140

• E •

earnings before interest and tax (EBIT), 245
Easy Searcher 2 (search engine), 80
EasyJet (budget airline), 34, 171
e-buying group, 217
eclipse (e-training supplier), 336
e-commerce
  business plan writeup on, 99
  customer trust and, 16
  defined, 111
  help resources, 110–111
economy
  changes to, 313
  forecasting cash flow and, 122
  preparing for business and, 34–35
  pricing products and, 169
  vision statement and, 154
education
  distance learning, 305
  importance of, 24
  learning new skills, 46, 319–320
effectiveness, 36
efficiency, 36
elevator pitch, 105
emergency leave, 205
Emplaw (employment law Web site),
    200, 205
employees
  benefits for, 199, 256, 261
  Business Link's help with, 110
  compensation for, 198–200
  confidence and, 92, 314
  contracts of employment, 202–203
  counseling service for, 116
  delegation and, 308–309
  difficult, 193–194
  discrimination issues, 205–206
  emergency leave, 205
  environmental safety for, 206–207
  finding, 69–71
  hours of work, 42–43, 203–204
  income tax, 261–262
  job satisfaction and, 309

• *F* •

Notes

Notes

Notes

Notes

FOR DUMMIES®

The easy way to get more done and have more fun

K EDITIONS

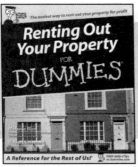

0-7645-7016-1

0-7645-7019-6

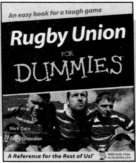

0-7645-7020-X

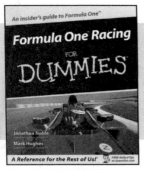

*   0-7645-7015-3

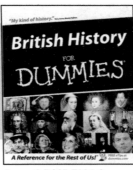

*   0-7645-7021-8

0-7645-7017-X

0-7645-7023-4
Due July 2004

0-7645-7025-0
Due July 2004

0-7645-7026-9
Due July 2004

FOR DUMMIES®

The easy way to get more done and have more fun

GENERAL INTEREST & HOBBIES

0-7645-5106-X

0-7645-5194-9

0-7645-5193-0

0-7645-5196-5

0-7645-5434-4

0-7645-1771-6

Also available:

Japanese For Dummies®
0-7645-5429-8

Architecture For Dummies®
0-7645-5396-8

Rock Guitar For Dummies®
0-7645-5356-9

Anatomy and Physiology For Dummies®
0-7645-5422-0

German For Dummies®
0-7645-5195-7

Weight Training For Dummies®, 2nd Edition
0-7645-5168-X

Project Management For Dummies®
0-7645-5283-X

Piano For Dummies®
0-7645-5105-1

Latin For Dummies®
0-7645-5431-X

Songwriting For Dummies®
0-7645-5404-2

Marketing For Dummies®
2nd Edition
0-7645-5600-2

Parenting For Dummies®
2nd Edition
0-7645-5418-2

Fitness For Dummies®
2nd Edition
0-7645-5167-1

Religion For Dummies®
0-7645-5264-3

Selling For Dummies®
2nd Edition
0-7645-5363-1

Improving Your Memory For Dummies®
0-7645-5435-2

Islam For Dummies®
0-7645-5503-0

Golf For Dummies®
2nd Edition
0-7645-5146-9

Stock Investing For Dummies®
0-7645-5411-5

The Complete MBA For Dummies®
0-7645-5204-X

Astronomy For Dummie
0-7645-5155-8

Customer Service For Dummies®, 2nd Edition
0-7645-5209-0

Mythology For Dummies
0-7645-5432-8

Pilates For Dummies®
0-7645-5397-6

Managing Teams For Dummies®
0-7645-5408-5

Screenwriting For Dumm
0-7645-5486-7

Drawing For Dummies®
0-7645-5476-X

Controlling Cholesterol F Dummies®
0-7645-5440-9

Martial Arts For Dummies
0-7645-5358-5

Meditation For Dummies
0-7645-5166-7

Wine For Dummies®
2nd Edition
0-7645-5114-0

Yoga For Dummies®
0-7645-5117-5

Drums For Dummies®
0-7645-5357-7

**Available in the UK at bookstores nationwide and online at
www.wileyeurope.com or call 0800 243407 to order direct**

Also available in the United States at www.dummies.com

FOR DUMMIES

The easy way to get more done and have more fun

FOR DUMMIES®

The easy way to get more done and have more fun

TRAVEL

0-7645-3875-6

0-7645-5478-6

0-7645-5455-7

0-7645-5495-6

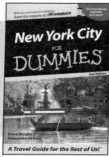

0-7645-5451-4

0-7645-5477-8

0-7645-5494-8

0-7645-5453-0

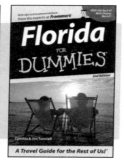

0-7645-1979-4

Also available:

Alaska For Dummies®
1st Edition
0-7645-1761-9

Hawaii For Dummies®
2nd Edition
0-7645-5438-7

Arizona For Dummies®
2nd Edition
0-7645-5484-0

California For Dummies®
2nd Edition
0-7645-5449-2

Boston For Dummies®
2nd Edition
0-7645-5491-3

New Orleans For Dummies®
2nd Edition
0-7645-5454-9

Las Vegas For Dummies®
2nd Edition
0-7645-5448-4

Los Angeles and Disneyland
For Dummies® 1st Edition
0-7645-6611-3

America's National Parks For
Dummies® 2nd Edition
0-7645-5493-X

San Francisco For Dummies®
2nd Edition
0-7645-5450-6

Europe For Dummies®
2nd Edition
0-7645-5456-5

Mexico's Beach Resorts For
Dummies® 1st Edition
0-7645-6262-2

Honeymoon Vacations For
Dummies® 1st Edition
0-7645-6313-0

Bahamas For Dummies®
2nd Edition
0-7645-5442-5

Caribbean For Dummies®
2nd Edition
0-7645-5445-X

France For Dummies®
2nd Edition
0-7645-2542-5

Maui For Dummies®
0-7645-5479-4

Chicago For Dummies®
2nd Edition
0-7645-2541-7

Vancouver & Victoria For
Dummies® 2nd Edition
0-7645-3874-8

**Available in the UK at bookstores nationwide and online at
www.wileyeurope.com or call 0800 243407 to order direct**

Also available in the United States at www.dummies.com

WILE